CW00969280

Ghost Patrol

A History of the Long Range Desert Group, 1940–1945

John Sadler

Oxford & Philadelphia

Published in Great Britain and
the United States of America in 2015 by
CASEMATE PUBLISHERS
10 Hythe Bridge Street, Oxford OX1 2EW, UK
and
1950 Lawrence Road, Havertown, PA 19083, USA

Hardcover Edition: ISBN 978-1-61200-336-8
Digital Edition: ISBN 978-1-61200-337-5

A CIP record for this book is available from the British Library

Printed and bound in the UK by TJ International

For a complete list of Casemate titles, please contact:

CASEMATE PUBLISHERS (UK)
Telephone (01865) 241249
Fax (01865) 794449
Email: casemate-uk@casematepublishers.co.uk
www.casematepublishers.co.uk

CASEMATE PUBLISHERS (US)
Telephone (610) 853-9131
Fax (610) 853-9146
Email: casemate@casematepublishing.com
www.casematepublishing.com

Non Vi Sed Arte ('Not by Strength by Guile')

This one is for Captain Rebecca Meadows RE

If you can keep your kit, when all around you
Are losing theirs and blaming it on you;
If you can scrounge a fag when all refuse you,
But make allowance for their doubtful view;
If you can wait, and not be tired of waiting,
Or, being pushed, let no man push you back,
Or, being detailed, waste no time debating
But force a British grin and hump your pack;
If you can drink, and not make drink your master,
And leave the thinking to your N.C.O.,
If you can meet with dear old Lady Astor
And treat her just as though you didn't know –
If you can bear to see your rations twisted
Into the weird concoction known as stew;
If neither knees nor face are ever blistered,
And neither flies nor fleas can worry you;
If you can face the other fellow's chinnings
And turn deaf ears to their unleashed abuse;
If you can force your heart and nerve and sinew
To serve on guard when you should be relieved,
And swear like hell with all the breath that's in you,
With all the curses ever man conceived;
If you can walk with blondes and keep your virtue,
Or ride in trams and keep your pay book safe;
If needle stabs and castor oil don't hurt you,
And rough angora shirts don't even chafe;
If you can fill a sandbag every minute,
Dream that your trench is Lana Turner's flat –
Yours is the blue my son, and all that's in it.
And what is more, you are a DESERT RAT.

—R.F. Marriott, *Crusader* (no. 37, 11th January 1943)

The desert was a small raider's paradise.

—General Sir John Hackett

Contents

Acknowledgements

When I was a boy, a maternal uncle who had served in the desert presented me with carved wooden models he'd made of a Sherman tank and a Spitfire, roughly 1/32nd scale, ideal for the size of toy soldiers I was campaigning with at the time, created in idle hours from spare pieces of timber and odd, redundant radio parts. My uncle, alas and like so many veterans, has died but the models remain, having made, over the last forty years, that hallowed transition from mere playthings to artefacts. Timpo I think was the toy manufacturer, along with Cherilea and Lone Star who produced desert war figures in 54mm and 60mm, Monty was there in his beret and flying jacket; Australians in a variety of stern action poses. The Germans were usually in the act of surrendering or expiring; either was good. In the modern world with its absurd, emasculating Puritanism, such things would doubtless be banned, for too much fear of children enjoying themselves and dreaming martial dreams.

Specific credits for verse and prose extracts are comprised of: Introduction, *Epitaph on a New Army* is reproduced by kind permission of the publishers of *More Poems of the Second World War.* Chapter One: *Blessing for the Traveller* is quoted in *G Patrol, A Cook's Thoughts on Bully Beef* is anonymous, *Code of Fellowship* is quoted in John Strawson's, *the Battle for North Africa, Ode to a Desert Flower* appears in *Crusader,* issue 57 and *Rare as Fairies* is Anzac doggerel, the author is unable to trace any copyright holder. Chapter Two: *I never see a map…* is from Kennedy Shaw. Chapter Three: *Streams of Blood* by Hanns Pfeuffer is quoted in Hargreaves, R., *Blitzkrieg Unleashed* (Barnsley, Pen & Sword, 2008). Chapter Four: *If* is included by kind permission of the trustees of the Fusiliers Museum of Northumberland. Chapter Five: the author is unable to trace copyright on *Desert Victory.* Chapter Six: *The Poor Bloody Infantry* is quoted in Mallinson, A., *the Making of the British Army* (London, 2011). Chapters Seven and Eight: the two poems by E. Yates are both included by kind permission of County Durham Record Office, Chapter Nine: *the D-Day Dodgers* is featured by kind permission of Mrs. Margaret Ward.

Thanks are due to Pen & Sword publishers for permissions to quote from the late Captain William Kennedy Shaw's *Long Range Desert Group* and the late Major-General David Lloyd Owen's *Providence Their Guide*, also to Sutton Publishing for permission to use extracts from Mike Morgan's *Sting of the Scorpion.*

Furthermore, this book could not have been written without the generous assistance of a number of organisations and individuals, particularly The Long Range Desert Group Preservation Society, Peter Hart and the staff of the Imperial War Museum Sound Archive, Richard Groocock at the National Archive and Amy Cameron of the National Army Museum, the archive staff of the Defence Academy of the United Kingdom at Shrivenham, Liz Bregazzi and Gill Parkes of Durham County Record Office, David Fletcher of the Tank Museum, Bovington, Roberta Goldwater of the Discovery Museum, Rod Mackenzie of the Argyll and Sutherland Highlanders Museum, Thomas B. Smyth of the Black Watch Museum, Paul Evans of the Royal Artillery Museum, Ana Tiaki of the Alexander Turnbull Library, New Zealand, Christopher Dorman O'Gowan for information concerning his late father Brigadier E. Dorman-Smith, John Stelling and Henry Ross of North War Museum Project, Dr. Martin Farr of Newcastle University, Barry Matthews of Galina Battlefield Tours, Trevor Sheehan of BaE Systems Plc, John Rothwell, James Goulty, Sir Paul Nicholson, Major (Retired) Chris Lawton MBE, Arthur W. Charlton, Colonel Anthony George, John Fisher, John Shepherd, Mary Pinkney, Brian Ward, Jennifer Harrison, Neville Jackson, the late Nigel Porter, Timothy Norton, Kit Pumphrey, Graham Trueman for his indefatigable and enthusiastic help with primary source material, and Chloe Rodham for the maps.

As the author I remain, as ever, responsible for all errors and omissions.

John Sadler,
Mid-Northumberland, summer 2015

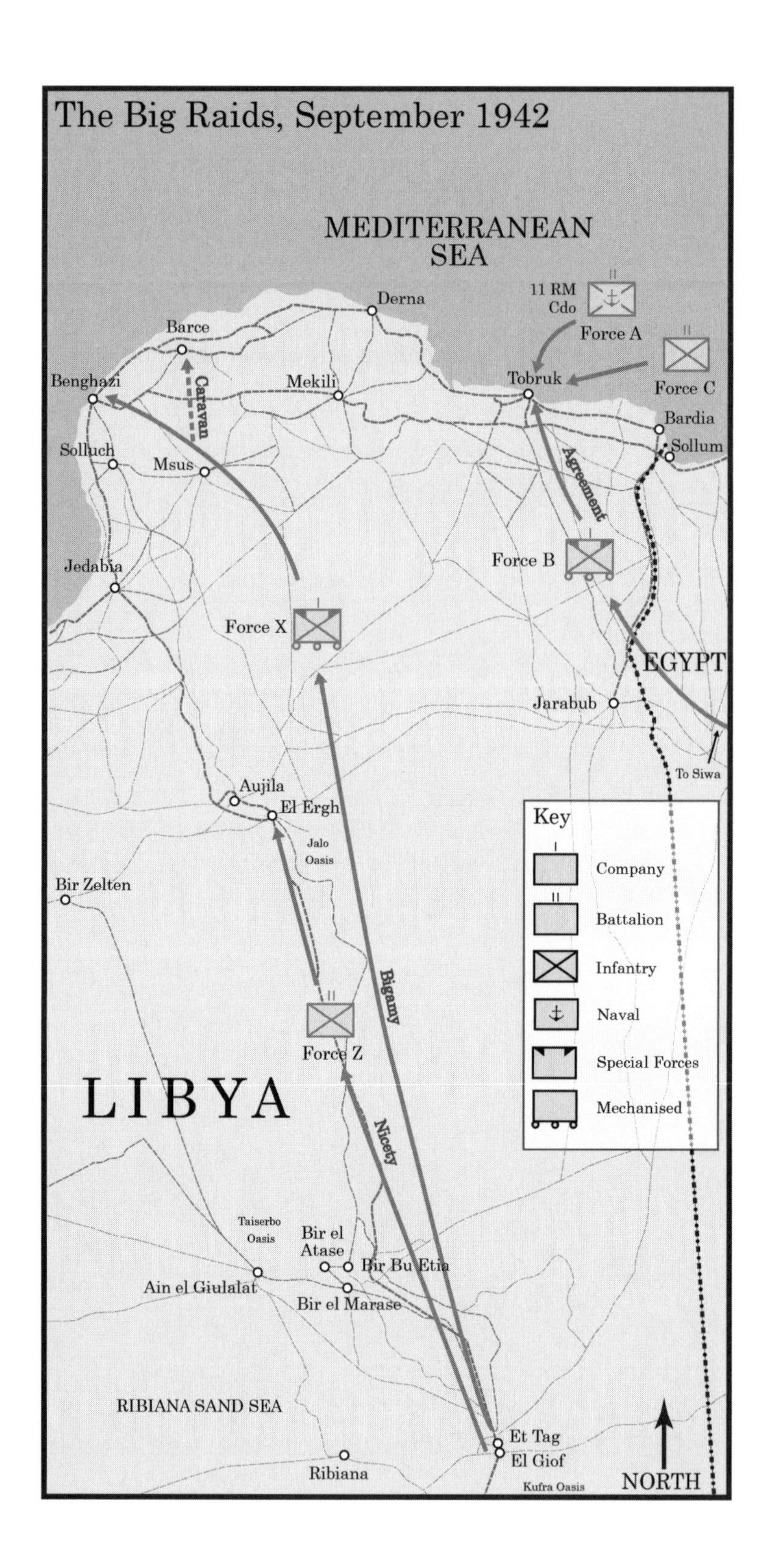
The Big Raids, September 1942
MEDITERRANEAN
SEA
11 RM
Cdo
Force A
Force C
Derna
Barce
Caravan
Benghazi
Mekili
Tobruk
Bardia
Sollum
Solluch
Msus
Agreement
Force B
Jedabia
Force X
EGYPT
Jarabub
To Siwa
Aujila
El Ergh
Jalo
Oasis
Bir Zelten
Key
Company
Battalion
Infantry
Naval
Special Forces
Mechanised
Bigamy
Force Z
LIBYA
Nicety
Taiserbo
Oasis
Bir el
Atase
Bir Bu Etia
Ain el Giulalat
Bir el Marase
RIBIANA SAND SEA
Et Tag
El Giof
Ribiana
Kufra Oasis
NORTH

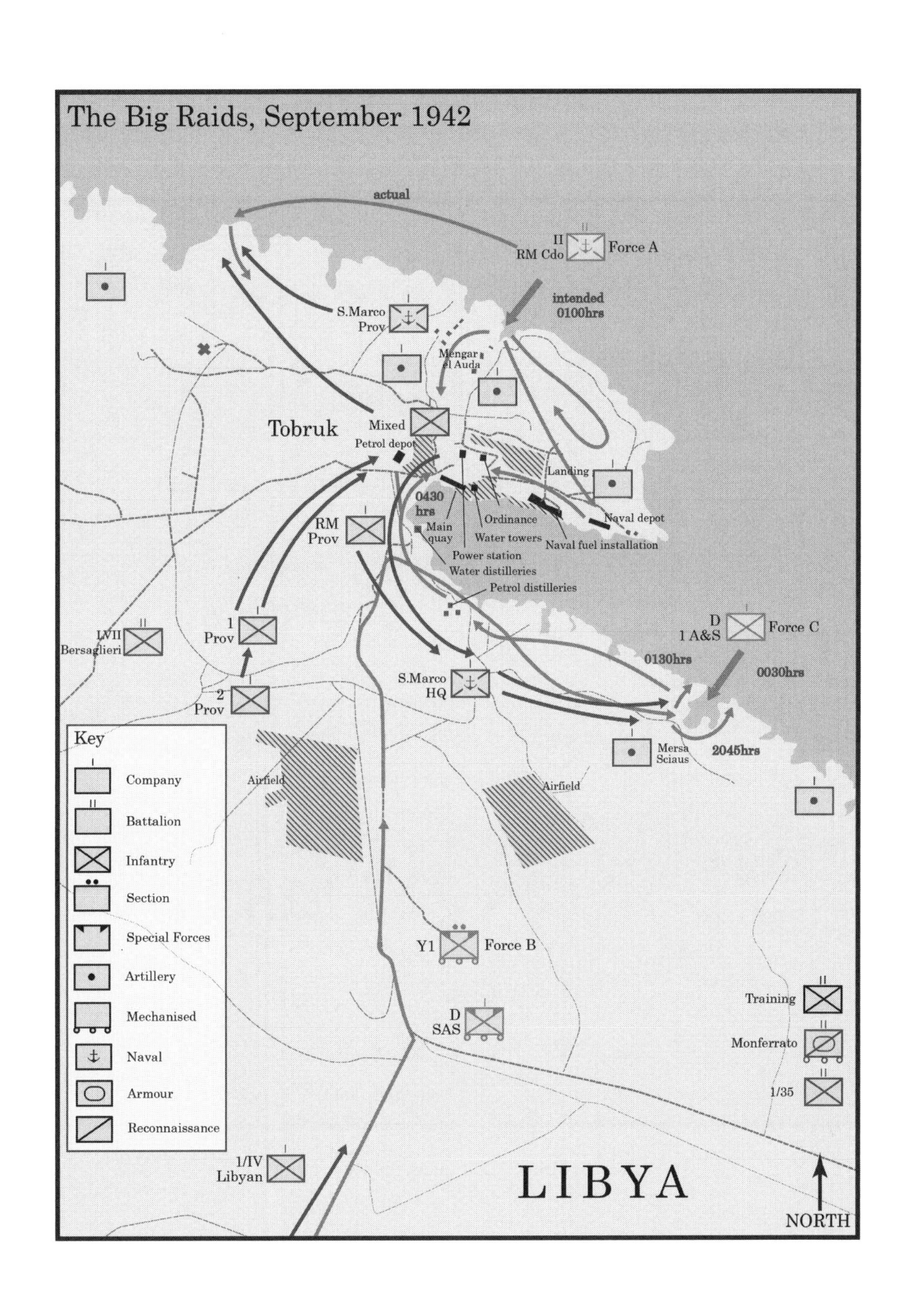

The Big Raids, September 1942
actual
II
RM Cdo
Force A
intended
0100hrs
S.Marco
Prov
Mengar
el Auda
Tobruk
Mixed
Petrol depot
Landing
0430
hrs
Ordinance
Naval depot
RM
Prov
Main
quay
Water towers
Naval fuel installation
Power station
Water distilleries
Petrol distilleries
D
1 A&S
Force C
LVII
Bersaglieri
1
Prov
0130hrs
0030hrs
S.Marco
HQ
2
Prov
Mersa
Sciaus
2045hrs
Key
Company
Battalion
Infantry
Section
Special Forces
Artillery
Mechanised
Naval
Armour
Reconnaissance
Airfield
Airfield
Y1
Force B
D
SAS
Training
Monferrato
1/35
1/IV
Libyan
LIBYA
NORTH

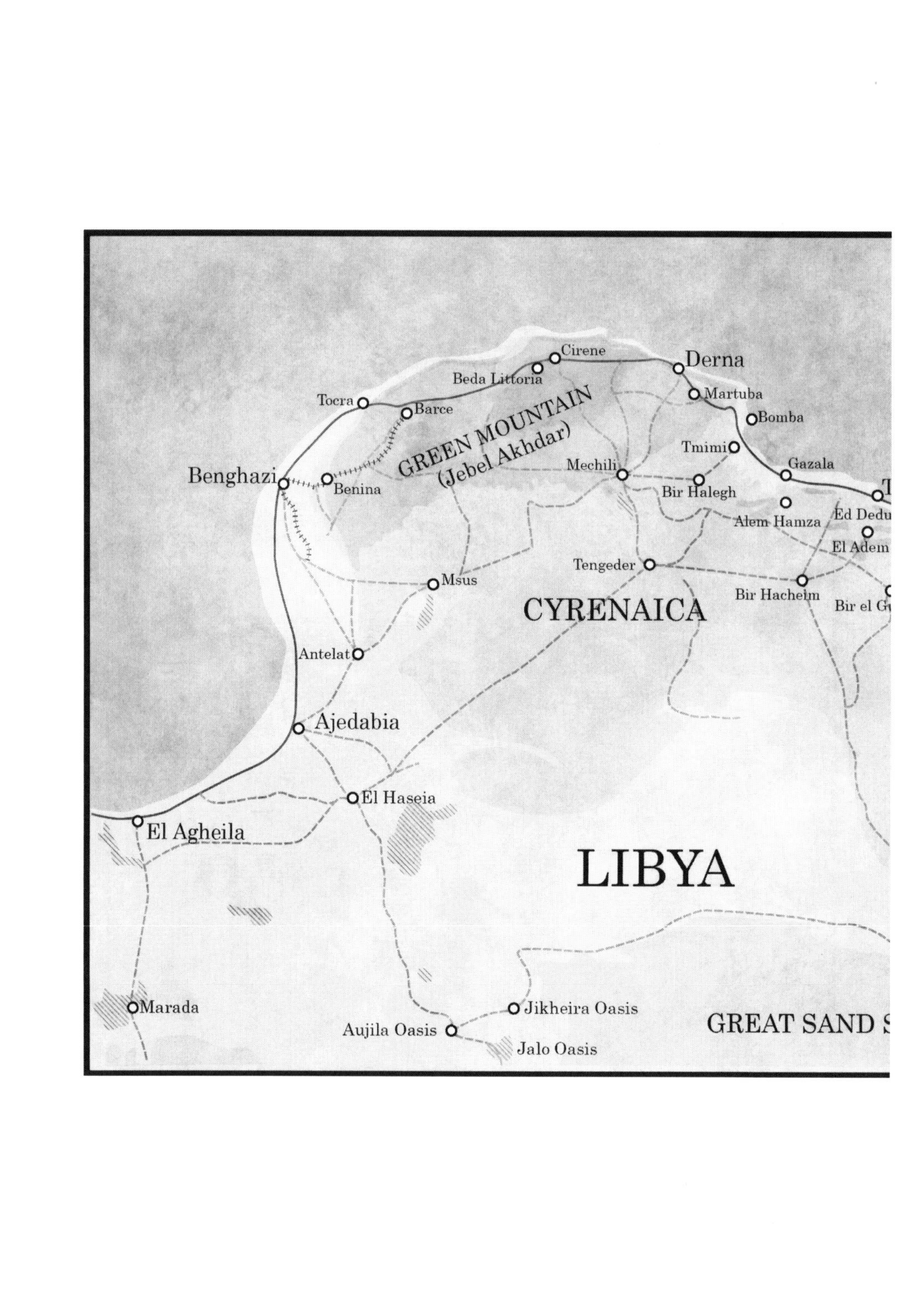
Cirene
Derna
Beda Littoria
Martuba
Tocra
Barce
Bomba
GREEN MOUNTAIN
(Jebel Akhdar)
Tmimi
Gazala
Benghazi
Mechili
Benina
Bir Halegh
Alem Hamza
El Adem
Tengeder
Msus
Bir Hacheim
CYRENAICA
Antelat
Ajedabia
El Haseia
El Agheila
LIBYA
Marada
Jikheira Oasis
Aujila Oasis
Jalo Oasis

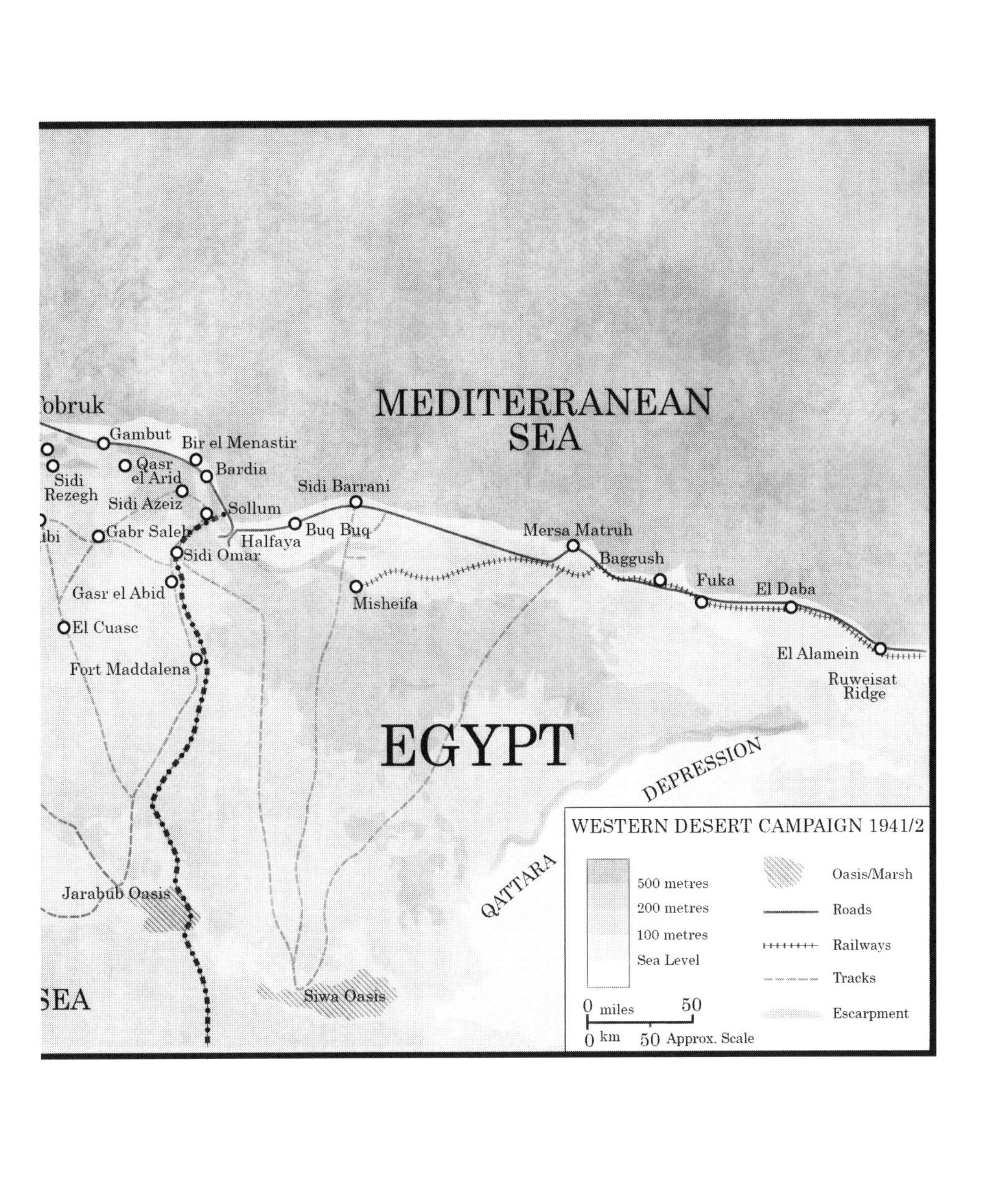

MEDITERRANEAN
SEA
Tobruk
Gambut
Bir el Menastir
Qasr
el Arid
Bardia
Sidi
Rezegh
Sidi Azeiz
Sollum
Sidi Barrani
Gabr Saleh
Halfaya
Buq Buq
Sidi Omar
Mersa Matruh
Baggush
Fuka
El Daba
Misheifa
Gasr el Abid
El Cuasc
Fort Maddalena
El Alamein
Ruweisat
Ridge
EGYPT
DEPRESSION
QATTARA
Jarabub Oasis
Siwa Oasis
SEA
WESTERN DESERT CAMPAIGN 1941/2
500 metres
200 metres
100 metres
Sea Level
Oasis/Marsh
Roads
Railways
Tracks
Escarpment
0 miles 50
0 km 50 Approx. Scale

Chronology

1939

3rd September – Britain declares war on Germany

1940

10th June – Major Ralph Bagnold suggests the concept of a desert patrol

11th June – Italy declares War on Britain; 11th Hussars involved in initial border skirmishes

23rd June – General Wavell, C-in-C Middle East, approves Bagnold's plan

10th July – the War Office approves formation of the LRP

17th – 19th August – LRP begins reconnaissance and observation along the Jalo-Kufra road

11th August – Italians invade British Somaliland

19th August – British withdraw fully from Somaliland

27th August – Wavell inspects the LRP; ready for duty

5th September – first LRP mission into Libya

13th September – Italians invade Egypt and occupy Sollum

17th September – the Italians occupy Sid Barrani

20th September – British open the Takoradi aircraft reinforcement route through West Africa to Egypt

29th September – WO authorises doubling the unit size

9th November – LRP becomes LRDG with HQ and two field squadrons, each of three patrol units

12th November – Germany's OKH issues the order to create a force to support the Italians in North Africa

23rd November – W & R patrols on 1st operation

5th December – G Patrol at the Citadel in Cairo

8th December – Wavell launches Operation 'Compass' under the command of General O'Connor

11th December – Sidi Barrani recaptured; British counter-offensive proceeds with less difficulty than anticipated
17th December – Sollum recaptured
27th December – G & T Patrols undertake the Fezzan expedition

1941

5th January – British enter Bardia
11th January – LRDG & Free French take Murzuk
22nd January – Australians enter Tobruk
29th January – British re-invade Somaliland
30th January – British enter Derna
31st January – Southern Rhodesian Squadron is formed
5th/7th February – British defeat Italians in Battle of Beda Fomm
25th February – British complete re-conquest of Somaliland
27th February – initial skirmishes with Afrika Korps
1st March – Free French capture Kufra
5th March – first British troops withdrawn from theatre to be deployed in Greece
9th March – Yeomanry Patrol is formed
21st March – RA gunners arrive
24th March – *Panzerarmee* takes El Agheila
31st March – Rommel attacks Mersah Brega
3rd April – Germans occupy Benghazi
7th April – Generals O'Connor and Neame captured; Germans occupy Derna
9th April – LRDG, minus A Squadron, locates to Kufra Oasis: A Squadron in spring and early summer ranges through Cyrenaica
10th April – Tobruk besieged, Rommel bypasses garrison to press eastwards
13th April – Tobruk surrounded, Bardia falls
14th April – Axis assaults on Tobruk defences repulsed
28th April – Germans occupy Sollum
May/June – British intervention in Iraq (effectively subdued by 1st June)
5th/12th May – 'Tiger' convoy brings much needed armour across Mediterranean
15th May – British launch Operation 'Brevity'
16th May – British complete conquest of Ethiopia

20th May/1st June – Germans launch Operation 'Mercury' to take Crete; Allied survivors evacuated by RN
June/July – British open campaign against Vichy French in Syria
15th June – British launch Operation 'Battleaxe'
22nd June – *Barbarossa* begins
1st July – Auchinleck replaces Wavell
10th July – LRDG at Kufra, relieved by Sudan Defence Force
25th July/8th August – British intervention in Persia
1st August – Colonel Bagnold receives promotion and hands over operational command to Lieutenant-Colonel Prendergast
14th/15th September – Rommel launches raid on Sofadi
1st October – LRDG comes under command of (what will be) Eighth Army
1st November – LRDG Patrols divided into two
9th November – LRDG, minus S Patrol, is concentrated at Siwa
18th November – British launch Operation 'Crusader'
18th November – all LRDG units bar a reserve deployed to support the 'Crusader' Offensive
19th November – British enter Sidi Rezegh
21st November – sortie by Tobruk garrison to effect link with forces around Sidi Rezegh
23rd November – Germans fare better in confused tank battles
24th November – Rommel makes a dash across Egyptian border
26th November – Auchinleck takes over direct command of Eighth Army from General Ritchie
30th November – Rommel tries to sever the corridor between British forces from Tobruk and Sidi Rezegh
6th/8th December – massed battles around and south of Sidi Rezegh
10th December – British relieve Tobruk
13th/17th December – Rommel's series of counter-attacks are eventually beaten off
19th/24th December – British occupy Derna (19th), Mechili (19th), Barce (23rd), Benghazi (24th)
23rd December – LRDG acts as pathfinders for SAS
28th December – ILRS is formed
30th December – Kufra base abandoned

1942

2nd January – British re-capture Bardia
6th/8th January – Rommel's offensive from Agedabia is beaten back
12th January – British occupy Sollum
17th January – British regain the Halfaya Pass
21st January – Axis offensive pre-empts Operation 'Acrobat' – British forces worsted and forced into retreat
23rd January – Germans re-take Agedabia
26th January – LRDG HQ evacuates Jalo
1st February – HQ set up at Siwa
2nd February – British occupy Gazala Line and lay plans for offensive – Operation 'Buckshot'
4th February – Axis re-capture Derna
2nd March – LRDG begins 'Road Watch'
26th May – Axis offensive against the Gazala Line
2nd June – Axis besiege Free French forces at Bir Hakim on southern flank of Gazala Line
3rd June – General Ritchie's attempted riposte founders, 150th Brigade destroyed
10th June – Free French ordered to abandon Bir Hakim
12th/13th June – Major tank battle ranges around 'Knightsbridge' position
14th/17th June – British withdrawal to Egyptian border
18th/21st June – Axis pressure on Tobruk which falls, followed by Bardia
23rd/26th June – LRDG retreats from Siwa
24th June – Axis forces enter Egypt
25th June – Auchinleck assumes personal command of Eighth Army
27th/28th June – Axis forces successful in Battle of Mersah Matruh
2nd/3rd July – 1st Battle of El Alamein begins
4th July – Eighth Army launches counter-attacks
10th July – Australian gains from Italians
26th July – further British attacks held off
26th July – official end of the battle – a limited British victory
18th August – Alexander replaces Auchinleck as C-in-C Middle East and Montgomery is appointed to Eighth Army following the death of General Gott
31st August – New Axis offensive opens; the Battle of Alam Halfa

3rd/7th September – unsuccessful attack by NZ division in Alam el Halfa area, battle ends as a limited British defensive victory

13th/14th September – Operations *Bigamy, Agreement, Nicety* & *Caravan* are launched

1st October – Eighth Army stages attack in the Deir el Munassib sector

1st October – ILRS (two patrols plus HQ) come under LRDG command

23rd/24th October – 2nd Battle of El Alamein opens after initial bombardment – the 'Break-in' phase

24th/25th October – the 'Crumbling' phase

26th/28th October – the 'Counter' phase

29th/30th October – Stalemate

30th October – LRDG again comes under direct control of GHQ ME

1st/2nd November – 'Supercharge'

3rd/7th November – Break-out and pursuit by Eighth Army

8th November – Allied landings in French North Africa: Operation 'Torch'

1943

14th/25th February – Axis offensives from Sidi Bou Zid to Kasserine, initially successful but finally repulsed

6th March – further Axis offensive – Battle of Medenine

20th/27th March – Eighth Army breaks through Mareth Line

23rd March – US forces defeat Axis at Battle of El Guettar

March – April – LRDG units withdrawn to Egypt

6th April – Eighth Army defeats Axis at Battle of Wadi Akarit

13th May – remaining Axis forces surrender at Tunis; end of the Desert War

June – the Allies prepare to invade Sicily

July – the Battle of Kursk ('Operation Citadel') begins; Palermo falls to the Allies and Mussolini is overthrown

August – the Quebec Agreement is signed

September – official surrender of Italian forces, Mussolini rescued by Skorzeny

September – British Dodecanese campaign begins

October – the Germans take Kos

November – Battle of Leros

November – the Battle of Tarawa opens; Red Army offensive in Ukraine

December – Tito declares a provisional government for Yugoslavia; Allies sink the *Scharnhorst*

1944

LRDG active in Italy and the Balkans

January – the Red Army Enters Poland; 1st Battle of Monte Cassino

February – 2nd Battle of Monte Cassino; 'Big Week' strategic bombing of Germany

March – beginning of battle of Imphal; 3rd Battle of Monte Cassino; Germany occupies Hungary

April – the British advance from Imphal; de Gaulle commands all Free French forces

May – the Red Army retakes Sevastopol, Monte Cassino is finally taken

June – Operation Overlord, D-Day

July – fighting in the bocage country in Normandy; attempt on Hitler, the July Plot fails

August – the Warsaw Uprising begins; German forces in Normandy nearly trapped in the Falaise Pocket, and Paris is liberated

September – Brussels is liberated, Operation market Garden fails, V1's and V2's land on England

October – the Moscow Conference; British enter Athens, Battle of Leyte – MacArthur returns

November – Operation Infatuate – clearing the Scheldt Estuary; at Auschwitz the gas chambers and crematoria are blown up

December – the Home Guard is stood down

1945

LRDG active in Greece, Yugoslavia and Albania

January – the battle of the Bulge ends in German defeat; destruction of Nuremburg; Auschwitz liberated

February – Russians close in from the east; bombing of Dresden

March – Allied crossing of the Rhine

April – Battle for Berlin begins; Belsen is liberated

May – death of Hitler and VE Day

21st June – LRDG officially disbanded

Dramatis Personae

Ralph Algar Bagnold (1896–1990)

Bagnold was the guiding spirit behind and first commander of LRDG, and one of the great pioneers of desert exploration during the 1930s. He laid the foundations for the research on sand transport by wind in his influential book *The Physics of Blown Sand and Desert Dunes* (first published in 1941), which remains an established reference in the field. It has been used by agencies such as NASA in studying sand dunes on Mars.

Herbert Cecil Buck (1916–1945)

Captain 'Bertie' Buck MC, was one of those classic British officers so beloved of post war stereotypes: dashing, eccentric and also a fluent German speaker. The unit he created was the most exceptional of all Special Forces – the Special Interrogation Group ("SIG"). Their purpose, like the LRDG and SAS, was to raid behind enemy lines but they did so in German uniforms, thus risking execution if captured. They trained, lived and thought in German. Most were also Jews who had escaped Nazi Germany in the 1930s to seek a new life in Palestine.

Patrick Andrew Clayton (1896–1962)

Clayton spent nearly twenty years with the Egyptian Survey department during the 1920s and 1930s, extensively mapping large areas of previously unmapped desert. At the outset of the war he was working as a government surveyor in Tanganyika. Bagnold had him brought back to Egypt because of his detailed knowledge of the Western Desert, and he was commissioned into the Intelligence Corps. Clayton was leading "T" Patrol in a planned attack on Kufra when the patrol was engaged by the Italian Auto-Saharan Company on 31 January 1941, near Gebel Sherif. He was wounded and captured.

Michael Duncan David Crichton-Stuart (1915–1981)

Crichton-Stuart was educated at Eton College. He subsequently graduated from Christ Church, Oxford with an MA. During the war he reached the rank of Major in the Scots Guards, serving with LRDG and was twice wounded, earning an MC in 1943. After the war he held a range of civic appointments in his native Scotland.

John Richard Easonsmith (1909–1943)

Easonsmith initially joined the 4th Battalion Gloucestershire Regiment. He then served in tanks before being commissioned, and joined LRDG in December 1940. His first command with the LRDG was with the New Zealand 'R1' Patrol which was the unit that collected the SAS after their first, unsuccessful mission. By August, 1941 he had been promoted to Captain, and in January 1942 was gazetted for a Military Cross. He was killed during the raid on Leros in December 1943.

Rupert Harding-Newman (1907–2007)

When he died at the age of 99, Harding-Newman's *Telegraph* obituary (11th December 2007) hailed him as *the last survivor of a handful of Englishmen whose professions had taken them to the Middle East between the First and Second World Wars and whose experience of desert travel and exploration led to the formation of the Long Range Desert Group (LRDG).* As a soldier he was commissioned into the Royal Tank Regiment in 1928 but became hooked on desert exploration, working with Bagnold both as mechanic and cook! Although he assisted Bagnold in equipping the group in 1940, he was not actually allowed to join.

John ('Jock') Haselden (1903–1942)

Jock Haselden was born in Ramleh, near Alexandria. Before the outbreak of war, he was employed by Anderson, Clayton & Company, a cotton trader. Haselden was fluent in several languages including Arabic, French and Italian. Initially, on joining up he was posted to the Libyan Arab Force. From July 13th, 1940, he served on the GR Staff Middle East, specializing in commando-type operations. He was then appointed as Western Desert Liaison Officer at Eighth Army HQ, working very closely with LRDG. He was killed in action during the final abortive phase of Operation *Agreement* on 14th September. His name is engraved on the Alamein Memorial at the Commonwealth War Cemetery in Alamein, Column 85.

Geoffrey Beresford Heywood (1914–2006)

'Tim' Heywood, who ran LRDG Signals, was born in Newcastle and educated at Eton. At school he became interested in wireless, then qualified as an accountant before being commissioned into the Royal Corps of Signals (Middlesex Yeomanry) in 1939. After the war, he inherited family land in Gloucestershire and became a farmer, very active in the Royal College of Agriculture. His passion was sailing. Lloyd Owen described him as an officer people respected, though they did not necessarily like him. A hard taskmaster, he was highly instrumental in the success of LRDG.

Robert Blair 'Paddy' Mayne (1915–1955)

Mayne was from Northern Ireland, a highly successful rugby union international and amateur boxer. He was an early recruit into David Stirling's fledgling SAS. Highly decorated and distinguished as a soldier, he had a dark and mercurial side exacerbated by heavy drinking. He worked as a solicitor after the war but never settled into civilian life, subsequently dying in a car crash.

Vladimir Peniakoff ['Popski'] (1897–1951)

One of the Desert War's more colourful and controversial characters, Vladimir Peniakoff was born in Belgium to Russian parents. He studied at St John's College, Cambridge and became a conscientious objector during the Great War. After a change of heart he volunteered to join the French artillery as a private; subsequently wounded, he was invalided out.

In 1924 he emigrated to Egypt where he worked as an engineer for a sugar manufacturer. During this time he learned the crucial art of steering motor vehicles through desert terrain, becoming a Fellow of the Royal Geographical Society. He spoke English, Russian, Italian, German, French and Arabic with varying degrees of fluency.

He was commissioned as a second lieutenant in October 1940, serving in the Libyan Arab Force. His buccaneering in the desert gained him an MC in November 1942 and a DSO three years later. In 1947 'Popski' was created a Belgian Officier de l'Ordre de la Couronne avec Palme and awarded the Belgian Croix de Guerre 1940 avec Palme.

David Lanyon Lloyd Owen (1917–2001)

Lloyd Owen was originally commissioned into the Queen's Royal Regiment. In July 1941 he joined the LRDG and took part in a number of operations, including the SAS raid on Tobruk in August/September 1942, which resulted in a Military Cross. He was badly wounded during an air raid on the base at Kufra in October 1942, nearly losing an arm, and did not rejoin till February 1943, in time for training in Lebanon before being sent to the Aegean. He took command of LRDG at the end of 1943 following the death of his predecessor, Jake Easonsmith.

Guy Prendergast (1901–1986)

Guy Lennox Prendergast was one of that elite body of British Saharan explorers in the late 1920s and early 1930s. In the war he was initially commissioned into the Royal Tank Regiment, before joining of Bagnold in the fledgling LRDG. After his promotion to Lieutenant Colonel he assumed command of LRDG between November 1941 and October 1943. Subsequently, he rose to be Deputy Commander of Raiding Forces and later Deputy Commander of the Special Air Service Brigade during 1944–1945 when he also led the Free French SAS Regiments with the rank of Brigadier. He gained a DSO and the Czechoslovakian Order of the White Lion III Class.

William Boyd Kennedy Shaw (1901–1979)

Between the wars Kennedy Shaw contributed to the exploration of the Libyan Desert in the area around the southwestern corner of modern Egypt with his particular interest and skills as a botanist, archaeologist and navigator. He made three major trips. Bagnold recruited him as the Intelligence and Chief Navigation officer for LRDG. Kennedy Shaw was transferred to the Intelligence Corps in 1940 and latterly served with the SAS. He wrote one of the earliest books on the LRDG, *Long Range Desert Group,* immediately after the war.

David Stirling (1915–1990)

Founder of the SAS, Stirling was indefatigable, bold and often brilliant. His style of aggressive raiding contrasted with LRDG's more low-key, intelligence-led approach. Nonetheless, in the fifteen months before his capture, the SAS had destroyed over 250 aircraft on the ground, shot up and bombed dozens of supply dumps, and sabotaged railways and all manner of enemy communications. Hundreds of enemy vehicles were put out of action. He ended the war in Colditz.

Moir Stormonth-Darling (1913–2002)

Born the son of a Writer to the Signet, Stormonth-Darling was commissioned into the 2nd Cameronians in 1935. Pre-war he served in Palestine then in India, Iraq and Persia. He became a ski instructor, which led to his introduction to LRDG. A born adventurer, he commanded two squadrons in the Aegean sector. His excellent logistical skills were as much in demand as his fighting spirit. He remained in khaki for a considerable period after the war before retiring to manage the family estates in Angus.

Eric Charles Twelves Wilson VC (1912–2008)

Wilson was commissioned into the East Surry Regiment but transferred to the Somaliland Camel Corps in 1939. It was during the Italian invasion of British Somaliland that he won the VC, having been presumed killed. He was released after the Italian surrender in East Africa and joined LRDG. He moved to the 11th (Kenyan) King's African Rifles. He subsequently served in Burma. After the war he served in the Overseas Civil Service, retiring in 1961 after Tanganyika gained independence.

Being Introductory

> No drums they wished, whose thought were tied
> To girls and jobs and mother,
> Who rose and drilled and killed and died
> Because they saw no other,
> Who died without the hero's throb,
> And if they trembled, hit it,
> Who did not fancy much their job
> But thought it best and did it.
>
> —Michael Thwaites: *Epitaph on a New Army* (November 1939)

> The concept of indirect operations, in the aftermath of Britain's sole commitment of a mass army in the First World War, had been forgotten in this country. It was revived in the struggle against the Axis in Egypt and Libya during the crisis of the Second World War. Among several Special Forces raised to carry war to the enemy's flanks and weak points the Long Range Desert Group was pre-eminent. Today, when Britain's mastery of Special Operations is universally acknowledged, it is appropriate to recognise the pioneering achievements of those who raised, led and served in the Long Range Desert Group.[1]

Most of us who were born some years after the end of the Second World War and who were children during the 1960s, grew up on a diet of British and American war films. Quite a number of these were set in the North African Campaign and the blistering sands enlivened many a dank northern afternoon even where, as was frequently the case, they were depicted in black & white. The exploits of what are now termed Special Forces, then more often referred to simply as commandos, thrilled us eager youths.

As early as 1958, the British movie *Long Range Desert Group* with Richard Attenborough, John Gregson and Michael Craig, offered an exciting but generally accurate view of the role of LRDG. They were our heroes really; the Special Air Service weren't anywhere near as popular, and it took till the 1980s and the storming of the Iranian Embassy to catapult SAS fully, and it seems now indelibly, onto the wider public consciousness.

For many of us of that generation, LRDG were the new musketeers, a wartime extension of Dumas or Henty. The desert was a vast, exotic expanse with no civilian casualties and a cause that was undeniably just. A whole genre of films glorified the desert commandos: *Tobruk, Raid on Rommel,* even the 'Dirty Dozen' version of *Play Dirty* with Michael Caine and Nigel Davenport.

After the end of the Second World War the LRDG was disbanded, as its post desert operations had not met with such resounding success. High command tends to look down on Special Forces and commando units as too costly, too maverick and of questionable value. Many operations had been unsuccessful. Operation *Agreement,* the ill-starred raid on Tobruk, for example, was a fiasco. However, nothing could detract from the fact that LRDG had shown the true potential for Special Forces if conceived, recruited and deployed correctly. They punched well above their weight throughout the desert war.

Though both LRDG and SAS had been disbanded, the 'Winged Dagger Boys' were resurrected with considerable success during the long counter-insurgency in Malaya and have gone on to become the very epitome of Special Forces, forming the model for such units worldwide. The dawn of asymmetric[2] and now hybrid[3] warfare has created a very different kind of battlefield.

This in part, forms the justification for this new history. There have of course been others, starting in 1945 with Bill Kennedy Shaw's *Long Range Desert Group*, Michael Crichton Stuart's *G Patrol*, and *Providence their Guide* by David Lloyd Owen, and Mike Morgan's *Sting of the Scorpion.* What I aim to achieve building on the excellent foundations prepared by these accomplished authors, most of whom were veterans of LRDG, is to reflect upon how their wartime experience has influenced modern Special Forces thinking. It is rumoured that the US army holds Lawrence's *Seven Pillars of Wisdom* as the definitive manual for low-intensity warfare. All modern Special Forces operations also owe a debt, freely acknowledged, to the LRDG, pioneers of modern irregular tactics.

As former UK Prime Minister Tony Blair tellingly remarked to the parliamentary Enquiry into his ill-judged latter-day crusade in Iraq in 2003: *9/11 changed everything*. In this he was undoubtedly correct. The consequential implications for the current use of Special Forces are discussed more fully in the final chapter, but 'the War on Terror' seems a very far cry from the wide, barren spaces of the Western Desert and a war where the enemy was clearly defined; where the Allied cause was patently right and the final objectives never in doubt. The War in the Desert lasted less than three years and ended in a resounding Allied victory. The involvement in Afghanistan required a full decade longer and fizzled out with a low-key withdrawal of UK forces. For those left behind of course, the war continues.

Seventy years and more from the events of the Desert War, we look back on the conflict with a brand of nostalgia. A war where the enemy was clearly perceived as being the very epitome of the forces of darkness, a war of pure and clear ideologies and easily defined aims – beat Hitler. And we did. This was 'our finest hour' and most of what has come after fails to measure up. Perhaps no single unit embodies that ideal more than the Long Range Desert Group with its famous Scorpion badge.[4]

Notes

1 Keegan, Sir John, in the foreword to Lloyd Owen, Major-General D., *Providence their Guide* (Leo Cooper London, 2000), p. xv.

2 Asymmetric warfare – essentially the irregular alternative to interstate war, a conflict where the two sides are vastly disproportionate in terms of strength and resources.

3 Hybrid warfare – a form of low-key total war where the use of conventional and irregular forces is blended with cyber-warfare, guerrilla operations, and the use of improvised explosive devices ("IEDs").

4 Trooper "Bluey" Grimsey was the soldier credited with designing the LRDG cap badge. The legend has it that a scorpion stung him and then promptly died (the scorpion, not the trooper!). The emblem is not entirely dissimilar to the Italian Auto-Saharan Company, which features a crab in a circle: http://lrdg.hegewisch.net/beret.html, retrieved 5th February 2015.

CHAPTER 1
Legends of the 'Blue'

God be thy guide from camp to camp; God be thy shade from well to well;
God Grant beneath the desert stars thou hear the Prophet's camel-bell

—*Blessing for the Traveller*[1]

The last days before Christmas were spent packing. 'Shorty' had turned out to be a splendid New Zealand quartermaster who allotted us rather over twenty tons of equipment and stores to load onto the '30-cwt' trucks and a light Ford scout car. Any pedantic ideas we had been taught about load limits were dissolved by simple arithmetic. Seven Lewis Guns, four Vickers, Boys anti-tank rifles, the Bofors and their ammunition; spare parts, with plenty of extra springs; rations and water cans; navigator's equipment; fitters' tools, medical stores, signaller's wireless and accessories, all had to be checked and loaded. But the bulk of every load was petrol, tons of it in four-gallon 'expendable' tins, two tins to a wooden packing case. Keep every scrap of wood we were warned.[2]

The Western Desert

The great swathe of the Sahara Desert covers a vast expanse. It has an enduring aura of romance and exoticism, experienced by very few of those who served in the Desert War. Armies have fought in desert conditions both before and after, but never on such a scale and of such duration. Desert ("the Blue") threw up a whole catalogue of factors to hinder military activity and increase the misery of individual combatants.

For these, British and Dominion, the Germans, Italians, French, Greeks and others, it seemed they had arrived in the very cauldron of a particular version of hell. *...my three strongest recollections are: the heat, sweat pouring and oozing from me, until I ached and itched with it ... the strange lack of fear ... the seemingly endless hours of utter boredom, observing a law ridge about 2,000 yards away with nothing moving, nothing happening, except the sun beating mercilessly down and one's eyes straining (as I remember our gunner putting it) "at miles and miles of f*** all".*[3]

The story of the Long Range Desert Group unfolds primarily in the Libyan Desert, a natural amphitheatre in which large armies wheeled and charged, stood at bay, gave and took ground. Men poured out their lifeblood over featureless, rock-strewn ridges barely showing above the scorched desert floor. Tanks, like dusty men o' war, cruised and fought, largely untroubled by the human landscape that defined other battlefields.

Along the Mediterranean coast, runs a narrow littoral of pleasant and cultivated land, the fertile coastal strip, along which most of the main settlements are located. This agreeable plain is bounded inland by a line of limestone cliffs, steep and bare, dragged through with narrow defiles or wadis. These create a formidable barrier, impassable to most wheeled vehicles. Atop the cliffs and running southwards in a gentle decline, is a bare plateau, scorched by the hot sun and scoured by millennia of harsh winds. The surface is comprised of rock and layered grit, like the topping on a primeval cake, varying in density from metres to centimetres. Where the base rock is denser, low hills have been left, insignificant humps or irregular ridges, possession of which was to be vital to the armies and demand a vast sacrifice in blood and materiel.

Where the limestone is more friable, depressions of varying size create undulations. These can form either obstacles or handy defences. Of all these pits in the desert floor the largest is the vast Qattara Depression which lies to the south of the plateau, forming an impassable inland sea several hundred metres below the escarpment, bounded by steep cliffs with salt-marsh below. As one moves southwards towards this great depression the unyielding surface of the plateau gives way to a rolling, almost dizzying series of dunes.

This, perhaps, is nearest to the classic image of the desert landscape so beloved of filmmakers. Theses dunes arise some half a hundred miles inland and the ground considerably restricts movement of large forces. Thus the armies were penned into the area between the coast and the dunes, a relatively narrow battlefield in so wide a landscape. This was never more than seventy miles in width but stretched for a thousand miles and more east and west, creating a very thin oblong.

Though unremittingly harsh, the desert was not devoid of either flora, fauna or, for that matter, inhabitants: … *there was virtually no animal or insect life. Just the occasional jerboa – the desert rat (a nice friendly little fellow) – the scorpion and an occasional gazelle. The Arabs and their camels kept well out of the way.*[4] Of manmade roads running east to west there was only one, the Via Balbia from Tripoli through Sirte, El Agheila, Benghazi, Derna, Gazala, Tobruk and Bardia, to Sollum. Westwards lay Sidi Barrani, Mersa Matruh, Fuka, the rail halt of El Alamein, and finally the great jewel of Alexandria and the fertile sweep of the Nile. Of these coastal settlements only Tripoli, Benghazi and Tobruk had significant harbours. For transit north to south there were only local track ways, ('trigh').

These were not hard-surfaced but beaten paths linking oases, hammered out by centuries of human and camel traffic.[5] Clearly these had never been intended for wheeled vehicles, and the passage of motorised convoys punished the surface, leaving a chaos of endless ruts. To avoid these, drivers tended to edge their vehicles to the side, thus beating an ever widening path. When winter rains deluged the trigh, surfaces turned into a glutinous, impassable soup. Where these routes crossed, the location naturally assumed a clear local significance often marked by a saintly burial, (denoted by the prefix 'Sidi').

Such places became natural foci for area defence or supply stations. Without wishing to push the naval analogy too far, fighting in the largely featureless desert placed a premium on navigation, demanding an exact use of the compass. *So five miles beyond Sidi Barrani we branched off into the open desert and bumped along over boulders and scrub as far as "Fred Karno's Circus". This was the name given to the gap in the wire on the Libyan-Egyptian frontier, at the southern end of the Halfaya ('Hellfire') escarpment. By this time we were beginning to realise just what driving in the desert meant. The sun was merciless, even at this time of year, and our loads were floating about the lorry, bursting open tin after tin of priceless petrol*[6]. In addition to the magnetic compass, often upset by the steel in vehicles, the sun compass[7] came into its own. *It was our first effort at movement, using only compass and sun compass. Fortunately, we had some guide in a row of telegraph poles that stretched away towards the forward area along the desert tracks.*[8]

In this, the pioneering work undertaken by pre-war cartographers was particularly useful. Mapping the desert had an appreciable provenance, beginning with Herodotus. Classical and medieval travellers were followed by British explorers such as Mungo Park and Major Laing who first crossed north–south to Timbuktu in 1826. During the inter-wars years much work had been done by an eclectic group including two Englishmen who were both to serve in LRDG: Bagnold[9] and Clayton.[10] One of the more colourful of this colourful bunch was the Hungarian Lazlo Almasy.[11] Due to their combined efforts the empty canvas of the desert was marked by the network of ancient trails, with every feature in an otherwise bare landscape plotted and surveyed. This included the white bones of escarpments, sunken depressions, oases, salt marshes and dry wadis that could spring to brilliant life after rains.

During the summer months, from May–October, the climate is scorching hot, a blisteringly and relentless sun, furnace bright and searing dry. Only in the evenings before the dark cold of night, before the sun sinks, is the broiling fire of day mellowed into evening cool. Winters are drear and damp with frequent heavy downpours. Torrents flow down the scree-riven wadis but water is soon soaked up by the parched and greedy desert.

Mainly in spring, an enervating wind shifts direction and can whip the sands into the abrasive fury of the *Khamseen*. The land is harsh and gives nothing, shows no mercy to the unwary and punishes all who toil there. Yet there is great beauty, and the desert can exert a powerful, almost obsessive pull. Dawn and sunset can be infinitely memorable and the stars glow with a clear cold light that conjures biblical images. Soldiers were thrown back on their recall of heroic conflicts as depicted in the *Iliad.*

> Wilfred Owen said that the poetry is in the pity; but that was in another war. This later war was one of great distances and rapid movement and for me the poetry came when least expected, in the interstices of a generally agitated existence, in the rush of sudden contrasts, and the recognition that, whatever else changes, one's own mortality does not.[12]

East of the emptiness lies Egypt, fertile valley of the Nile, a cradle of civilisation, the jewel in successive empires. Britain's interest in Egypt stemmed primarily from her need to safeguard the vital passage of the Suez Canal. This concern had led Britain to perceive a need for intervention in 1882, when nationalist sentiment in the Egyptian army simmered. After the native military were suitably chastised at the Battle of Tel-el-Kebir (1882), Britain became the dominant force. Egypt remained vital to Britain's strategic interest during the Great War, even though the land was still nominally an Ottoman possession.

A popular uprising broke out in 1919 and, in November 1924, the British representative to Sudan, Sir Lee Stack, was murdered. King Fuad, a British puppet installed in 1922, died in 1936 and his youthful successor, Farouk, was minded to enter into an Anglo-Egyptian Treaty. It was agreed that the British would withdraw from Egypt, save for a garrison of 10,000 who would remain for a certain period to defend the Canal. Fear of Italian aggression following Mussolini's invasion of Abyssinia was an influential factor. When war broke out again in 1939, Egypt once again assumed a key strategic role. Many in the local opposition would not have been unhappy to see the Axis powers victorious.

Waging war in the Desert

> Q. Were they good days for you?
> A. Oh yes. Happy days with my men … I have always longed to meet them again. Where are all the Geordie men I loved and commanded now?[13]

> You can stew it, you can fry it
> But no matter how you try it
> Fundamentally it remains the same,
> You can hash it, you can slash it,
> With potatoes you can mash it,
> But when all is done you've only changed the name.
>
> —'A Cook's thoughts on Bully'

Herodotus chronicles the dire warning offered by the unfortunate experience of King Cambyses II of Persia (d. 522BC). The despot dispatched an army, said to be 50,000 strong, to punish the Oracle of Amun at Siwa Oasis. This entire force vanished in a sandstorm of suitably biblical proportions and was never seen again. Over centuries the legend flourished, and many explorers since (including Count Lazlo Almasy), have sought to solve the riddle of this lost army.

Wartime infantry who fought in the Desert would never forget the hardships the terrain imposed. In addition to the normal perils of being under enemy fire and the hidden hazard of landmines, there were flies in abundance, numerous forms of disease, plus the odd poisonous snake or scorpion. Ground was barren, scorched, featureless, waterless and invincibly hostile to man. It must at times have seemed almost unbelievable that such titanic efforts were exerted by both sides to win these arid, seemingly endless acres. …*In the desert, men asked "Why?" again and again. There had to be some good and justifiable reason for fighting in such inhospitable climes. No men fought merely for the sake of fighting.*[14]

For the most part infantry inhabited trenches, much as their fathers had done on the Western Front, though these were less permanent affairs. To dig down into sand was not difficult but, where the surface had been whittled away by wind and the limestone was exposed, powered tools were necessary to gouge out shallow trenches and foxholes, supported by a rough parapet of stones, or 'sangars'.[15]

Battles were large and terrifying, though relatively rare. Smaller actions at platoon or company level were far more common and there was a constant need for patrolling, either light reconnaissance or the beefier and bristling fighting patrol.

> Recce patrols were messy affairs if we had to go through the pockets of some poor devil who had been killed and had been left lying out in the sand for a couple of days. People talk about rigor mortis, but after a day or two the limbs were flexible again and indeed, after a week or so, a quick pull on an arm or leg would detach it from the torso. Two-day-old corpses were already fly blown and stinking.
>
> There was no dignity in death, only masses of flies and maggots, black swollen flesh and the body seeming to move, either because of the gases within it or else the thousands of maggots at work. We had to take documents, identity discs, shoulder straps, anything of intelligence value. Pushing or pulling these frightening dead men to reach their pockets was sickening. Of course, we couldn't wash our hands – one rubbed them in sand – sometimes we rubbed them practically raw if it had been a particularly disgusting day.[16]

'Desert Rose' sounds like an attractive form of flora. To the Allied army however it denoted an altogether more basic convenience – the field latrine. For temporary arrangements the hollow shell of a petrol container was buried with another laid on top at a suitable angle to form a urinal. Where more creature comforts were needed a deep trench was sunk with a hessian sheet on timber frame arranged above. Chlorine was applied liberally.[17]

Cleanliness was essential in the Desert climate where dysentery and other horrors stalked. Personal hygiene and liberal application of AL63[18] were equally emphasised. Opportunities for washing one's person or attire were often limited, the soldier coated in a caked carapace of stale, dried sweat and dust. Cuts and scrapes could swiftly become infected and morph into most unpleasant weeping ulcers.

For the majority of the young men who served in these campaigns, any form of overseas travel, indeed any travel at all was a novelty. To such innocents the Levant appeared a distant and exotic place: *Waiting for a taxi, he breathed the spicy, flaccid atmosphere of the city and felt the strangeness of things about him. The street lamps were painted blue. Figures in white robes, like night shirts, flickered through the blue gloom, slippers flapping from heels. The women, bundled in black, were scarcely visible.*[19] Few could deny that their apprehensions were overlaid by a sense of adventure: *We sailed along the Red Sea for a century, it seemed. The heat was insufferable. Sleep an impossibility. Tempers were frayed and fights developed freely. … Curiosity replaced apathy. Stage by stage, and those men who had been to Egypt before found themselves in popular demand and frequent visitors to the canteen.*[20]

At first their destination appeared almost delightful. *As we clambered ashore we stamped and rubbed our feet delightedly.… We ran the sand slowly through our fingers; it was warm and real and comforting. I could never have believed then that I would hate this self-same sand so bitterly; the crumbled, remorseless rock that sucked at the lifeblood of us who tried to master her vastness in the following months.*[21] They would find that the epithet 'Desert Rat' was not accorded to novices as of right. It had to be earned, the recognition of an apprenticeship in desert warfare and survival.… *The name given to themselves by the soldiers of the Eighth Army … it became an expression of pride among the men. It soon became the entitlement only of experienced desert fighters and could not be claimed by any newcomer to the desert.*[22]

In such surroundings the comradeship of war was inevitably heightened. Men might express fine sentiments and extol the nobility of sacrifice but such poetic expressions soon wilted in the face of reality. Endless hours of tedium, dirty, sweaty, beset by a constant and ravenous horde of flies, troubled by looseness of the bowels and all the other complaints that add endless misery to a soldier's life, enlivened only by odd moments of sheer terror. The code of behaviour which evolved was dictated by pure pragmatism:

> Your chief concern is not to endanger your comrade.
>
> Because of the risk that you may bring him, you do not light fires after sunset.
>
> You do not use his slit trench at any time.

> Neither do you park your vehicle near the hole in the ground in which he lives.
>
> You do not borrow from him, and particularly you do not borrow those precious fluids, water and petrol.
>
> You do not give him compass bearings which you have not tested and of which you are not sure.
>
> You do not leave any mess behind that will breed flies.
>
> You do not ask him to convey your messages, your gear or yourself unless it is his job to do so.
>
> You do not drink deeply of any man's bottles, for they may not be replenished. You make sure that he has many before you take his cigarettes.
>
> You do not ask information beyond your job, for idle talk kills men.
>
> You do not grouse unduly, except concerning the folly of your own commanders. This is allowable. You criticise no other man's commanders.
>
> Of those things which you do, the first is to be hospitable and the second is to be courteous ... there is time to be helpful to those who share your adventure. A cup of tea, therefore, is proffered to all comers ...
>
> This code is the sum of fellowship in the desert. It knows no rank or any exception.[23]

Discipline was essential, though the fire of combat tempered the parade ground bellowing of peacetime and the drill sergeant into a more businesslike focus.

> Discipline such as we had formerly known disappeared. In its place came a companionship. Officers no longer issued orders in the old manner. They were more friendly and more with the men. They realised that this was a team. We, for our part, never took advantage of this new association. While orders were given, except in emergency, more in the nature of requests, they were obeyed even more punctiliously than under peacetime conditions. It was a case of every man pulling together, willingly. From what we had seen of the German Army, so such relationship existed, and it was not long before we discovered this was our strength.[24]

Krieg ohne Hass[25] was a description attributed to Rommel himself and insofar as war can ever truly be said to represent chivalry then it was here. The British had a high regard for the Desert Fox, both as a fighting soldier of the highest calibre and a man of impeccable honour. Some years after the war Lieutenant-General von Ravenstein[26] observed: *If the warriors of the Africa Campaign meet today anywhere in the world, be they Englishmen or Scots, Germans or Italians, Indians, New Zealanders or South Africans, they greet each other as staunch old comrades. It is an invisible but strong link which binds them all. The fight in Africa was fierce, but fair. They respected each other and still do so today. They were brave and chivalrous soldiers.*[27]

Humour, as ever, was the soldier's balm. *A typical example of the sort of thing that amused us was the story that Hitler had secretly contacted Churchill with the offer to remove Rommel from his command in return for Churchill retaining all his generals in theirs.*[28] Though the soldiers in the line observed a strict blackout procedure, the sky to the east was lit up with the rich glow of the Delta cities. The brightness and gaiety of easy living these represented could not have contrasted more tellingly with the drab but dangerous austerity of the front. The contrast between the rigours of the line and the luxury of Cairo, the 'Unreal City', could not have been greater:

> To an outsider like Alan Moorehead coming upon Cairo early in the summer of 1940, a world of Edwardian privilege seemed to define the city's ambience. "We had French wines, grapes, melons, steaks, cigarettes, beer, whisky and an abundance of all things that seemed to belong to rich, idle peace. Officers were taking modern flats in Gezira's big buildings looking out over the golf course and the Nile. Polo continued with the same extraordinary frenzy in the roasting afternoon heat. No one worked from one till five-thirty or six, and even then work trickled through the comfortable officers borne along in a tide of gossip and Turkish coffee and pungent cigarettes."[29]

Though Cairo might be a cushy billet, some at least were very much aware of what awaited me preparing to deploy 'up the Blue' or on leave. The Countess of Ranfurly was one: *It is always the same. These young men come on leave or for courses in Cairo or Palestine, or for a while they are on the staff. They take you out to dinner and talk of their families and what they are going to do after the war; they laugh and wisecrack and spend all their money in the short time they can be sure they are alive. Then they go down to the desert leaving their letters, photographs and presents to be posted home. So often they never come back.*[30] If the beauties of the desert could move this generation of war poets then even the simple army convenience could raise an ode:

Of all the Desert flowers known
For you no seed is ever sown.
Yet you are the one that has most fame,
O Desert Rose – for that's your name.

There's thousands of you scattered around,
O' Desert Rose, some square, some round,
Though different in variety,
At night you're all damned hard to see.

Although you're watered very well
You have a most unfragrant small;
And just in case you do not know,
O' Desert Rose, you'll never grow.

For you are not a Desert Flower,
Growing wilder every hour;
You're just a bloomin' petrol tin,
Used for doing most things in.

—Ode to a Desert Flower[31]

The Pendulum

It could be argued that the fall of France and the evacuation at Dunkirk, apparently catastrophic, did in fact confer an element of strategic advantage upon Britain. Freed from the dire attrition of obligations to continental allies, such as had enmeshed Imperial forces during the Great War, Britain could fall back upon her traditional strengths. These were an all-powerful navy and a resolute air force that had, in the summer of 1940, successfully defied the *Luftwaffe*'s best efforts.

Germany's failure to crush Britain presented the Nazi high command with a limited range of strategic options. To all intents and purposes the war in the West was won. As Hitler intimated when writing to Mussolini, all that remained was the final push against a moribund and defeated England. The key question for Berlin was whether they could afford to turn the swollen and victorious Wehrmacht east to settle with Russia whilst the British Empire, technically at least, was still in the ring.

There was also the question of the oil, which in war, as Clemenceau pronounced, *is as necessary as blood.*[32] Without an adequate and continuous supply of crude oil no state could meet the huge demands of modern warfare. In 1939 Britain was importing some nine million tons of crude, the bulk of which flowed from Iran, Iraq and the USA. By early 1941 oil reserves had fallen to alarmingly low levels. A failure of supply would force Britain to seek terms as surely as a renewed and successful air offensive.

It was estimated by the Petroleum Board that between the spring of 1940 and 1941 some 14 million tons of oil would be required. The USA could be counted on to supply less than half of this, and oil producers were not swayed by Anglophile considerations. They wanted cash on the barrel. Precious dollars that Britain could ill afford to disburse. The Shah of Iran had seized on the urgency to extort fresh concessions. Supplies from the USA were subject to sickening wastage through U-Boat attacks. As the Vichy administration in Syria stood adjacent to the vital oilfields in the Middle East and the key but vulnerable refinery at Haifa, their sympathies were of some concern.

If French naval power, based in the North African ports, was to be added to that of the formidable Italian fleet then the balance of naval power in the Mediterranean would be upset, dangerously so. Oil tankers sailing from Iran would be vulnerable, and Britain's entire position in the Middle East under serious threat. Already Mussolini was massing troops in Cyrenaica for a thrust into Egypt, their numbers vastly exceeding those of the defenders. In November 1940 the Fleet Air Arm sallied against Italian capital ships sheltering in Taranto and scored a signal success. A further engagement off Cape Spartivento on the 27th of that month reinforced British superiority, but the threat from a compliant Vichy remained.

Aside from possible British aggression, the other factor that alarmed Hitler was the likely intentions of his Italian ally. Il Duce was steadily becoming disaffected with the relegation of his country's role in the war. Where were the great gains he had hoped for, the triumphal marches of Fascist armies through captured Allied dependencies? Now very much the junior partner in the Axis alliance, Mussolini was hungry for spoils.

The relationship between the two states was further strained by a clear element of mistrust. The Germans, or at least some in the high command, were deeply suspicious of their ally's competence in the intelligence war, to the extent that outright treachery was mooted.[33] Aware that Italy was looking covetously at Greece, Hitler took pains to ensure that his fellow dictator was aware that Germany was steadfastly opposed to any military adventure.

Mussolini, however, was hungry for laurels. At the same time Sir Archibald Wavell, C-in-C Middle East, and General O'Connor, commanding Western Desert Force (from September 1941 this became the legendary Eighth Army), scented an opportunity. In December 1940 Wavell unleashed Operation Compass. This offensive achieved prodigies. By the time it was ended Il Duce's legions had been significantly trashed: 3,000 were dead and a staggering 115,000 captured. British & Commonwealth fatalities were in the order of five hundred. The Italians also lost vast quantities of materiel.

By the time the dust had settled over Bardia on 5th January, Hitler had taken the momentous if inevitable decision to intervene on behalf of his crumbling ally. He could not countenance a total collapse of the Italian position in North Africa. Major-General Hans von Funck was sent to carry out an analysis, and gloomily reported that the proposed injection of German forces would not suffice to stem the rot. Hitler had already issued Directive no. 22 of 11th January determining that Tripolitania must be held and that a special military 'blocking force' would be deployed: Operation 'Sunflower'.

This infusion of German troops would enjoy air support from *Fliegerkorps X*[34] which was to be moved to Sicily. This formation was already trained in air attack upon shipping and quickly made its presence felt, inflicting considerable damage on the aircraft carrier *Illustrious*. These *Luftwaffe* squadrons could also strike at British depots and targets in North Africa. If the British could strike at the Axis in the Eastern Mediterranean, then deprived of any other opportunities in the West, Hitler could riposte. In February, the Fuhrer appointed Lieutenant-General Erwin Rommel to command his African contingent. The 'Desert Fox' thus enters the stage, a player who would tax the hounds rather more sorely than his Italian predecessors.

Logistics were the determinant of success in the desert war. Life and campaigning in the arid expanses were only possible because of mechanisation and a supply chain that could move, deliver and maintain the vast stocks of every element that was needed to keep a modern, mobile force in the field. The further an army advanced the more tenuous the supply chain, and rapid advance brought a risk that the army might completely outrun its own supply, thus severing that vital umbilical cord and grinding to a fatal halt.

Clausewitz observed, and this long before mechanised warfare, that the advantages accruing to an attacking forced diminished over time. Surprise, morale, concentration of resources and initiative cannot be maintained indefinitely. Those advantages enjoyed by the defender are not so susceptible to attrition, and the closer he is forced back upon his own base areas the easier his re-supply becomes. This 'seesaw' or 'pendulum' effect was never more apparent than in the desert where the armies fought over such vast, sterile areas, habitually never more than fifty miles inland from the coast. Troops dubbed such violent swings of fortune the 'Benghazi Stakes'.

Wavell was a brilliant leader and Compass became the first successful British offensive of the war. It would be some time before the Allies scored another. Rommel's arrival in the theatre should have sounded louder than it did, but Churchill and Eden were then much perplexed by matters in the Balkans. Greece had successfully blunted an Italian invasion, fighting the attackers to a standstill, even taking the offensive.

A decision to intervene in Greece was taken wholly on political grounds. Churchill did not like Wavell, who lacked flamboyance, and the C-in-C, despite deep misgivings, felt he had no choice but to comply with his Whitehall masters. As predicted, the Greek campaign was a costly fiasco. As truculent Aussies caustically observed:

> We marched and groaned beneath our load,
> Whilst Jerry bombed us off the road,
> He chased us here, he chased us there,
> The bastards chased us everywhere.
> And whilst he dropped his load of death,
> We cursed the bloody RAF,
> And when we heard the wireless news,
> When portly Winston aired his views –
> The RAF was now in Greece
> Fighting hard to win the peace;
> We scratched our heads and said 'Pig's arse',
> For this to us was just a farce,
> For if in Greece the air force be –
> Then where the Bloody Hell are we?[35]

Operation *Marita*, the Axis intervention, cost the Allies just under a thousand dead but fourteen times that number became prisoners. Vast numbers of guns and vehicles were also lost. Next, the action shifted to Crete. Paratroop General Kurt Student's grand concept of 'aerial envelopment'[36] led to a pyrrhic victory. The battle raged between 20th May–1st June 1941, and though costly to the German airborne arm, the Allies again lost heavily. Nearly 7,000 were left dead or wounded with a further 17,000 as prisoners. Such dire losses in personnel and equipment weakened Wavell, just as 'the Desert Fox' prepared to bite.

Rommel owed his appointment to a personal relationship with the Fuhrer and the perceived charisma observed by Josef Goebbels. The exploits of his 'Ghost' Division in France and his own fondness for self-promotion had contributed to the general's rise. His tactical abilities, relentless and ruthless energy, boldness and decisiveness were qualities that would ensure his desert legend. In addition to being hampered by the fact he was outside the patrician loop of staff-college generals, his unwillingness to tolerate fools or abide by orders he considered incorrect won him few friends at OKW. As the Official History correctly observes:

> The [*Axis*] chain of command creaked from time to time, but the firm hand of General Rommel made up for its many weaknesses. He was not the C-in-C, it is true, but he was emphatically the man whose views mattered, for he did what he felt to be militarily right in spite of the frequent protests of his superior, General Bastico. And then, having made up his own mind on the policy, he had a habit of becoming a tactical leader, and by taking command personally at the most important spot, ensuring that his ideas were carried out.[37]

Both Von Brauchitsch[38] and Halder[39] had made it perfectly plain to Rommel that his role was defensive and subordinate to the Italian C-in-C, General Gariboldi.[40] The forces he had were all that he would get. There would be no more and he must not consider plans for an offensive until 15th Panzer was deployed in theatre. His superiors, unlike Rommel himself, were privy to the plans for *Barbarossa* – the invasion of Russia, compared to which North Africa was the merest of sideshows. The deployment was strictly a blocking move, *sperrverband.* Despite these stern admonitions the Fox was keen to make his gambit and had already determined *to depart from my instructions to confine myself to a reconnaissance and to take the command at the front into my own hands as soon as possible.*[41]

Weakened by the pointless and immensely costly diversion to Greece and with his forces strung out, Wavell was caught wrong-footed by Rommel's first lightning strike. In the middle of May a British response, Operation Brevity, despite an encouraging start, fizzled out. Its bigger brother Battleaxe, launched the next month, fared little better. Tobruk was heavily besieged and remained leaguered for an epic span of 240 days. Its Australian defenders became legend.

The failure of Battleaxe proved the final nail in Wavell's coffin. Churchill reacted ruthlessly and he was replaced by Auchinleck. The 'Auk' found himself under immense political pressure. Churchill and the war cabinet needed signs of victory to bolster lukewarm US confidence. The new C-in-C's offensive, 'Crusader', did not sally forth till 18th November and blazed till the year's end. British and Axis tanks brawled in the dust-shrouded melee of Sidi Rezegh. Rommel did well overall but was eventually forced back, first to Gazala then all the way to El Agheila.

'Crusader' was a British victory, in that Tobruk was relieved, the enemy was driven from Cyrenaica with heavy losses, and all Axis troops holding positions on the Egyptian frontier were destroyed or captured. This all took longer than expected, however, and in doing it the British exhausted themselves. Winter quarters in the Western Desert were generally disagreeable:

> Flies produced more casualties than the Germans. It is impossible to describe, without suspicion of exaggeration, how thickly they used to surround us. Most of us ate a meal with a handkerchief or piece of paper in one hand and our food in the other. While we tried to get the food to our mouths, free from flies, we waved the other hand about wildly; even so we ate many hundreds of flies. They settled on food like a cloud and no amount of waving about disturbed them. They could clean jam and butter from a slice of bread much quicker than we could eat it … it can be realised how serious the menace of flies was considered when I say that, even in remote parts of the Desert, one came across notices saying 'Kill that fly, or he will kill you'.[42]

The pendulum had indeed swung but this placed fresh difficulties in Auchinleck's path. As a direct result of this strategic shift, Eighth Army was that much further away from its supply base and its communications were that much more attenuated. Conversely, the army which had retreated was so much closer to its base, thus supply and replenishment was that much easier, the 'pendulum' effect again.[43] Technically, Eighth Army had won the day but it was dearly bought. Allied losses in killed wounded and missing, were in the region of 18,000, whilst the Axis lost 20,000 more. Both lost heavily in tanks and guns.

Barbarossa altered the entire global, strategic position. Hitler's decision to fight on two fronts was the tipping point of the war. Immediately, this was far from apparent. In the summer and early autumn of 1941, the *Wehrmacht* stormed through White Russia, the Baltic States and Ukraine. The Red Army suffered defeat after defeat with calamitous casualties. In spite of all these successes the offensive was ultimately a failure as it failed to crush the Soviets. War in the east would continue into 1942 and suck the life blood of Axis resources. Rommel was the poor relation. His victories disguised but could not ultimately conceal the fact that the odds were beginning to stack against him.

None of this was necessarily apparent in the first half of 1942. Rommel bounced back from his retreat at the close of Auchinleck's offensive and sprang forward like a tiger, driving the British back, often in rather unseemly haste. Tobruk, the totemic bastion, fell. Expressions such as the 'Msus Stakes' and 'Gazala Gallop' entered Eighth Army's vocabulary, synonymous with near rout. The Gazala line was outflanked and forced, and the Allies hurled back towards El Alamein, a bare threescore miles west of Alexandria. There could be no further retreat, nor was there. In July Rommel came again, pounding the line for almost all of July. He did not break through but British counter-attacks exposed serious flaws. It was a stalemate.

The Long Range Desert Group was a child of opportunity blended with necessity. Britain and its Allies were extremely lucky to have men like Bagnold and Clayton with all their vast knowledge and daring. Alastair Timpson was with the Scots Guards who found himself in an altogether more unconventional unit: *The Long Range Desert Group in Africa provided an efficient service behind the enemy lines for the 8th Army (and its predecessor the Western Desert Force) and Middle East headquarters. The main functions were: Intelligence, 'Taxi-Service' and 'beat-ups'. Of these functions intelligence was the most important.*[44]

Intelligence was indeed the key task. Attacking the enemy, however satisfying, was far less important than providing HQ with a clear picture of what was going on 'over the hill' and equally vital, *were reports on the 'going' – the terrain, whether it was good enough to enable a force of all arms to make a left hook around the enemy when on the offensive.*[45] One of the most famous examples of LRDG opening up strategic possibilities was the discovery by Nick Wilder's T2 Kiwi Patrol of a backdoor which would enable Eighth Army to outflank the formidable pre-war Mareth Line. Wilder found a narrow gap between the Matmata Hills, which lay to the east, and the sand sea. The passage was named 'Wilder's Gap in honour of its finder. So a small reconnaissance patrol actually influenced the overall strategic balance at a critical juncture and saved Eighth Army the heavy casualties which would have certainly been incurred in a grinding battle of attrition[46].

Ever since Britons had first ventured into the desert, its vast and lonely expanses of sand had exerted a strong pull. The wartime generation had, in many instances grown up with Lawrence's classic *Seven Pillars of Wisdom*. Ron Hill who served with LRDG was one of these: *I had always been fascinated by stories of the desert since reading T.E. Lawrence.... But I had also picked up copies of Bagnold's 'Libyan Sands' and Wilson MacArthur's Road to the Nile when on leave in Cairo which reinforced my interest.*[47]

Many volunteered because they were sick of the boredom, 'bull' and general 'mucking about' that formed regular Calvaries in the life of the desert soldier. John Shute found himself stuck in Iraq in 1943 having disobeyed the old dictum of 'never volunteer for anything' – *so when a call came for volunteers for the LRDG, I – with several hundred other bored young men – put my name down and wondered whether I could possibly measure up to the exacting tests to which I could expect to be subjected.*[48]

'Blondie' Duncalfe was another young hopeful who, having listened to his father's tales of comradeship in the previous war, saw that the LRDG could be *the ultimate dream, of any soldier.*[49] Archie Gibson MM was a driver in the Guards. Several of his mates had already volunteered for service with LRDG. Archie had all his worldly goods and possessions including *a beautiful set of German spanners*[50] in his truck, which the *Afrika Korps* disobligingly blew up, capturing him in the process. He was rescued by a patrol from 11th Hussars as his captors stopped for a brew. The Germans left hurriedly and Archie, once he'd convinced his deliverers he was not an enemy prisoner, which he managed by abusing them roundly and with such an excellent command of English no doubts remained, he was re-united with his unit. *Then they said the magic words, 'we've had an application for a driver/mechanic from the LRDG. Are you interested?'* [51]

By summer 1942, Churchill had lost patience with Auchinleck, though a great deal of his and his staff's hard-earned theory went into the planning of 2nd El Alamein. 'Strafer' Gott was to have replaced the Auk but died in a plane crash. Alexander now became C-in-C and Bernard Law Montgomery took over leadership of Eighth Army. Rommel knew the sands of time were running out. In late August he attacked again at Alam Halfa and was seen off with loss. The battle scarcely lasted a week. Montgomery did not immediately stage a counter-offensive. Despite the urgings of his critics, he was determined to prepare his forces for a knockout blow. He would not be hurried. The PM had found a general as obstinate and opinionated as himself!

That summer, Hitler had dreamed of a combined drive to the oilfields of the Caucasus as Rommel burst through towards Iran and Iraq. Mussolini had even prepared his white charger for a triumphal entry into Alexandria. Rabid nationalists in the Delta dusted off their German dictionaries. However, the horse stayed in the stables and the phrase books on the shelf. One of the most profound phenomena of the Desert War was the manner in which the Delta was transformed into one vast industrial estate. Its sole output was war supplies.

The British created this flourishing and versatile infrastructure which fed a very large part of the Allies' needs, avoiding a necessity to bring everything in by ship. Rommel had no such comparable resource. For fuel and materiel he was dependent on his Italian allies. These tried and failed to supply him. Enigma decrypts provided Allied planes and warships with dates and coordinates. A vast tonnage of Axis shipping went to the bottom of the Mediterranean.

In the opening stages of the Desert War, the British suffered badly from material deficiencies. Their two-pounder ant-tank gun, whilst a clever and handy weapon, was largely ineffective. Most British tanks carried this same two-pounder which afforded very limited firepower at best. German armour was faster, better armed and considerably more reliable.

Lumbering Matildas, fickle Crusaders and even the nimble Honey (Stuart) sallied forth like medieval knights 'balaklavering' onto screens of lethal 88mm Axis flak guns, drawn into one-sided melees. By mid 1942, however, the balance had begun to shift. Allied forces now had the vastly improved six-pounder anti-tank gun. New tanks, US Grants and latterly Shermans, achieved parity with the Axis workhorse the Mark IV Panzer. Progressively, the Desert Air Force (RAF) eroded Axis supremacy and achieved near hegemony in Saharan skies.[52]

The Desert presented other opportunities. Britain's imperial dominance had been built upon a powerful navy able to place land forces pretty much at any spot on the globe. This led to an essentially peripheral strategy, avoiding costly continental confrontations between mass armies and striking at the enemy's soft underbelly. Britain had done very well indeed from the Seven Years War (1756–1763) when surgical military strokes delivered at key points, such as the taking of Quebec in 1759, bled France white whilst boosting Britain. The defeat of Napoleon in 1815 had ended any dreams of French hegemony in Europe. Wellington's great victory ushered in a century of British imperial growth with increasing if ultimately unaffordable splendour.

On 1st July 1916, British army corps attacked along the eighteen mile front of what would become the battle of the Somme and, on that terrible day suffered nearly sixty thousand casualties. The Great War left little room for swashbuckling, amidst a grim, relentless, sapping battle of attrition that left all the combatant nations prostrate. Britain, for the first time committed mass armies, and victory in 1918 was entirely pyrrhic.

The war, for all the horrors of the Western and other fronts, was not completely devoid of derring-do, however. T.E. Lawrence had shown the potential offered by well led indigenous guerrilla forces striking at the conventional enemy's supply and communications. For the first time since then in an interstate war, the Desert offered opportunities for that type of behind the lines buccaneering action in which the Long Range Desert Group ('LRDG') would come to excel.

Notes

1 Crichton-Stewart, M., *G Patrol* (London 1958) p. 19.
2 Ibid. p. 31.
3 Warner, P., *Alamein, Recollections of the Heroes* (London, 1979), p. 39.
4 Crawford, R.J., *I Was an Eighth Army Soldier* (London, 1944), p. 21.
5 The trigh had previously only been trodden by human and camel traffic.
6 Crawford, p. 21.
7 Possibly a Norse invention.
8 Crawford, p. 21.
9 Ralph Algar Bagnold (1896–1990) a noted desert explorer in the 1930s, he later founded LRDG.
10 Patrick Andrew Clayton (d.1962) another inter-war desert surveyor, served with Bagnold in LRDG.
11 Count Lazlo Almasy (1895–1951), real life version of the fictional character immortalised in *The English Patient* whose life was, if anything, more colourful.
12 From de Manny, E., 'Silver Fern Leaf up the Blue' in *Return to the Oasis* (1980).
13 Lucas, J., *War in the Desert* (London, 1982), p.9.
14 Crawford, p. 86.
15 Sangar – from the Northwest Frontier denoting any small temporary fortification made up of stone and perhaps sandbagged walls.
16 Lucas, p. 74.
17 Ibid. p. 74.
18 AL63 – anti-louse powder.
19 Crawford, p. 20.
20 Ibid.
21 Ibid., pp. 19–21.
22 Ibid.
23 Strawson, J., *The Battle for North Africa* (London, 1969), p. 8.
24 Crawford, p. 27.
25 Literally 'war without hate'.
26 Johann Theodor von Ravenstein, 1889–1962, post war he became director of traffic for Duisburg.
27 Strawson, p. 10.
28 Warner, p. 30.
29 Alan McRae Moorehead (1910–1983), Australian born war correspondent and latterly, historian, quoted in Warner, p. 30.

30 Hermione, Countess of Ranfurly (1913–2001), her wartime diaries were published as *To War with Whittaker* (London, 1994), p. 135.
31 *Crusader*, issue no 57, May 31st 1943.
32 Quoted in Simpson, R., *Operation Mercury, the Battle for Crete* (London, 1981), p. 22.
33 The Germans found it easier to blame failure on Italian incompetence than face the possibility that the British might have cracked Enigma.
34 The 10th Air Corps, specialising in coastal operations.
35 ANZAC doggerel.
36 'Aerial Envelopment' was the strategic notion that an enemy held island in this case could be taken entirely by means of air assault. In the circumstances this proved deeply flawed and virtually ended Student's career.
37 Playfair, Major-General I.S.O., *Official History, UK Military Series, Campaigns: The Mediterranean and Middle East* (London 1962–1966), vol. 3, p. 152.
38 Heinrich Alfred Brauchitsch (1881–1948), Field-Marshal and army commander (*Oberbefehlshaber des Heeres*) in the early stages of the war, relieved after the failure of Barbarossa.
39 Franz Halder (1884–1972) was Chief of the Army General Staff from 1938 to September 1942.
40 General Italo Gariboldi (1879–1970) replaced Marshal Graziani but was later removed due to his poor relationship with Rommel.
41 Parkinson, R., *The War in the Desert* (London, 1976), p. 40.
42 Crawford, p. 34.
43 The Defence Academy, Shrivenham, TRDC 13711.
44 Timpson, A. & A. Gibson-Watt, *In Rommel's Backyard* (Pen & Sword, Barnsley 2000), p. 6.
45 Ibid.
46 Ibid., p. 7.
47 Morgan, M., *Sting of the Scorpion* (Sutton, Stroud 2000), p. 75.
48 Ibid.
49 Ibid., p. 74.
50 Ibid., p. 73.
51 Ibid.
52 The Defence Academy, Shrivenham, TRDC 02954, 05407, 05408, 05889.

CHAPTER 2
Piracy on the High Desert, 1940

> Somehow one feels unfettered by any of the harsh, restricting influences of human existence as we live it these days. There are no buildings, no roads, no street lights, no artificial or even natural noise, no hustle and bustle, no need for anyone to shout or to have money or to pretend about anything: those human beings who are with you are probably fairly well known to you, and are there for the same reason you are – they know the dangers and delights of solitude just the same as you do, and they will react to the unblemished and staggering loveliness of a huge desert sky, deep blue by day and of a marvellous purple at night, sprinkled haphazardly with hundreds and thousands of stars silently lighting up that great canopy of night-time that drifts down with the close of day.
>
> —David Lloyd Owen

In the central hall of the Imperial War Museum in London, stands a true veteran of the LRDG, a 30 cwt Chevrolet[1], discovered intact in the Libyan Desert in 1980 and presented in its recovered state to the IWM three years later by the LRDG Association. The words 'iconic' and to a lesser extent 'totemic' have been much abused in recent years, to the extent their impact has largely drained away. It would however, be quite right to apply either to this remarkable survivor.

This really is the image of the LRDG; the chariot of myth, stripped and scoured by the harsh wind. It offers a palpable connection to that eclectic group of pioneers who together made up what would now be branded as Special Forces in the Western Desert. 'Heroes' is another much abused expression, applied with such grapeshot effect as to include anyone who does anything praiseworthy from winning the Victoria Cross to rescuing next door's cat. Nonetheless, that or perhaps the term 'Homeric' sums up those who fought Rommel and, as he conceded, punched way above their weight.

Though these Special Forces actions were, in relative terms, mere pinpricks, they did reduce the numbers of Axis aircraft and forced Rommel to divert resources into defending his airfields. Their intelligence gathering was of prime significance. Besides, this was precisely the type of Henty-esque derring-do the Prime Minister adored. Not only Churchill was impressed; soldiers of Eighth Army were not immune to the charisma of these fabled desert warriors:

> Of course, the super-saboteurs were our long range desert patrols. These were the super 'Desert Rats'. Stories were legion about their exploits.... No men were braver or fitter than those in these groups. Occasionally we actually saw them move out into 'the blue', but mostly they were as legendary as Lawrence of Arabia. They stayed out behind enemy lines for months at a time.... They were led by men of unrivalled knowledge of the Desert, and did untold material damage to German supplies, but their main contribution was in boosting our morale and lowering the German morale correspondingly. Whenever news came round of their exploits, our tails went up like anything.[2]

Special Forces were by no means a novel concept, though the vast sweep of the desert provided a perfect, bespoke canvas. One commentator, speaking of a much later conflict, the First Gulf War, echoing General Hackett, referred to Iraq as a 'Special Forces Theme Park'.[3] This observation, outwardly flippant, might be said to have been true of Libya. The British have or are perceived as having a form of mythic attachment to these empty spaces, from Doughty and Burton through T.E. Lawrence, Gertrude Bell, Glubb and Thesiger.

Their enemies did not. In the main, the Italians found the sands distinctly unappealing, whilst the Germans simply got on with it and made the best they could.[4] The comment by Driver Crawford who was writing in 1944, only two years after the events he describes, highlights the less tangible value of Special Forces operations. The fact that the Allies were still taking the fight to the Axis, even when fortunes overall were dire, afforded a much needed boost to morale.

Beginnings

We tend to associate Special Forces operations in the Western Desert very much with the Second World War, but the genesis of these dashing cavaliers of the sands originated a generation earlier during the Great War. In that conflict Italy was an ally but the Senussi Arabs sided with the Turks. A series of border bickerings escalated in late 1915 into a more dangerous incursion into Egypt. Such a highly mobile foe, fighting in his very specialist environment, proved a sore trial to hard-pressed Imperial cavalry, hamstrung by supply constraints and a hostile terrain. Mobility and firepower were provided by motor vehicles, yeomanry patrol groups, driving customised Model T Fords.[5] Active only between 1916 and the following year, the trucks proved highly successful and their crews learnt much about desert travel. They mapped as they went.

Although the need for a constant military presence disappeared, the lure of the sands survived the onset of peace. Organisations such as the Sudan Forest Commission or the Egyptian Desert Survey, together with various archaeological digs provided a platform for those who felt the tug.[6] The Light Car Patrols which, like the exploits of T.E. Lawrence, had offered a dash of chivalric glamour amid the horror of industrialised warfare on the Western Front, attracted a series of intrepid desert explorers. Prominent amongst these was Ralph Bagnold, a major in the Royal Signals. He turned desert travel from a challenging recreation into a navigational science.[7]

Bagnold was aware that the eastern flank of Italian Libya, the dead straight line of the frontier, ran south–north and Mussolini had set up a series of garrison outposts and desert landing strips. To cover these isolated bases, the Italians had created 'Auto-Saharan Companies' (see Appendix 6), mechanized patrols supported by limited air cover. The French too had formed such flying columns, and even before hostilities, as early as May 1939, some form of aggressive action in the event war did break out had been mooted.

This southwest corner of Libya is known as the Fezzan (in Berber, 'Rough Rocks'), an expanse of deep desert. To the north, this region is traversed by the Ash-Shati Valley (*Wadi Al Shatii*) and in the west by the Wadi Irawan. Only these parts, together with reaches of the Tibesti Mountains straddling the Chadian border plus a scattering of remote oases and outposts, are capable of sustaining settled communities. The vast dune seas ("ergs") of the Idehan Ubari and the Idehan Murzuq cover much of the remaining ground.

This string of isolated Italian posts snaked south through Jalo and Kufra to Uweinat, some six hundred miles inland. Here was real *Beau Geste* country. The closest garrisons of Mussolini's ramshackle empire of Africa were over a thousand miles away over the great swathe of the Sudan. The narrow umbilical of a single track linked these far-flung bases.

A random accident at sea meant Ralph Bagnold fetched up in Alexandria and, during the hiatus, went off to visit his many friends in Cairo.

> Although most of us were young army officers, not one of us in the 1920s dreamed for a moment that war would ever come to the vast, waterless and lifeless Libyan Desert. We simply enjoyed the excitement of pioneering into the unknown. But the Second World War was declared almost as soon as the physics book ['*The Physics of Blown Sand and Desert Dunes*'] was finished.... Now, as a reservist, I was recalled to the Army in the autumn of 1939 and posted to East Africa. It was by the pure accident of a convoy collision in the Mediterranean that I was landed at Port Said to await another troop ship.[8]

The diversion to Cairo happily resulted in Bagnold being re-assigned to Egypt. For a long while HQ British Troops in Egypt ("BTE") had been focused purely on internal security. The threat, fast becoming a reality, of external invasion had not featured in pre-war planning. HQ in Cairo did not seem overly keen to get involved in the hot arid wastes, so the long frontier with Libya was effectively wide open. Those pioneering light-car patrols of 1916 had since been consigned to the tactical waste-basket and few current British military vehicles were suitable for a mechanised revival.

Bagnold initially struggled in vain against such ingrained languor. He penned a skeleton argument for a revival but was brusquely turned down ... *even the idea of driving out into the desert seemed to appal them as impossible, insane or at least reckless.*[9] Only the arrival of General

Archibald Wavell as C-in-C Middle East Forces and the subsequent side-lining of BTE created a window – that and the clear implications of the forces Italy was building up in Libya. The indefatigable Major rescued his earlier memo and, with some hasty additions, arranged for it to be laid on the great man's desk… *I was sent for within an hour.* Things had changed.

Wavell was ready to listen and Bagnold outlined the risks of a potential enemy raid on Aswan coming out of Uweinat. The distance was no greater than five hundred miles and he himself had covered this in only a day and a half. The potential for damage was enormous, and in their Major Lorenzini (an enterprising officer Bagnold had encountered during his desert explorations), the Italians possessed a capable leader who had openly boasted he could achieve just this. As a counter, the English Major proposed raising a small, specially equipped band of volunteers who would have the capability to cross 1,500 miles of ground without re-supply. Bagnold knew the desert like his own back-garden. For him and men like him it held no terrors. The key requirements for the Long Range Patrol ("LRP" as it was first known), were quite straightforward:

- Ability to make the 130-mile crossing of the dune barrier of the Sand Sea.
- Sufficient firepower to deal with enemy convoys and their escorts.
- A reasonable amount of AA Defence.
- Adequate W/T communications between detachments of the force and with Cairo at least once a day.
- Low, inconspicuous vehicles with good camouflage which could be easily concealed from aircraft.
- Leaders with experience of the desert country; and navigators trained in dead reckoning by compass and speedometer, and in astronomical position finding.
- Steady and self-reliant personnel.

It was also decided that the organisation must be such as to provide two independent patrols to work the 'police trap' method of ambushing convoys on a road, with a third party in identical vehicles to provide immediate reinforcement of men, trucks and technical equipment. Each of these three parties was organised in four troops. The establishment decided on comprised:

- HQ., OC., Adj., QM., a
- Two fighting patrols: each including a major (or captain) intelligence officer, 1 subaltern and 23 Ors.
- 'A' Echelon Supply Party of 2 subalterns, 1 MO, and 19 ORs.
- 'B' Echelon Supply Party of 2 subalterns, 1 MO and 19 Ors.

> The two patrols and 'A' echelon supply party had each ten Lewis guns, four Boys AT Rifles, one 37 mm Bofors gun (at that time Bren guns were not available in Egypt; and the transport in each case consisted of ten 30-cwt trucks and one 15-cwt pilot car.[10]

The new unit's primary function would be to carry out deep reconnaissance and intelligence gathering. Wavell then asked what would happen if the group discovered little of interest. 'How about some piracy on the high desert?' Bagnold suggested. *At the word piracy the rugged face that had seemed a bit stern suddenly broke into a broad grin. 'Can you be ready in six weeks?' – I said, 'yes'.*[11] Before the end of June 1940, the Major's revised scheme was approved and the basic building blocks assembled.[12]

The Major was next handed a potent talisman: Carte Blanche signed by Wavell himself. This was a magician's wand that cut through all of the normal laborious and highly uncooperative channels. A cadre of able volunteers was not hard to find. Many of Bagnold's pre-war contacts were straining at the leash as soon as the green light was given. Experienced hands such as Bill Kennedy Shaw[13] and Pat Clayton (surveying in Tanganyika), were rescued from mundane assignments and threw themselves into the herculean task with vast enthusiasm.

As Barrie Pitt points out, the mere fact that the Italians appeared supine did not mean they were totally incapable – after all their dominion stretched back two full decades.[14] Key to the Fezzan is the remote Kufra Oasis in south-eastern Cyrenaica. Sacred to the Senussi and fringed on three sides by depressions, Kufra dominates the ancient east-west route over the hostile sands. Jebel 'Uweinat is a bloc of high ground forming a nub on the borders of Egypt, Sudan and Libya. Mussolini's forces had both troops and aircraft there which, in addition to threatening Egypt, gave them a handy balcony for a strike inside Chad, where the administration was potentially pro-Gaullist. As well as for a raid on Aswan, the oasis was well placed for a blow against Wadi Halfa.[15]

It must be stressed that, from the outset, Bagnold's commandos saw their prime role as intelligence gathering rather than offensive action, or 'biffing' the enemy. Across this limitless expanse, knowledge of the enemy's strength and likely intentions was invaluable. To undertake such a vital function, both the right men and the right kit were absolutely essential. Regular soldiers, drawn from the urban sprawl, were not ideal; too rigid, too conformist, too unused to so alien and harsh a battleground. Countrymen and farmers, gamekeepers (and poachers), hunters and marksmen were to be found amongst Kiwis and Rhodesians, from British Yeomanry regiments and even within the august ranks of the Guards.[16]

> Within six weeks we'd got together a volunteer force of New Zealanders. The New Zealand Division had arrived in Egypt but had yet to be supplied with arms and equipment because of shipping losses. So they were at a loose end. Apart from that, I wanted responsible volunteers who knew how to look after and maintain things, rather than the ordinary British Tommy who was apt to be wasteful. They were a marvellous lot of people, mostly sheep farmers who'd had fleets of trucks of their own and were used to looking after them.[17]

Bill Kennedy Shaw had not encountered any Kiwis before this:

> all the knowledge I had of them were my father's words of the last war – that they were the finest troops from the dominions. Closer acquaintance showed that one should always believe one's father.... Most of the first New Zealanders were from the Divisional cavalry – the 'Div. Cav' – farmers or the like in civil life, and with a maturity and independence not found in Britishers' of similar age. Physically their own fine country had made them on the average fitter than us, and they had that inherent superiority which in most of a man's qualities the countryman will always have over the townsman.[18]

These beginnings would become the LRDG, still, until 9th November 1940, the Long Range Patrol ("LRP"). Bill Kennedy Shaw as an English officer, even though highly experienced in the desert, was aware that commanding these independently minded colonials would constitute a significant test of leadership skills. You had to work very hard indeed to earn their respect, and the highest praise you might get would be a grudging *not such a bad sort of bastard after all.*[19]

Kennedy Shaw drew up a balance sheet for life in the LRP, pros and cons: On the credit side there were excellent rations, no chance for boredom, blessed relief from normal army 'bull' and little or no 'mucking about'. Desert soldiers were always very aware of just how much they were in fact 'mucked about'. On the debit side of the balance-sheet, there was that constant stress of behind the lines action, tiredness, frequently to the point of exhaustion, and all the natural hazards of daily life in the desert, including 'cafard' (literally 'cockroach', a condition of apathy and depression brought on by exposure to the sun).[20]

> The creation of a completely unorthodox force in six weeks was quite a feat. And it was great fun. There was an awful lot to do. Everything was new. Clothing and footwear had to be redesigned. Army boots were no good at all because they got filled with sand. So I had sandals made – the Indian North-West Frontier chappali, which was very tough with an open toe so that if sand got into it you could shoot it out with a kick. All we wore was a shirt and shorts and Arab headgear. The advantage of wearing a shemagh or shawl which goes round the head, was that it flaps in the wind and keeps the face cool.

For security reasons, Bagnold cannily decided to avoid putting in a bulk order for new shawls so he simply raided the Palestine Police stores![21]

The Chevy 30-cwt truck was the backstairs child of compromise. Begged or borrowed from local dealers in the Delta or from the Egyptian Army, these were standard commercial vehicles that could be heavily customised for the harsh rigours of desert warfare. Stripped down to bare skeletons, their load carrying capacity beefed up to a couple of tons by additional springs, fitted out for weapons and ammunition, wireless and medical gear, rigs welded on to take heavy and medium machine guns and the ingenious adaptation of the radiator condenser, the Chevy went to war (see Appendix 1). Surveyor's instruments, binoculars and the all essential sun-compasses were cadged or scrounged from any and every source:

> We had this wonderful means of conserving water from the radiator. When the water boiled, instead of it being lost through the overflow pipe, it was blown off into a can on the side of the truck which was half full of water where it

would condense. When the engine cooled it would be sucked back into the radiator again. If everything was right and there were no leaks you could go the whole life of a lorry and never put any more water in after the first filling.[22]

Those Great War and inter-war geographers had produced some highly accurate and detailed maps, but enormous areas were simply blank. Italian cartographers were not well regarded as Bill Kennedy Shaw, newly appointed as Intelligence Officer (he'd been working as curator of the Palestine Museum), observed: *There was no nonsense about the petty details of topography on these* [Italian] *sheets. Many of them were obviously based on air observation...after a few flights over the country the cartographer had roughed in a range of mountains here and a sand sea or two there. The mountains were all as high as became the dignity of Fascist Italy....*[23] In due course the appropriately named Captain Lazarus and his hardy volunteers provided LRDG with a first rate map-making section.

Navigation in the desert is often likened to being upon the ocean, rather a lot of nothingness, unchanging, implacably hostile. Navigation skills would be at an absolute premium (see Appendix 1). Bill Kennedy Shaw divided the desert, in cartographer's terms, into four areas:

- A little well mapped terrain but all within Egypt
- A lot of badly mapped ground and all in Libya
- Poor, very poor and very bad maps, some virtually blank
- No maps at all

He took the rather sneering view that Italian maps of Libya *reflect the Italian national character in its aspects of bombast and self-assurance....* This was translated into Tommy's anonymous doggerel as:

I never see a map but I'm away
On all the journeys that I long to do
Over the mountains marked in grey,
Up all the rivers which are shown in blue,
And into those white spaces where they say.[24]

Discipline in the LRDG was considerably less formal than in regular units. It had to be. These men were independent specialists as well as fighting troops. In the desert everyone had an assigned role, and survival of the group depended upon both self-discipline and innate cohesion. As one volunteer explained it:

> We never had parades or rifle inspections, like we'd been used to in the Army; your common sense told you to keep your gun clean, one day you might want to use the damned thing! No one pulled rank either. When dinner was served at night, the cook would shout, 'grub up!' and you got in the queue. If you were in front of an officer, there was none of this, 'I'm an officer, therefore I go first' business. We were a very democratic unit, and it worked very well.[25]

Campaign life in the Western Desert, especially the exacting role of LRDG, demanded a level of austerity and self-denial that harks back to the warrior monks of the crusades. It isn't hard to see Bagnold, Clayton and the others as natural successors to Hospitaller knights. Water was more precious than gold. Bagnold reflected on the Spartan ethos:

> We had a water ration of three pints in winter and four in summer. It was really enough if one was careful and lived at the bottom of one's spare gallon of water, instead of at the top like most people. Everybody has a spare gallon of water in their bodies. Most people in hot weather want to drink and they over-drink. They perspire freely and waste water which does no good and doesn't cool you at all. But if you keep to the bottom of the spare gallon your perspiration only moistens the skin to provide evaporation and cooling. If you don't sweat so much you don't lose salt. We had no trouble with lack of salt whereas on the coast they did.[26]

The Major recruited one of his former co-explorers, Rupert Harding-Newman, who was already on hand in Cairo, and Newman managed to scrounge the first thirty 30-cwt Chevy trucks (Harding-Newman's military mission to the Egyptian Army was deemed too vital to permit his re-assignment to LRDG). The initial establishment would comprise three patrols, each intended to be fully self-reliant. GHQ's slender stores were pillaged to provide weapons and communications; sandals were preferred to boots and the traditional Arab head-dress adopted. This gave far greater protection against blown sand. They would be encountering a great deal of this.

As noted earlier, New Zealand provided the first batch of zealots. Bagnold had first fancied Australians but the home government would not allow their men to serve outside the regular units, and General Blamey felt his hands were tied.[27] Happily, this did not apply to the Kiwis, and General Freyberg put out a suitably vague call for volunteers. Two officers and 150 men came forward and, providentially these turned up at the same time as the modified trucks were emerging from workshops – *tough, reliant and responsible people with many useful skills.* On the job training was combined with regular forays to Ain Dalla (an ancient stopover on the caravan routes to Siwa), to create a forward operating base ("FOB"). The Kiwis were quick learners.

One of the pioneers of the LRP was Teddy Mitford, a Northumbrian from the colourfully contentious Mitford clan. He'd also explored in the desert pre-war and latterly commanded an armoured brigade:

> It was decided to form a small HQ and three patrols each of two officers and thirty men carried in eleven vehicles, also a small supply section of three large trucks for building forward dumps.... The armament was one Vickers machine-gun per patrol and some Lewis guns, First World War type as seen on television's 'Dad's Army'. I think I was the only one to know anything about the Lewis gun, having been taught its use at Sandhurst twelve years before. My patrol was also given a Polish 37-mm gun with little ammunition and dubious sights. We managed to discard this after our first training run.... Our vehicles had painted on them the 7th Armoured Division red rat to disguise our real purpose. Ralph produced a camouflage pattern of very broad dark and light stripes, different for each truck, which would help in areas of rock and scrub.[28]

Ralph Bagnold was a demon for detail. The Vickers, when used in an anti-aircraft role, tended to jam as rounds slipped out of the canvas belt, so he had an additional section of plate welded onto the belt box carrier, which kept the canvas taut and aligned. One tale concerns Bagnold berating a Kiwi driver that his tyres were not blown up to the correct pressure, which ended with the disgruntled squaddie muttering (polite version), *the trouble with that joker is that he's always right.* In late 1940 when the unit was re-branded as LRDG, three further patrols, Guards, Yeomanry (regular British formations claiming descent from volunteer cavalry) and Rhodesians were to be created.

Good and reliable communications would clearly be vital. Tim Heywood began his war as a Wireless officer with 1st Middlesex

Yeomanry. His father, recalled to the colours and assigned to MI5, based, of all places, in Wormwood Scrubs, attempted to recruit him. He was tempted to join but the War Office had other ideas and he found himself, with his unit, in Palestine at the start of 1940. Nonetheless, his potential value to more clandestine branches had not been forgotten, and he found himself being interviewed by both Bagnold and Bill Kennedy Shaw.

Bagnold didn't waste words and Tim Heywood found himself slightly off guard: *Do you know the Number 11 set? Yes Sir,* his reply. *What is their range?* The young officer proudly announced he'd been able to communicate up to a distance of 120 miles. *That's nothing,* snapped the Major. *I expect you to manage over 1,000 miles.* Lieutenant Heywood had just joined the LRDG. This sudden shift didn't go down well with his colonel who was furious but the divisional commander was more accommodating ... *some thought me mad, others were envious.*[29]

Bill Kennedy Shaw observes, quite rightly, that nobody but Ralph Bagnold could have created LRP/LRDG. To do so required an intimate knowledge both of the desert and of the British Army, both of which have many secret ways! In summer 1940, getting one to fit into the other represented a Sisyphean task. It was particularly helpful that General Wavell was a man of both vision and practicality.

The First Patrols

On 27th July 1940, Pat Clayton came to Cairo. The desert explorer was in his mid-forties and by no means medically A1. He'd been promised a desk job but what Bagnold offered his old friend was no sinecure. Still, he didn't refuse. On 7th August Clayton led the first patrol. *Care had to be taken to leave nothing behind to disclose to the Italians that invasion had begun, so army toilet paper was refused and old Italian newspapers garnered from our lady friends in the censorship to whom was said 'if I told you what it was for, you wouldn't believe me!'* [30]

Both of the trucks and all six Kiwis were borrowed as the recruits were still in training. From Siwa, where he picked up a party from the

Egyptian army, Clayton pushed southwards motoring over the drear expanse of the Great Sand Sea. By 11th August he was through and established a supply point by the two 'Mushroom Hills'. It was here that the Egyptian contingent had to turn back, much to their chagrin – orders forbade them crossing the border. Despite encountering a previously unknown belt of sand-sea, they reached the Jalo-Kufra road without incident. There were no signs of any enemy moves towards either Aswan or Wadi Halfa. By the 16th, Clayton's patrol was safely returned to Siwa Oasis.

> We had, as hoped and intended, not fired a shot or seen the enemy ... but we had proved that LRDG could go and come back to a strict timetable and general Wavell, who sent for Bagnold and me on 20th August, made up his mind then and there to give us his strongest backing ... That was the LRDG's first trip, 1600 miles in 13 days.[31]

Clayton also wanted to have a peek at those Italians based at Uweinat. Using vehicles would be to give the game away, but the searing heat made any reconnaissance on foot virtually impossible. A camel was the obvious natural compromise but, due to the distance, this appeared equally tricky. Clayton then bought a camel, recruited two of his former herdsmen, and manhandled the beast into the back of a truck. This unusual portee method worked. The camel was transported to the sector, used for the job and then bundled back in the lorry, peering out with a fine show of disinterest over the tailgate!

This first foray was a relatively modest affair and yielded no practical gains aside from very useful experience. Supply, the lifeblood of desert raiders, was paramount. A series of major and ancillary dumps were established along all main axes leading south and west from the Delta. One of the most important of these was that at Ain Dalla on the edge of the Sand Sea. When Bill Kennedy Shaw arrived there in his small convoy of 6-tonners, he found the place pretty much as he'd last seen it a decade earlier with Bagnold: *There were the same stunted palms, the same rickety wooden hut where we had stored our spare petrol in 1930, and the same pipe tapping the warm spring water half-way down the slope.*[32] Even their original tyre tracks were still clearly visible.

It wasn't just the sweet water that was welcome. Ain Dalla was the LRPs' back door into Libya. Any patrol motoring south from Cairo could be sure of eyes tracking their every move. Once beyond the ancient, looming bulk of the pyramids and over the shoulder of Gebel Khashab, the raiders disappeared, were swallowed up. Ain Dalla was not just the staging point for crossing into Libya, it was the junction of roads to Kufra and Uweinat, these approaches handily screened by belts of sand sea the Italians considered impenetrable.

These were not offensive operations; enemy territory lay westwards. Mundane as these runs were, they formed a first rate training ground. Large stocks of ammunition, medical supplies, foodstuffs and, above all, petrol, were cached. It was time to move westwards onto enemy ground, over the wide, lunar waste of the Great Sand Sea, so nobly described by Bill Kennedy Shaw: *There is nothing like these sand seas anywhere else in the world. Take an area the size of Ireland and cover it with sand. Go on pouring sand on to it till it is two, three or four hundred feet deep. Then, with a giant's rake score the sand into ridges and valleys running north-north-west and south-south-east, and with the ridges, at their highest, five hundred feet from trough to crest.*[33]

By day this is an inferno, parched, scoured and scorched; when evening falls, as swiftly as a cloak, the dying, iridescent light shows a scene of desolate, unearthly beauty. God had not sculpted the desert to facilitate vehicular traffic. Crossing was a grinding attrition of exertion, sweat and thirst, unendingly harsh on men and vehicles alike.

Ralph Bagnold was, of course, an old hand at this with over a decade of desert travel behind him: *If one was bogged down, the nose of the car would tip right forward, axle deep in the sand. The problem was to get it out. Going round the junk shops in the slums of Cairo we found these heavy metal channels which had originally been used in the First World War for roofing dugouts. They were about five feet long and you could carry one under each arm, just. You scooped the sand away from the back wheels and pushed the channel under the wheel. Directly it gripped the car would be shoved forward and hopefully you'd get out of the soft patch on to harder ground.*[34]

For the LRP to cover those 150 miles from Ain Dalla in the east to Big Cairn (erected by Clayton in 1932), astride the Libyan border in the west, involved two full days of constant purgatory. Once across, a supply line and advanced landing strip could be established and, from this nodal point, patrols could venture forth. Kennedy Shaw, driving those heavy 6-tonner Marmon-Harrington trucks, was kept gainfully employed ferrying fuel and gear across the Great Sand Sea.[35]

The desert was a unique and harsh environment. Yet many who rode out with LRP/LRDG patrols were intensely moved by its qualities, the harsh, primeval purity. Though now largely denuded of humanity, the raiders were constantly reminded that man had once lived here: *Ten thousand years ago the climate was kinder, there was more rain and men lived in what is now desert, hunting ostrich and antelope and keeping milk cattle. Often we found traces of them – paintings and engravings on the rocks and stone implements at their camping places. There must have been many places which we passed through on LRDG journeys where no man had been for five thousand years.*[36]

On 5th September three LRP patrols set out from Cairo, just ahead of the major Italian offensive in the north which would kick-start the desert war. Marshal Graziani didn't advance further that Sidi Barrani, more of a *Sitzkrieg*. There remained the fear he might try and be more adventurous in the south, as Bagnold had originally warned. LRP was tasked to check the lie of the land, ascertain enemy intentions, hopefully netting some prisoners and generally beat up any targets of opportunity that might cross their sights.

Teddy Mitford, with Bill Kennedy Shaw, was to check out a couple of landing strips on the Jalo-Kufra route. They dealt with fuel reserves there before bumping a small Italian convoy a couple of days later. Only two trucks, swiftly cowed by a burst from a Lewis gun, and LRP had its first haul of captives, including a goat! A modest if satisfying encounter, yet this single rattle of fire persuaded the Italians they had to escort their convoys in future, a significant diversion of resources.[37] LRP activity would never open gaping wounds in the enemy's flanks but could create persistent ulcers, draining out precious reserves, taking away from offensive capacity further north.

Neither of the other patrols met any enemy but accomplished much useful intelligence gathering. By the end of the month all three were safely back in Cairo. General Wavell was still ready to be impressed. An important benefit conferred by these early patrols was in myth-busting. Most of the staff in Cairo and most of Middle East Command shunned the deep desert to the same fearful extent as their Axis adversaries. Bagnold was demonstrating that the Allied forces could trump the enemy by learning to operate effectively in all conditions.

To us now this seems an obvious role for Special Forces; however, at the time it was something of an epiphany. *Bagnold's patrols had covered 1,300 miles completely self-contained. They had impressed everyone, and even the most doubtful of their critics had begun to see what possibilities there were if the exposed southern flank – which was thought to be quite impenetrable – could be used with impunity by the LRDG.*[38]

Success brought expansion and the unit was increased in size to two full squadrons, each of three patrols, with a HQ section and a lieutenant-colonelcy for Bagnold. General Freyberg was making increasingly loud noises for the return of his Kiwis though Wavell was able to persuade him to grant an extension while new volunteers, primarily from Rhodesian and British units, were being trained up. Having tested the crust of the Italian defences in the south and detected no appetite for offensive action, LRP could continue to make life uncomfortable for these nervous frontier outposts. The year 1940 had been a very bad one for the Allies but at least, as the autumn drew towards winter, the British were attacking somewhere, if on a very small scale.

The replacement scheme which had received War Office approval on 25th October had provided for six new patrols to be formed, one from each of the Guards, South Rhodesians, Highlanders, Yeomanry, Rifles and Home Counties Regiments. This was rather ambitious at the time as the whole theatre suffered from a chronic lack of both good officers and men. Regiments were understandably loath to part with their bravest and best for what many regarded as a maverick and madcap formation.[39]

Bagnold, again in October, found he had competition from the brilliant if unorthodox Orde Wingate, later famous for the formation of the Chindits. Wingate wanted an all-arms, mechanized raiding force far larger than the LRP, virtually at divisional strength. This was plainly impractical, and Wingate had no real appreciation of the distances and ground involved. Bagnold, who understood both, countered with a watered-down proposal suggesting a gradual build up of all-arms capability. The prevailing shortages of men and materiel and the dearth of desert-worthy vehicles doomed Wingate's scheme. By the time these shortages had been, to a degree at least, overcome, LRP/LRDG had more than proved itself as the ideal solution.[40]

During the last week of October the LRP launched another sortie. The objectives were:

- To harass the enemy by mining the Uweinat-Kufra-Jedabia track.
- To gain intelligence of enemy strength and movement in this area.
- To recover and utilise the two lorries captured earlier (these had been left hidden).[41]

T Patrol, led by Clayton, moved out from Cairo on 23rd October; mine laying its primary function. The raiders passed via Ain Dalla, over the surreal reaches of the Sand Sea to Big Cairn where Clayton levelled an ad hoc airstrip. No. 26 (Bomber Transport) Squadron was detailed to carry out re-supply. Next, they drove towards Jalo, 260 miles northwest, and by 30th October were planting mines along the roadway. On 1st November, after only token resistance, Clayton easily subdued the fort at Aujila whose garrison fled at the first burst. In all, the patrol covered 2,140 miles in 15 days.[42]

T and R patrols with HQ and N troops were equally active. Italian stores together with a Savoia-Machetti S.79 (a three-engine, medium bomber) were destroyed. Though enemy aircraft did make an appearance, no casualties or damage were sustained. These raids were textbook examples of what the LRP had been raised for.

Results were not overly dramatic, as these were pinpricks rather than body blows, but the cumulative effect was telling: enemy communications were disrupted and his transport damaged or destroyed, but the main value was psychological. After so many bruising defeats, the Allies were taking the initiative and getting the better of the enemy. The Italians suffered a consequential slump in morale. Nowhere was too remote to escape the raiders' intention. All movement was fraught. This was not a defeated army, a tottering empire. Britain still had teeth.

The Free French

One obvious potential connection was with the French garrisons in Chad. Not all Frenchmen had been prepared to side with Vichy and there was a clear possibility for joint action and the creation of a viable Free French force. In the course of a busy October, Ralph Bagnold had proposed a plan to occupy Kufra as a springboard for operations even further west. This would disrupt any notions the Italians themselves had of attacking Kano. The Northern Touaregs were their potential allies and by no means averse to a spot of pillaging.

The settlement at Toummo on the borders of French West Africa and the Fezzan, had potential for a westward FOB. The Free French themselves ranging up from Chad could strike at Toummo but the region itself, the Tenere District, was nominally held by Vichy. 'Baggers' proposal was that British forces, the LRP, could operate in partnership with the Free French to disrupt and threaten the Italian outposts and deter them from any offensive action of their own. The British representative in West Africa, the Hon. Francis Rodd, was tasked to broker a meeting at Fort Lamy (in Chad).[43]

Bagnold, never backward at grasping an initiative, travelled to Khartoum of Gordon fame to confer with Douglas Newbold, the British resident there. Newbold knew the provincial governor in Chad, M. Eboue, and felt that he, or at least the younger officers there, could be persuaded, though he could do nothing through official diplomatic channels. These were altogether too sensitive. Bagnold of course was not a diplomat and Newbold just happened to have a plane standing by![44]

Bagnold was not prone to hesitation, and on the 8th November flew to Fort Lamy where he was suddenly struck down by a savage bout of tropical fever. The official purposes of his mission were to contact Colonel Marchand, who commanded the Chadian garrison, and test the water for offensive spirit. Bagnold was to ascertain if the Free French would entertain a formal military mission from GHQ, ME. Crucially, from his own point of view, he was to find out if Marchand was interested in working with the LRP (officially the LRDG from 9th November), in beating up Italian outposts.[45]

He was still laid up in bed as he received a delegation consisting of the governor himself and Lieutenant-Colonel d'Ornano, a *beau sabreur* straight from the pages of P.C. Wren. Ill as he was, Bagnold sensed this was a significant moment: *I told him* [d'Ornano] *frankly exactly what I wanted – petrol, rations and water to be carried by camel through the Tibesti mountains to a point near the Libyan frontier, where we would rendezvous with them.... Then d'Ornano turned to the Governor and said 'This is it. You must decide now – now', he said, thumping the table. 'I can't hold my officers much longer....*[46]

This was an historic moment, 'game on' in the modern sense. The French would help, on the one condition that d'Ornano himself, a junior officer and NCO went in with the British raiders and the Free French flag flew alongside. Bagnold had no hesitation in accepting. A formal agreement was concluded and General de Gaulle, hearing of the initiative, had little choice but to agree, though he did send Major (later General) Philippe Leclerc de Hauteclocque (nom de guerre "Leclerc") to assume overall command. Bagnold had already identified the Italian outpost at Murzuk as an objective. Too remote and inaccessible for LRDG from its base in Cairo but, with aid from Chad, the garrison there was now a prime target.

Colonel Marchand was equally enthusiastic. The Free French were itching to have a crack at the enemy, who they generally despised as Hitler's jackals. Moreover, bold, offensive action could, at this juncture, have a marked effect on waverers further west who might otherwise incline towards Vichy and the sour path of collaboration. These proud colonial warriors had seen their country crushed and humiliated, and the unthinkable – German jackboots resounding down the Champs-Elysees, and the historic railway carriage at Compiegne used to snort Hitler's triumph, then hauled away to Germany as booty. Time was ripe for *la revanche.*

Happily, the formidable General Freyberg, a man easily as brave as any lion and much decorated in the Great War who, one suspects, would have heartily approved of the LRDG, was turning a blind eye to the prolonged absence of his soldiers. New volunteers from the 3rd Coldstream and 2nd Scots Guards (collectively known as 'G' – for Guards Patrol) were forming. Their training was to be very much 'on the job' as, with Pat Clayton and his Kiwis, they left just after Christmas, on 27th December, for the planned raid on Murzuk.

G Patrol was commanded by Michael Crichton-Stuart with Martin Gibbs, a Coldstreamer, as 2 I/C. Bill Kennedy Shaw would be their navigator over the vast, bare distance they had to travel. In total, the force mustered 76 soldiers in 23 trucks.[47] The attack on Murzuk was more than a raid. It would represent the first active cooperation between Western Desert Force and the Free French. Success could not only persuade waverers in Niger to throw in with the Allies, it would show the Italians conclusively that nowhere in the Fezzan was immune.

Just beyond Cairo, they picked up the Senussi Liaison Officer with their guide, Sheikh 'Abd el Galil Seir en Nasr, a legendary warrior with a long history of fighting the Italians. His was still a name to conjure with, *a big man, sixty years or more which reminded me of pictures in the 'Seven Pillars of Wisdom' and with one claw-like hand shot to pieces in some desert battle.*[48]

Even while action in the Fezzan was being planned, the LRDG, in the shape of R Patrol, led by Captain Steele, was prowling in the northern sector with Teddy Mitford, commanding W Patrol, operating further south towards Uweinat. The indispensible 'B' echelon trucks were busy building up supplies at the Ain Dalla dump. These were classic deep reconnaissance forays, livened by mine-laying. Mitford's patrol was bombed and strafed on 29th November. Despite being stonked with over 300 small bombs, dispersion and evasion tactics proved highly successful. Undeterred, on 1st December, the patrol attacked Ain Dua.

After a lively exchange of fire the small Italian garrison was hounded from its positions and fled to higher ground. Mitford himself went to ground when enemy planes appeared, but once they'd passed, laid into the survivors, blasting from both flanks. Though some enemy were killed, they could not be dislodged and the raiders made off in the gathering dusk.[49] LRDG had suffered no casualties and the patrol returned safely to Cairo on 6th December.

By early January the hounds were drawing close on the fleeing Italian armies. In the north, General O'Connor's counter-offensive was achieving prodigies, Bardia had fallen. By the time the LRDG and Free French forces made their approach to contact, the British were some 1,500 miles south of their base! T and G Patrols had moved out from Cairo on 27th December, motoring through Ain Dalla and north of Taizerbo. Clayton had his RV with the Free French at Kayugi. He found them to be as good as their word, supplies having being brought up by camel. Colonel d'Ornano was accompanied by Captain Jacques Massu, who would fight throughout the Second World War, reach the rank of general and earn some notoriety in Algeria. The Free French party numbered ten in all.

By this time the LRDG had already covered 1,333 miles and, in the course of its marches had only seen three people, all natives with their camels and not the least bit interested. Whilst a lonely statistic, this at least suggested very strongly the enemy was unaware of their presence.[50] On 11th January in the early afternoon Clayton's force motored into Murzuk. All was calm, the enemy blissfully unaware. The local postmaster, complete with mailbag, was nabbed from his round and pressed into unwilling service as a guide. In the centre of the settlement the imposing fort, a true colonial relic, could not be successfully attacked without heavy weapons.

G patrol kept the garrison occupied with harassing fire whilst the rest had a crack at the airfield. A considerable amount of damage was inflicted and one of the fort's towers set alight, though an LRDG trooper, Sergeant C.D. Hewson, was killed and three more wounded in the exchange of fire. The Italian commander and his wife, who'd been out to lunch, came barrelling back in his staff car and ran into a hail of fire. Both were killed.[51]

At the airfield the Kiwis shot up three light bombers and torched their hanger. The score or so Italians did put up some resistance and Clayton's truck got stuck in a firefight with a resolute machine gun post. His Vickers jammed at the most embarrassing moment and gallant d'Ornano was killed. He did not live to witness the full success of the raid as the airfield defenders capitulated soon after.

There was no point in lingering. Enemy aircraft could soon be on the prowl from their nearest base at Hon, some 250 miles away. Aside from the fort, all of the enemy facilities at Murzuk were destroyed and the raiders withdrew. Ten Italian soldiers were left dead with another fifteen wounded and two useful prisoners. The rest who'd surrendered were released as there was no transport available. They were fortunate as the LRDG's Free French allies were all for putting them more permanently out of action![52] The victory, in the vast scale of the desert pendulum, was a small one, but it sent a clear message both to those wavering over the attraction of de Gaulle and to the Italians. Literally, nowhere was safe.

After the adrenalin rush of action, the burial of the two dead would be sobering, as was the thought they were still very far from safety with the imminent prospect of retaliation coming out of the blue desert skies. Despite this, Clayton wasn't done. Heading south towards the Chadian border, he resolved to mop up any small outposts, and the first of these was the garrison at Traghen, some thirty miles south of Murzuk.

On 12th January, just outside the settlement, a pair of camel-mounted Libyan policemen were captured. The place had no wireless communications and a threat of imminent destruction persuaded the few carabinieri there to surrender without a shot, though not without noise and some pomp: *With banners flying and drums beating, the Mudir [Mayor] and his elders were coming out to surrender the village in traditional Fezzan manner....*[53]

The next target was Umm el Araneb, a further twenty miles or so northeast. This time the defenders were prepared and the fort looked substantial. The unfortunate Murzuk postman, still gainfully employed as a go-between, came pelting back after being fired on. Other tempting targets were about but so was the *Regia Aeronautica.* Happily, their aim was no better than their army's, but Clayton wisely took the hint and headed back towards Chad. By now Leclerc was installed at Fort Lamy, and he was an energetic, aggressive commander. Bagnold was already liaising with him, and Kufra was very much on their joint agenda. Clayton's two patrols would act as the vanguard for a Free French column, and LRDG left Faya on 26th January.

Leclerc also moved out of Faya the same day but his forces had little experience of motorised desert warfare and suffered accordingly. Clayton left Ounianga on the 29th, advancing to Sarra where he found the enemy had slighted and blocked the well. They pushed on to Bishara two days later and found the same had been done there.

It was now that their enviable run of good luck ended abruptly.[54]

Escape and Evasion

By 11.30 hours on 31st January, Clayton's Patrol (G Patrol being left in reserve), had got as far as Gebel Sherif, sixty miles or so short of their intended target. Enemy aircraft had been prowling and, realising he'd been spotted, Clayton slid his eleven trucks into a defensive laager amongst rocks. The planes hadn't given up and the patrol was soon contacted by ground forces. From 14.00 the LRDG was under sustained and heavy fire from 20 mm Bredas'. Clayton attempted to deploy and take the fight to them but was bounced by more enemy planes. One man had already been lost and Clayton himself was wounded and captured. This was a grievous blow which the Italian Press modestly described as a *masterstroke.*[55] For once they weren't far off the mark. The luckless postman of Murzuk was another fatality. There's an interesting anecdotal postscript to the history of this fight related in chapter ten.

Most of the survivors made it back to rejoin G Patrol, and Leclerc realised he's have to reshape his plans for the assault on Kufra. The bulk of the LRDG component returned to Cairo, arriving on 9th February 1941. They had covered a total of 4,500 miles since late December! Four men missing from the fight at Gebel Sharif were unaccounted for: Trooper Moore, Guardsmen Easton and Winchester, together with fitter Alf Tighe[56] from the ROAC. These four had, in fact, suffered neither death nor capture.

Having dodged the Italians, who had, happily, shown little inclination to search the ground, abandoning even their own dead, the four escapees decided they would follow the LRDG vehicle tracks south till they were, hopefully, rescued. Both Moore and Easton had minor but troubling wounds, they had very little water and no food. On 1st February they began their lonely trek.

An Italian prisoner they still had with them wandered off and was eventually picked up by his own side. For three hard, relentless days they slogged south. Tighe weakened and had to be left lagging behind (though he was able to continue at a much slower pace). The others gave him the last of their precious water. After an exhausting tab of 135 miles, half-blinded by a sandstorm, they reached the original jumping-off point of Sarra. The place was abandoned and thoroughly wrecked by the enemy. There was no sustenance whatsoever. Tighe stumbled in, utterly exhausted, the next day but after the others had left. Providentially, he was rescued by a French patrol that immediately set off after the other survivors.

Easton too was now struggling and had fallen behind the other two. A French aircraft spotted Moore and Winchester and attempted to drop food and water. The bag burst on landing, they barely managed a mouthful each. On 10th February, the patrol from Sarra found Easton who had, even in his terrible state, managed a further 55 miles. Despite frantic efforts the wounded man, dehydrated and exhausted, nearly emaciated, could not be saved. Barely moments from death, when the French gave him some hot, sweet tea, he could still quip *I like my tea without sugar.*[57]

Ten miles on they found Winchester, nearly delirious but still on his feet. Another ten and they found Moore, some 210 miles from the ambush site and with no water for another 80 miles. Still going strongly, he was perfectly convinced he *could* have reached the water. These men embodied the very spirit of the LRDG, and their sublime courage and resourcefulness were beacons in a very dark hour. The Axis might be advancing but the fight was far from over.

Leclerc then moved on Kufra. The Italian motorised formations used their vehicles only to speed their withdrawal and, on 1st March the fort there surrendered. Bill Kennedy Shaw relayed the grandiose message sent out from the commander before striking his colours, a typical piece of overblown operatic bravura. As he pithily observed, *positions are not held on such stuff as this.*

Notes

1 This can be viewed on YouTube.
2 Crawford, R.J., *I was an Eighth Army Soldier* (London, 1944), p. 52.
3 Associated Press, 3rd March 1991–http://articles.baltimoresun.com/1991-03-03/ne retrieved 24th August, 2012.
4 An exception was Count Friedrich Gerhard Rohlfs (1831–1896) and of course Almasy (see Appendix 6).
5 Pitt, B., *The Crucible of War–Western Desert 1941* (London, 1980), p. 223.
6 Ibid.
7 Ibid., p. 224.
8 Morgan, p.3.
9 Ibid., p. 4.
10 Wynter, Brigadier H.W., *The History of the Long Range Desert Group June 1940–March 1943* (National Archives, CAB 44/151, 2008 edition), p. 15.
11 Morgan, p. 5.
12 Pitt, p. 224.
13 Major William Boyd Kennedy Shaw (1901–1979).
14 Pitt, p. 225.
15 Pitt, p. 225.
16 Ibid., p. 224.
17 Ibid., p. 225.
18 Kennedy Shaw, W.B., *The Long Range Desert Group* (Greenhill Press, London, 1945), p. 19.
19 Kennedy Shaw, p. 20.

20 Ibid., p. 21.
21 Pitt, p. 226.
22 Quoted in Gilbert, (ed.) *The Imperial War Museum Book of the Desert War 1940–942* (London, 1992), p. 192.
23 Quoted in Pitt., p. 227.
24 Kennedy Shaw, p. 24.
25 IWM, p. 191.
26 Ibid., p. 192.
27 O.H., Volume One, p. 295.
28 Morgan, pp. 9–10.
29 Ibid., pp. 13–14.
30 Ibid., p. 15.
31 Ibid.
32 Kennedy Shaw, p. 35.
33 Quoted in Pitt, p. 229.
34 IWM, p. 193.
35 Lloyd Owen, Major-General D., *The Long Range Desert Group–Providence their Guide* (Pen & Sword, Barnsley 2000), p. 27.
36 Kennedy Shaw, p. 32.
37 Lloyd Owen, p. 27.
38 Ibid., p. 28.
39 Wynter, p. 24.
40 Ibid., p. 25.
41 Ibid., p. 26.
42 Ibid., p. 27.
43 Ibid., p. 31.
44 Lloyd Owen, p. 29.
45 Wynter, p. 31.
46 Bagnold quoted in Lloyd Owen, p. 31.
47 Lloyd Owen, p. 30.
48 Kennedy Shaw, p. 55.
49 Wynter, pp. 34–35.
50 Ibid., p. 38.
51 Lloyd Owen, p. 31.
52 Ibid., p. 30.
53 Ibid., p. 33.
54 Wynter, p. 40.
55 Lloyd Owen, p. 36.
56 Tighe was awarded the MM before being killed in action in Greece in 1944.
57 Lloyd Owen, p. 36.

CHAPTER 3
A Year of Dangerous Living, 1941

Streams of blood must run over the earth,
The ground trembles, the world shakes;
Where over de-composing, shot-up heaps
The last men run, hounded by fear
Fire mercilessly strikes the field.
There's drumming and drumming, rumbling and crashing!
The enemy has now got to know us!
For we have provoked this hell,
In which the victor of every battle –
Death – reaps his grim harvest.

—*Gefreiter*, Hanns Pfeuffer

After sixteen years in the Middle East I was beginning to think that I knew something about heat. I had some experience – five years in the Sudan, the Red Sea in the hot weather; a summer at Beisan in the Jordan Valley 300 feet below sea level; Cairo to Khartoum by train in June – all these had qualified me to lie against anyone about the temperatures I had known. But I had not before this met a Libyan 'qibli'.[1]

Raids on Rommel

By any standards the LRDG was a remarkable and utterly professional fighting force, a perfect complement to regular operations. Yet Bagnold and his buccaneers were not completely alone. A slew of other units jostled for a place in the unconventional underbelly of desert warfare.

First amongst these were the commandos. Colonel Robert ('Bob') Laycock commanded Nos. 8 & 11 Commando. Laycock was born into a military family and then commissioned into the Horse Guards. His first wartime appointment was responsibility for chemical warfare during the battle for France, an inauspicious beginning. David Niven[2] later claimed to have been the facilitator for Laycock's transformation to commando.

The Middle East Commandos were what might most kindly be described as a mixed bunch. Some had fought in the Spanish Civil War on the losing Republican side and so had a strong personal motive for fighting Fascism. Others volunteered for less idealistic reasons as Terence Frost, a yeomanry trooper who joined because he wanted some real fighting, found out: *I didn't know that the volunteers from the regulars hadn't actually volunteered at all. They had been kicked out for getting drunk or socking the sergeant-major, and I had the shock of my life when I found this out. I was amongst a real shower of tough blokes…*[3]

On the night of 19th/20th April 1941, the commandos mounted an amphibious raid on the Axis port of Bardia. The assault was a partial success as considerable damage was inflicted on German stores and materiel. Nonetheless, not all the commandos could be got off by the single landing craft which pitched up to extract them, and the rest were left on the beach. Inevitably they were forced to surrender. The prisoners were inspected by the Desert Fox himself who pronounced them *very foolish but very brave.*[4] Many in the Allied camp would have agreed wholeheartedly with this pithy analysis.

After the Bardia raid, Laycock's unit ('Layforce') was dispatched to Crete as a strategic reserve during the Axis invasion of the island. This was hardly a Special Forces role. Wavell had thrown in the commandos largely because there was simply no one else. By this time the fight was virtually lost and Layforce's job was simply to provide a rearguard as the Allies withdrew over the bare spine of the high mountains towards the south coast. Evelyn Waugh was Laycock's aide-de-camp and along with his CO was one of the last to be lifted from the beach at Sphakia. This conventional action cost the unit some 600 casualties, around 75 per cent of its fighting strength. Many commandos, fearing capture, wisely dumped their array of fighting knives and knuckle dusters![5]

From the Boer War onwards the Lovat Scouts[6] had formed the kernel of Special Forces within the British Army. Brigadier Simon Fraser, 15th Lord Lovat, was one of the war's most distinguished commando officers. His first cousin was David Stirling of the Scots Guards, initially attached to Layforce. The immensely tall and charismatic Guards officer was the very stuff of Hollywood derring-do. He attempted a self-taught course of parachute training which very nearly brought his career to an end, resulting in two months hospitalisation.[7] His convalescence, enthusiasm undimmed, was spent in preparing ideas for a parachute force, descending from the skies upon unsuspecting enemy targets. Neil Ritchie, Auchinleck's Deputy Chief of Staff and a long-term friend, proved receptive.

Stirling's plan was simple. Operations should be undertaken by a mere handful of specialists rather than company-sized or larger raiding parties. The Scot was deeply unconventional and wary of the Army's byzantine and frequently obstructive ways. He reported only to the Commander-in-Chief and his fledgling force was designated as 'L' Detachment, Special Service Brigade. Latterly the Special Air Service (SAS), this was indeed the birth of a legend.

Gainful employment was soon forthcoming. As a curtain raiser to 'Crusader' two particularly daring raids were conceived. In the first, Lieutenant-Colonel Geoffrey Keyes, at 24 the youngest officer to hold so senior a rank, would lead No. 11 Commando in an attack on the former Italian prefecture at Beda Littoria. This lay 250 miles behind enemy lines and was believed to by Rommel's HQ. 'Jock' Haselden,[8] an experienced desert hand, had been dropped in by parachute to confirm that the Fox was actually in his lair. He was convinced this was indeed the place and that he had sighted Rommel himself.[9]

On the night of 13th November, Keyes led a force of raiders whose intention, put quite simply, was to kill or capture the Desert Fox. The rather oddly branded Operation *Flipper* got off to a bad start and fared worse. Keyes was fatally wounded in the initial stages of the assault.[10] Aside from nearly the entire British force then being scattered or captured, casualties on both sides were light, but there was no sign of Rommel. In fact he wasn't even in the theatre at that point. Haselden had indeed sighted him but only on a routine visit; his actual headquarters was far nearer the front line.

Stirling led the second attack. His objectives were the two Axis airfields at Timini and Gazala. Bad weather, which had already contributed to Keyes' failure, scattered the drop. One planeload actually came down onto an enemy runway and all aboard were captured. Another crew were pitched out over the wastes of the Great Sand Sea and none survived. Stirling's group lost most of their kit including vital explosives and detonators. When survivors limped back to the RV with LRDG, only 21 out of 54 had made it.[11] The raid was a costly fiasco but Stirling was undeterred. He did, however, decide that his commandos, following the example set by LRDG, would now travel by vehicle.

By the summer of 1942 the SAS had some 15 customised jeeps in action in North Africa. The ubiquitous term 'jeep' may have originated with the designation 'GP' for General Purpose. These light but tough, durable 4WD vehicles were primarily manufactured by Willys and Ford, and several hundred thousand were produced during the course of the war. SAS jeeps were stripped, like their Chevy predecessors, of all superfluous features including the windscreen, most of the radiator grille bars and even sometimes the front bumper to increase effective load carrying capacity. Condensers, following LRDG precedent, were fitted, and the durable jeep could cart an impressive payload of ammunition, kit, fuel and supplies.

They were ideal, fast moving gun platforms, bristling with a formidable array of Browning and Vickers K machine guns. The latter were stripped from aircraft, generally mounted in pairs. Their combined firepower was phenomenal, a cyclic rate of nearly five thousand rounds per minute. A potent mix of ball, armour-piercing and tracer could devastate lines of parked enemy planes – as many as a dozen were destroyed in a single-five minute raid.

It was against vulnerable enemy aerodromes that the SAS proved its worth, not just in the total of enemy aircraft destroyed (this amounted to some 400 by November 1942), but because of these sudden strikes the Axis were obliged to allocate more and more troops to purely defensive roles. This is perhaps the most enduring image of SAS/LRDG – a patrol of heavily armed jeeps, crewed by bearded, piratical commandos, storming along lines of parked Axis aircraft. Engines racing and jeeps spewing fire, a volcano of noise and fury, planes shuddering and sagging, a brief exultant burst of satisfying destruction, and the raiders roar off into the desert night.

One of the leading lights in these operations was Robert Blair 'Paddy' Mayne,[12] a pre-war sportsman of renown, brave to the point of foolhardiness, and often in trouble as a result of drunken brawling. When Stirling recruited him he was in the guardhouse after striking Geoffrey Keyes, his CO! Despite his instability and propensity for binge-fuelled violence, Mayne was formidable. His leadership of a jeep-mounted raid on Tamet airfield on the night of 14th December 1941 did much to re-establish the unit's credibility after the initial fiasco, and at a time when disapproving regulars would have been happy to see the SAS fold. Mayne was to claim he'd personally destroyed nearly a quarter of the regiment's total score.

Success earned Stirling promotion to major and inspired a stream of recruits. Inevitably, such an unorthodox unit attracted unorthodox soldiers, including Free French and members of the Greek Sacred Squadron,[13] all united by a hatred of the Axis and a burning desire to make an impact. From an inauspicious beginning, Stirling built a highly professional force, able to complement the LRDG with whom it often worked in tandem. Captain Pleydell, the unit's MO, commented on this very unconventional brand of warfare:

> Although life was free and easy in the mess, discipline was required for exercises and operations. On the operations in which I was involved, our patrol would make long detours south of the battle line and then loop up north to within striking distance of an airfield or similar target. Camouflage had to be expert, so that when you hid up you couldn't be detected – even at close distance, slow flying enemy aircraft could follow our tracks to our hiding places and they represented a real threat. It was a hit-and-run, hide-and-seek type of war.[14]

One of the more colourful characters in the Allied order of battle was Vladimir Peniakoff. 'Popski', as he was nicknamed, was an émigré who had fought for the French in the previous war and then worked in Egypt as a civilian. He managed to secure a British commission and began his clandestine career by stirring up anti-Italian sentiment amongst Libyan Arabs. Teaming up with LRDG he graduated to demolition and with some success: one of his raids destroyed 100,000 gallons of enemy fuel. However, none of these ad hoc Special Forces units was more remarkable or unlikely that the Special Interrogation Group, a highly unorthodox crew, drawn mainly from German-speaking Jews recruited in Palestine.[15]

Patrol Life

> When the dawn comes, and the stars have all gone away, there is something sharp and exhilarating about the smell in the air. It is fresh and clean and tantalisingly different to the atmosphere which will pervade the day once the sun has come up over the distant horizon. Then there will be no escape from its merciless and desiccating heat, which drains you of energy and leaves you burned and incapable of any prolonged activity.[16]

Members of LRDG would never have won any commendations for spit and polish; most had joined to escape just such subservience to 'bull'. On a patrol, the men might go without washing or shaving for days, burnt by the relentless, omnipresent sun, scoured by harsh corrosive winds, coated in cloying layers of dust thrown up by the vehicles. Patrols were a team effort; officers, NCOs and men were all equally important cogs in a very small and tight machine. Each depended on the other; informality was a badge of efficiency, not slackness. David Lloyd Owen came close to the dreaded RTU on his first patrol: *Guy* [Prendergast] *was never the sort of person to beat about the bush and he made it quite clear that Eric* [Wilson] *had not reported very favourably of me.*[17] Happily, Guy Prendergast took a longer view!

Very few Allied units can have featured a more eclectic and mongrel military attire. Obviously, patrols were drawn from several continents and brought their own kit with them. Some of this was vintage Great War issue. Headgear was varied in the extreme, from colonial style pith helmets to the distinctive Arab *keffiyeh,* held in place by the traditional band or *agal.* This gave wearers a suitably Beau Geste look, was ideal for protection against dust but rather less suited to the range of mundane tasks which made up a large portion of the desert raider's daily life, such as kit and vehicle maintenance – chores which had not affected the Bedouin! Woollen cap comforters and, latterly, black RTR berets became more commonplace.[18]

Conditions in the desert varied radically from day to night, from stifling, almost crushing heat to stark, penetrating cold. Standard battledress with heavy serge greatcoats alternated with KD shirts and shorts with personal gear carried in '37 Pattern canvas webbing. Peculiar to the desert was the kapok-lined Tropal coat. This was a very heavy and stiff item of kit that was unsuitable when moving but very warm for static or sentry work. Leather sandals or *Chaplis* – much easier for moving over soft sand – often replaced standard infantry boots.[19] The South Africans had introduced a lightweight durable form of footwear, descended from their Voortrekker ancestors' design, the 'desert boot' – eventually and enduringly turned into a fashion item by shoemakers Clark.

Life for the desert raider was very far from representations depicted in action movies or the boys-own style of graphic comics, beloved of this author's generation. It was gruelling, unceasing, uncomfortable, monotonous, frequently unhealthy and occasionally very dangerous. Hitler's infamous *Kommandobefehl* wasn't issued until October 1942, and LRDG units in the desert, unlike some which came later, were not affected. LRDG was fortunate that throughout the war, even in the Aegean and Adriatic sectors, whilst captured patrolmen were sometimes threatened with summary execution, none was ever actually shot. LRDG personnel were also notoriously proficient escapers! The main risks in Libya were from air attack and bumping into enemy ground forces.

To add to the normal discomforts, sandstorms could blow up, seemingly from nowhere and blot out the world in a frenzied, abrasive shroud. A hot, enervating *qibli* whispered distractingly from the deep, empty expanses of the desert, sapping energy, draining the will to continue. Libya also hosted any amount of local wildlife that was apt to do you harm, a whole cornucopia of insect varieties, harbingers of many ills, plus poisonous snakes and scorpions that made unwelcome and very dangerous bedfellows. Desert oases or Bedouin encampments were havens for innumerable and voracious plagues of flies. Desert sores and the spectre of *cafard* lurked in the shadows.

Patrols had to be largely self-sufficient and every item of equipment, every drop of fuel and water, was measured. As the vehicles moved out, a lighter command car probed ahead, choosing routes and keeping a trained eye open for unwelcome visitors. Flags were used for communicating changes of plan or alterations to route. Trucks would always attempt to remain within eyesight of each other. Behind the command vehicle came the radio truck (which couldn't operate its wireless on the move), then the rest of the patrol in three troops, each having a trio of trucks, travelling in as wide dispersion as the ground would permit. As a rule, the heavily laden mechanic's or fitter's vehicle drove with the rear troop, ready to attend on stragglers or breakdowns. It was the 2 I/C's job to act as rear-end Charlie.

Somebody was always on the lookout for prowling Axis planes. Patrols threw out great plumes and swathes of dust, unavoidable and horribly visible. It was often possible for the LRDG to simply brazen it out, masquerading as 'friendlies' when the unfriendly were overhead. If enemy aircraft were sighted, the alarm was raised by sounding trucks' horns and then the patrol would halt, scattering the vehicles over a wide area, at least 100 yards between each.

Clever dispersal using natural cover, augmented with camouflage, would often do the trick. If the hunters proved persistent and aggressive, the patrol would disperse at speed. Only one truck could be strafed at any one time and the driver would 'jink' and swerve to confuse the fighter's aim; speeding off after a lightning turn at ninety degrees to the angle of the attacker's run. Over hard going the vehicles could crack along at a fair rate, perhaps as fast as 50 mph, a very tricky target.[20]

Such adrenalin pumping moments were mercifully rare. The trooper's day started early, before first light, as the cook toiled over an open fire to get a brew and breakfast on. Though LRDG generally fared better than their regular army comrades, water was strictly rationed to six pints per man per day. The first of these was served as a mug of hot tea, Tommy's universal benison. He might also begin his day with porridge, bacon fried from the tin, or biscuits with marge or jam. Working off excess calories was never likely to be a problem.

There was nothing to be gained by moving off before the sun had climbed to at least 20 degrees above the horizon, sufficient to activate a sun-compass. Everyone packed stores and kit; vehicles, gear and weapons had to be checked. Guns, constantly getting fouled by blown sand, would have been stripped and cleaned the night before; a blockage could easily become a death sentence. This was the time for the W/O to radio HQ, for the commander to brief all troopers on the intended day's travel, plus RV's in case of dispersal. On sensitive ground or near the coastal littoral, all traces of the overnight camp would be systematically eliminated. Attention to detail was the measure of survival.[21]

As the sun climbed, heat building to a furnace filling the noon sky, a halt was called. Navigation using the sun compass and driving generally became near impossible. The blinding white glare flattened the ground, hiding a multitude of evils. Men lolled beneath the shelter of their trucks, metal so hot it must surely melt. A cold, sparse meal of cheese and biscuits, another precious pint of warm water, barely enough to replace sweat; the signaller would be busy with his midday call. Heat was everywhere, a molten universe; colour drowned out by the harsh, unyielding, unwavering light, no dark, no contrast, no shadow. As the afternoon began to wane, heat moving from unbearable to just manageable, the patrol would move off, towards, as Wilfred Owen would have said, *their distant rest.*

As dusk approached, a suitable camping ground had to be identified. This needed easy concealment and all round defence with good fields of fire. Like a cowboy's wagon train, the vehicles laagered around the hub of the comms truck; circled and parked for a fast getaway should any inconsiderate foe appear to disrupt a night's well-earned rest. Though the patrol carried its daily sustenance onboard the vehicles, rations might be supplemented by fresh game. Gazelle were sighted from time to time and a decent shot could boost the pot. The trick was not to panic the animals into flight.

The trooper's working day was far from over. As cavalry looked after their mounts, so the LRDG cosseted their vehicles. The ground was murderously hard on the trucks. Jerry-cans (so called as these were a pre-war German steel design that held 4.4 gallons or 20 litres of fuel), were used for re-fuelling, oil and hydraulics checked, tyre pressures checked and, if necessary, adjusted. Stores were counted, loads sorted. There was no scope for waste or sloppiness.

The ubiquitous jerry-can was a gift from Rommel, far superior in robustness and design to the two-gallon British tin. The design made the container easier to lift and to store. A fit man could carry one in each hand in the open, and while heavy when full, it was easy enough to fill up from. LRDG trooper Jim Patch recalled that transferring fuel from two gallon British to the larger German jerry-can in an enclosed space got everybody high on fumes. American-type cans, copied from the Axis model, were found to be much inferior in design. Finally, Britain did start producing her own, exact copies and these were very successful, though they didn't begin to arrive in theatre, some two million of them, till early 1943.[22]

Time for an evening brew, over an open fire built with used packing cases, a primus or improvised stove; the evening meal was served hot and the daily tot of grog was given out. This was the social highlight and could be swilled neat or diluted in tea to suit. The Rhodesians created a cocktail variant, mixing the raw spirit with Rose's Lime Juice, the 'sundowner' or 'anti-*qibli* pick-me-up.

Men bedded down in improvised pits, shoveled from soft sand, nastily reminiscent of shallow graves. Those on sentry duty stayed awake as would the W/O and navigator. He had to finish up his dead reckoning, which was checked by an understudy. He'd then use his theodolite for an astrofix, again checked by his junior, so an exact location for the camp could be determined and agreed. Only with this level of scrupulous care could the LRDG hope to function. Bill Kennedy Shaw relates how the theodolite was used: *Before the war I had spent many desert nights sitting for hours cramped on an empty petrol tin before the car's headlights, working out the elaborate formula which ended, if all went well, in a latitude and longitude.*

What made life easier by 1940 had been prompted by advances in the science of aviation. Obviously, in a moving plane, a lengthy calculation is pretty hopeless as the plane has already moved on a considerable distance. Pilots had then come to rely on books of tables which drastically cut back on the time needed to work out a 'fix'. This also greatly eased the burden on LRDG navigators.[23]

On the Trail of the Fox

The Desert Fox had arrived. Irwin Rommel proved to be a very different class of opponent to his Italian predecessors. Nominally subordinate to them, he pursued an aggressive war under his own direction. LRDG was, as the Murzuk Raid unfolded, undergoing yet another phase of re-organisation. 'S' Patrol, the new South Rhodesian detachment, went live on 31st January. Despite the name, not all recruits were Rhodesian; some were Scots and others Northumbrian. Happily General Freyberg agreed to his Kiwis (T & R Patrols) staying with LRDG.

On 23rd February the Yeomanry Patrol was formed, most of the recruits drawn from 1st Cavalry Division then in Palestine. Not all proved to be of the right sort, some far from it, and the patrol's official 'start' date was put back by a couple of weeks.[24] The failure to blast the Italians out of the stone-walled Murzuk fort had clearly demonstrated the need for a heavier 'punch' and so a small artillery sub-unit was formed to beef up LRDG's potential firepower.

Ralph Bagnold gained his lieutenant colonelcy with a full group HQ and two squadrons. Teddy Mitford led 'A' Squadron: G (Guards), S (Rhodesian), & Y (Yeomanry) patrols; while 'B' Squadron would be comprised of both Kiwi patrols.[25] The unit was also to move to a new base. British successes against the fleeing Italians meant that Cairo was now too far to the east. So far west had the Allies advanced that El Agheila began to seem attractive. Rommel's arrival in Tripoli and a more active German presence led to a second think and Kufra came up as clear favourite.

On 9th March, Bagnold with the Rhodesians took a close look at Kufra and its surrounding outposts. His brief was to establish contact with the Free French and to provide acclimatisation for officers and men. The overall tactical situation was complex in that the several oases around were not garrisoned, they were controlled by native populations who, while not a threat, were not necessarily any form of asset. Kufra is sacred to the Senussi and the Italians had wrested it from them in 1931, since when they'd constructed a fort at Et Tag. The oasis is around forty miles in length, less than half that in width, nestling in a bowl of shallow hills. There are four separate lakes lying in the bowl with the settlement of El Tag built on its northern rim, a dun coloured riot of earth brick buildings, seemingly as old as time.

> From the high wireless masts in the Italian fort at Et Tag, built over the ruins of the Senussi 'zawiya' [*religious centre*], you could see the whole oasis – thousands of date palms, thinly scattered on the upper slopes and thicker around the salt marches; the mosque and market places at El Giof; the two sapphire-blue lakes as salt as the Dead Sea, though you could dig a well of sweet water five yards from the margin; tiny patches of cultivation, laboriously irrigated by donkey-hauled leather buckets from shallow wells.[26]

The French at Kufra were mainly colonial troops without any heavy weapons. There was a viable airstrip at Tazerbo and this had to be secured, a task for the Rhodesians, who like the Kiwis were learning on the job. By 9th April LRDG had occupied the oasis and aerodrome.[27] Kennedy Shaw describes Kufra as 'the secret of the Sahara', even with its ancient romance stripped bare by Italian conquerors. Before then, the great Senussi warlord Mohammed el Mahdi es Senussi had brought his people to the pinnacle of their local power.

By early April, Rommel was on the move, displaying levels of aggression and energy far greater than ever evidenced by the Italians.

Very soon the Allies were on their back-foot. LRDG, less G & Y Patrols, was to concentrate at Kufra. Bagnold was given overall charge of Allied forces in the Kufra sector, under the direct orders of the C-in-C himself. The local free French forces were effectively under his control. As a caveat, no additional air or ground support was available.[28] On 9th April, LRDG, in four columns, set off for distant Kufra, the heavier transport, much burdened, made hard work of the desert travel and didn't reach the oasis till the 25th (see below). Patrols, stationed at the outlying settlements, formed a mobile perimeter defence while the Free French held the ring closer to Kufra.

Kufra itself is guarded, in strategic terms, by the Zighen gap. This meant that both Tazerbo and Bir Harash needed garrisoning. Life in these outposts of a remote garrison was not altogether congenial: *Life in Tazerbo was not pleasant. The thermometer climbed steadily towards 120 degrees in the shade. From dawn to dusk the flies were beyond belief; every afternoon it blew a sandstorm. Scorpions and snakes added to the hazards of existence. The story of the Sand Viper, Libya's deadliest snake, found gargling in its hole after biting a South Islander, is encouraged in Auckland but rejected by reliable authority in Christchurch!*[29]

Since hostilities began, civilian life had been disrupted and the oases' trade had declined. The overall population didn't exceed six thousand but civil administration had also withered. LRDG's setting up acted as a tonic for the local economy which began to revive as British political officers got the wheels of civic life moving again.[30] Keeping the garrison fed and fuelled became the responsibility of Sudan Command.

For a while fuel shortages became quite critical until the regular convoy route was established. The RAF was extremely stretched in the spring of 1941 and LRDG struggled to win any measure of cooperation. It was at this point Bagnold effectively solved the problem by privately acquiring the two WACO planes that were to form LRDG's diminutive private air force (see Appendix 1). Grudgingly, the RAF did relent and a modest squadron of Gladiators and Lysanders was made available. Happily, the enemy showed little inclination to be overly active through late spring and into summer.

Throughout the history of warfare those who maintain the sinews have often been overlooked. Driving convoys of unwieldy 10-tonners loaded to the gunnels, vehicles totally unsuited for desert travel at the best of times, was no mean feat. Dick Croucher who had departed from Cairo at the same time as Bagnold and the rest, should have arrived with his vital supplies shortly afterwards. He didn't. After three days Bill Kennedy Shaw flew in one of the Lysanders to find him.

This was not club class: *We took off at dawn in one of the decrepit Lysanders, Mahe piloting and I in the back separated from him by the long-range petrol tank and squatting on a green enamel bath plundered from the Italian officers' quarters in the fort.* The plane's internal comms weren't working so the French-speaking pilot was steered by Kennedy Shaw as navigator with a ribbon around each arm which he jinked appropriately to indicate changes of direction![31]

Locating the lost party, a needle in the proverbial haystack, proved both arduous and perilous. Happily, they were eventually found, almost literally down to their last pint of water. Kufra is 650 miles from Wadi Halfa and resupply remained a constant headache. When Guy Prendergast began flying the two WACOs, the RAF was not at all pleased, *very sticky* in fact. The Air Force was inevitably hostile to the notion of private enterprise and wasn't at the outset even prepared to allow the LRDG to paint roundels on their aircraft, an invitation to suicide in the skies.

Teddy Mitford and his two patrols of A Squadron were working for General Neame and based at Jalo. By this point the Germans had occupied Marada, some 80 miles south of El Agheila. Mitford's job was to watch and learn. Crichton-Stuart with fifty percent of G Patrol strength was detailed to have a good close look at Marada Oasis. In the event, there was very little to report. The calm was deceptive; on the night of 6/7th April the Guards discovered the enemy was very close indeed and fuel stocks were alarmingly low.

Crichton-Stuart had decided to make a dash for Jarabub, over 200 miles east. With only 54 gallons of petrol left, there would only be enough for one vehicle. This had to be the wireless truck of course and the rest were abandoned. Much of the kit was salvaged as the grossly overloaded vehicle struggled across the desert. A hard and fairly fraught march ensued, enlivened when the Jarabub garrison began shooting at these wild desert figures. However, all were got in safely.[32]

Meanwhile, Teddy Mitford, with the bulk of A Squadron, was moving inland from the Gulf of Sirte, heading towards Msus, a place Western Desert Force – latterly Eighth Army – might later care to forget, scene of the infamous 'Msus Stakes'. There were some alarms and it was obvious the enemy was in the general vicinity. A recce along the Trigh-el-Abd showed little signs of life but, on 6th April, Mitford's Patrols had to be deployed in a conventional role to assist the army in seeing off an Italian attack on Mekili.

Next day and there was more fighting, though this time the opposition was clearly Germanic. On 8th April the Allies were driven out of the Mekili position. Mitford was also obliged to fall back towards Jarabub. For once a sandstorm arrived at just the right moment to assist in LRDG's escape. During the retreat, an enemy column was beaten up and the whole force, Mitford's and Crichton-Stuart's detachments, were safely re-united at Jarabub by 10th April.

Nearly all that is. Trooper ('Titch') Cave had been left behind in Mekili, waiting for his truck to be repaired at the IAOC depot there. He missed the action but found himself, along with 1,500 Allied soldiers, as a POW. Like many others, he was dumped in a makeshift camp at Derna, neglected and abused by his Italian captors, whose attitude was in marked contrast to that of the far more civil Germans. He decided to remove himself from these uncongenial lodgings. On the night of 21st April, he and an Aussie escaper made a run for it, slipping past their guards and several MG nests. Trooper Cave experienced a series of fraught adventures as he with a small band of other escapees sought to dodge Axis patrols, short of water, food & footwear.

Their objective was Tobruk, many miles distant but still in Allied hands. Cave experienced a whole myriad of dangers; hunted, permanently hungry, at one point near delirious from drinking foul water. It was almost at the end of May when he finally reached a friendly position, and three days later he was in Alexandria. Less than a week after that, he had rejoined Y Patrol at Siwa.[33]

By 1st July General Wavell had been replaced by General Auchinleck ('the Auk'), a commander much respected by his troops but, like his predecessor, under constant badgering from Churchill to produce dramatic gains. The pressure was understandable. Britain's hoped for allies in the USA were getting disappointing reports from their man on the spot (whose codes the Italians had already cracked). The Auk would not be rushed, much to the PM's irritation, but Churchill for all his great genius had little real idea of the difficulties of warfare in the Western Desert.

As A Squadron had lost so many vehicles in the retreat to Jarabub, Guy Prendergast carried out a temporary re-organisation at Siwa, splitting the unit into two small patrols, one under Crichton-Stuart, the other led by Lieutenant Gibbs. In mid April, the former took his team out in an attempt to recover the vehicles he'd had to abandon. None could be found except for the patrol car which was suffering from busted suspension and of little value to anyone. It seemed the enemy must have netted everything salvageable.[34] The Germans, particularly, were very good at re-cycling.

Road Watch

From 18th–24th April G Patrol kept watch on the Gardaba Track, over fifty miles west of Jarabub. The mission was to take note of any enemy activity coming from Aujila or Jalo, now in Axis hands. Road Watch was to become an activity LRDG would soon come to know, not necessarily with affection. Keeping tabs on enemy movement was an essential function of intelligence gathering; precisely what LRDG had been set up to do. It was also dangerous, tedious, exhausting and uncomfortable. Nobody would ever want to make a movie about road watch.

Undertaking what amounts to a traffic census is about as unglamorous as it ever gets. As time went by, LRDG patrols would become far more skilled in identifying and recording details of Axis traffic, noting types of vehicles, troop movements, armoured as opposed to soft skin, the nature of convoys and amount of stores etc. This was far more detailed information than even the best aerial reconnaissance could hope to pull off. Patrols were not to know, since none of them or any of their officers were in the charmed loop of ULTRA Intelligence (see Appendix 7), that their work was in some ways deemed less valuable than ULTRA, but it was very useful nonetheless. As they became more skilled, LRDG observers learned to compile a veritable encyclopaedia of data on enemy traffic.

Every detachment would (once the process became more standardised late in 1941, early 1942), be watching for say a fortnight. The patrol would approach via an RV some way back from the target highway. They would then be guided into the camp ground by the outgoing watchers. This was carefully concealed and fully camouflaged; tyre tracks and all incriminating signs were swept away. As the handover progressed, the first brace of observers plus another man from the incoming patrol were led down to the hidden OP. Both the outgoing host and spare patrolman returned to camp, the new boys now knew their way around.

Each pair of observers worked for twenty-four hours. They'd be woken very early before first light, fortified with tea, then they'd tab the mile and a half or more down to the OP, relieve the last shift and set up – all before dawn. The OP would be a shallow trough, well screened with just enough room for the two observers with their kit. For the whole stint they would lie prone with only minimal movement possible. They might be, say, three hundred yards from the road itself, observing with the use of glasses, through a narrow aperture in the hide.

The work was unimaginably boring and extremely uncomfortable, like being inside a pressure cooker in midday sun, a fridge by dark. Scarcely any movement was possible, blown sand and insects a constant irritation, with the ever present possibility of discovery, if not by the Axis then by wandering Bedouin whose loyalties couldn't be relied on. For those immured in the bivvy, life was equally uncomfortable.

Movement was again almost impossible by day and long hours in a stifling blanket of heat and flies had to be endured.[35]

After G Patrol was withdrawn from road watch on 25th April, following a terrific sandstorm, Lieutenant Gibbs took over and remained watching till 11th May, by which time quite a few men were laid out with heat exhaustion. Road watch was gruelling, nerve-wracking and sapping. On the coastal battlefield, a limited Allied riposte had recovered Sollum, and Crichton-Stuart was detailed to work with the 11th Hussars (the 'Cherry-pickers' of Light Brigade fame). On 14th May as the LRDG reached the RV at Sheferzen, they abruptly discovered that the column approaching was very far from being friendly.

An unequal if mercifully short fire-fight ensued, followed by a high speed chase. High by desert standards, as Crichton-Stuart dryly observed – *it was found that a really frightened truck could get up to 50 miles an hour.*[36] The hunt was kept up for 30 miles but aside from two trucks lost and one guardsman wounded, there were no other casualties. At the time Crichton-Stuart thought it might have been our own 11th Hussars doing the shooting but subsequent reports confirmed these attackers had indeed been from the enemy. For a while G Patrol was immured on mundane duties at Siwa; attrition of vehicles had been considerable and more men were now laid low with malaria.

In early June the depleted Squadron was re-organised into three patrols, G, Y & H, each made up of six trucks. Most active patrolling was undertaken by Y & H whilst G was recovering. Equipment and vehicles had both taken a pounding and repairs were difficult. Colonel Bagnold had been pressuring HQ to make more systematic and structured use of LRDG. Part of the new brief would be to act as a 'taxi-service' for agents being infiltrated into Cyrenaica. Patrols would also find out as much as possible about the ground south of the Jebel-el-Akhdar, the hills which rose just inland between Bomba and Barce.

Jake Easonsmith led H Patrol on an agent-ferrying mission, departing on 9th June. Having deposited his human cargo, he kept an eye on a section of the Bardia-Tobruk highway. A suitably unsuspecting Axis convoy was heavily attacked. A number of vehicles were put out of action and Easonsmith returned to the scene of carnage on foot that evening to account for a few more. On 14th June, H patrol successfully rescued Pilot Officer Pompey whose Hurricane had been shot down at Bir Bidihi, a couple of miles south of the Trig-el-Abd track.[37]

H Patrol had a very busy month. Their next task was to ferry more agents and have a look around Mekili to ascertain if any significant convoy traffic was passing through the place, east to west. The recce went largely undisturbed except that one man died and another was wounded while they investigated a shot up Bedford truck. No damaged vehicle in the desert could be inspected with impunity. The unwary were apt to be suddenly taken off by a well concealed booby trap.[38] Jake Easonsmith led H Patrol on another taxi run at the start of July and recce'd the Trigh-el-Abd again; this was noticeably quiet.

Michael Crichton-Stuart had been ill with malaria and G Patrol had, temporarily, been commanded by Lieutenant Hay, a Coldstreamer. By 26th July Crichton-Stuart was back in the driving seat and took out a patrol – this time with a US observer, Major David Lair. He had a look at Jarabub airfield and located some enemy fuel dumps, destroying about 2,000 gallons of fuel and 500 of oil.[39] He was out again toward the end of July, his troopers battling a fearsome *Khamseen.* Both he and Lieutenant Gibbs were struck down with fresh bouts of malaria. To date, G Patrol had lost one guardsman KIA, a second had died of wounds, and three others had been wounded.[40] Y Patrol under Jake Easonsmith was equally busy throughout late July and early August, taxiing 'spooks' and sniffing out potential airstrips around Bir Hacheim.

Siwa

Though LRDG HQ was now firmly dug in, at and around Kufra, the enemy showed no interest, Bagnold had drawn up a full plan for all round defence, looking at axes of attack, but this remained theoretical. Success, however, had spurred strategic thinking towards beefing up Allied raiding capacity. Wingate's rather grandiose and impractical scheme still had its attractions. The more realistic approach of duplicating LRDG in other sectors, deeper into Africa and across the sea in Syria (held by Vichy and distinctly not Allied-friendly), was being actively considered.

From a command and control point of view, leaving Bagnold immured in deep desert was self-defeating. He couldn't really control his far-flung patrols or advise on wider strategy. Guy Prendergast, promoted to Lieutenant Colonel, held the magic wand of a pilot's licence, and the sturdy WACOs would give him the wings he needed. Bagnold was thus 'moved upstairs' to the special section of the Operations Staff back in Cairo to pursue the wider goal of recruiting new units.

In practice this was far easier said than done. LRDG was successful precisely because its founding fathers, Bagnold himself, Clayton and Bill Kennedy Shaw were old desert hands. This was a very small pool and there were few others. Vehicles, kit and the right breed of men were also in short supply. Prendergast was given the redoubtable Major Eric Wilson VC as 2I/C. The Major had in fact been awarded a posthumous medal after the fighting in Somaliland; happily he was in fact a prisoner![41] On 24th September, Eighth Army came into being, commanded by Sir Alan Cunningham, who also assumed control of LRDG. The proposal to form further units disappeared back onto the shelf, though the Indian Long Range Squadron ("ILRS") was formed during that winter.[42]

Guy Prendergast was an ideal choice. General Wavell had remarked that the most important quality in a senior commander was what the French might call *le sense du practicable* – we'd call it common sense. This core element revolves around an understanding of ground, movement and supply. Knowledge of strategy and tactics is secondary because without a sound logistical base, rooted in familiarity with the ground, no tactics, however brilliant, will ever have a chance to work. Prendergast could leave much of the day-to-day jobs to his patrol commanders. His priority was to ensure there was fuel in the tanks and tins in the cupboard. At this he excelled.[43]

By 10th July orders had come for the garrisoning of Kufra and its environs to be taken over by the Sudan Defence Force ("SDF"), and whilst LRDG continued to use the Oasis as a base, its role reverted fully to long range reconnaissance. Prendergast had a pretty broad brief – he was to monitor enemy activity around Zella, Marada and Jalo; survey potential routes across the Sirte desert, between Kufra and the Fezzan; and to investigate the hills of the Haruj.[44] To help draw better maps of these largely blank areas, two surveyors, Lieutenants Lazarus and Wright, were dispatched to Kufra. Between them they achieved remarkable results. Ken Lazarus would have a very active career with LRDG.

Guy Prendergast was given responsibility for his own 'turf', which was bounded by a line drawn from El Agheila to Jikerra, then along the northern rim of the Sand Sea as far as the Egyptian border. Eighth Army would be responsible elsewhere, though Prendergast was given a watching and advisory brief beyond his geographical remit. As LRDG was relieved of the tiresome business of garrison duty at Kufra, some of its men, particularly those from overworked G and Y Patrols, could benefit from some much needed R & R. The troopers were exhausted and many had suffered malarial symptoms – the abundant fleshpots of Cairo would be a very welcome balm.

Before July was out, T Patrol was active in the Sirte Desert. Prendergast was explicit in that their role was reconnaissance and intelligence gathering. Beating up the enemy, diverting as such actions were, had to be avoided. Prisoners could be taken if opportunities arose, but without giving the game away. Existing intelligence sources suggested the Italians were maintaining garrisons at Jalo, Marada, Tagrifet, Zella, Hon and Bou Njem.[45]

On arrival, the patrol split into three detachments, one under Captain Ballantyne (with Wilson who was fluent in Italian), a second led by Lieutenant Ellingham (with Kennedy Shaw as navigator), and a final reserve section remaining at Bir Zelten. The two forward patrols roamed freely within the target zone, coming in sight of the sea and learned much about the topography. There was little sign of Axis presence other than an abandoned training camp, and the patrols returned safely to base. This was unspectacular but solid work, precisely what Bagnold had intended his creation to perform.

During the first week of September, S Patrol, operating from Kufra, set out to recce the line of Jalo–Jedabia with a broad swath around.

This would be for a conventional force so LRDG needed to check out the going for heavy transport and armour, identify viable landing sites and identify sources of water. The patrol split into two detachments to cover more ground. The enemy, aside from the odd stray aircraft, were absent. Natives appeared friendly and reported some Axis patrolling from Jalo.

R Patrol was active in the Jebel-el-Akhdar sector during August. Again this was in part a taxi run to insert agents, to collect from a dead letter drop and to recce an area of dunes at Medwar Hassan. Though the agents failed to reappear, no enemy units were contacted. Towards the end of that month R Patrol was out again ranging west of Jarabub in search of possible landing strips. A round half dozen were roughly identified, though as the patrol had no theodolite, exact positions were impossible to determine. A marauding Italian plane fired a couple of half-hearted bursts at the patrol, happily inflicting no damage, and no other foe was sighted.

As summer waned, both G & Y Patrols, 'A' Squadron were withdrawn to Cairo for R&R and a general makeover. The desert as ever exacted a high toll from men and vehicles. R Patrol stayed at Siwa with a further HQ section under Major Steele. This now became a new 'A' Squadron whilst the old was designated as 'B'. T Patrol, at this point also in Cairo, formed part of the Siwa Squadron which reported directly to HQ Western Desert. Prendergast, from his fiefdom at Kufra, ran General HQ, S Patrol, the heavy supply section and the bulk of the signallers, less a sub-unit up at Siwa.[46]

Bagnold was concerned that levels of necessary vehicle servicing and repair weren't being carried out, and lobbied successfully for a separate mechanical unit, prised from the RAOC. His wish was granted and a suitable section was formed under Captain Ashdown. Heywood's signallers were also re-organised as a separate entity with him commanding. The pair of WACO aircraft was still doing good, essential service. Both were feeling the strain of age and air miles, but it was the planes which allowed Prendergast to survey his far-flung dominions. Air routes were carefully plotted and regularly adhered to with emergency stores of fuel and supplies stashed at key intervals.

Throughout the autumn on 1941, LRDG served two masters – patrols from Kufra under the hand of LRDG HQ and GHQ, and from Siwa reporting to HQ Western Desert Force. In September John Olivey took S Patrol with one 15-cwt and four 30-cwt trucks from Kufra up towards the coastal section west of El Agheila. His primary purpose was an extension of road watch, to gain intelligence on the volume and type of Axis traffic. This was all about stealth and guile, a true ghost patrol. He was to be neither seen nor heard. From 18th–25th September they kept watch from a small mound not far from the grandiose triumphal arch, a typically flamboyant piece of fascist mummery dubbed 'Marble Arch', if nothing else a handy landmark. As ever, road watch was laborious and infinitely tedious.

As a traffic census, Olivey's report was impressive as a very significant amount of enemy vehicle traffic was noted: motorcycles, light cars, trucks, artillery, armoured cars and tanks. At this point LRDG watchers were not really trained in recognising specific Axis vehicles, though they did note that trucks were often under tow, not it seems as a result of mechanical failure but in an attempt to conserve fuel – clearly then this was in short supply.[47] Jake Easonsmith with R Patrol from Siwa was providing additional taxi services, ferrying agents west of Mekili.

In October, Captain Holliman with S patrol was back near Marble Arch. This time to refine the information gleaned, GHQ had drawn up a regular questionnaire which posed a whole series of specific questions about the types of heavier armour and the nature and likely calibres of guns. To finesse details of troop types the watchers were tasked to identify formations from headdress. This time the watch was kept up for a week 9th–16th of the month, using Olivey's previous harbour.

As unglamorous as it was, road watch was yielding significant results, including pinpoint information on Axis strength and movement. Future patrols would be far better prepped. They received improved training in identifying different types of enemy vehicles, and were given tours of captured or wrecked Axis transport. They were furnished with notes and photos, boosted by the formidable intellectual gifts of Captain Enoch Powell.[48] He had enlisted in the Royal Warwicks in 1939 but was soon moved to Military Intelligence where his impressive powers gained considerable respect. Patrols were given a handbook with technical descriptions and silhouettes to aid recognition, plus plenty of clear pages for note taking. Traffic census was now fully industrialised.[49]

By 9th October, John Olivey was out again, leading S Patrol, scouting around Jalo and looking to net a talkative prisoner. The garrison was thought to be comprised of a hundred and fifty soldiers, trucks and a couple of planes; personnel billeted throughout principal buildings in the settlement. The old fort boasted a pair of 75-mm guns. The Italians at Jalo were more active than others with regular patrols, and it proved impossible to get close undetected.

S patrol was probably given away after being spotted by natives. This attracted unwelcome attention from the clear desert sky but, undeterred, Olivey managed to infiltrate the oasis on the night of the 15th/16th.[50] He couldn't manage to nab any prisoners but he did learn that provisions were short and water had to be brought in. From Siwa, Jake Easonsmith was still providing a taxi service for Allied agents. Leaving on 30th September he saw no enemy but did locate a crashed Wellington. No trace of the crew could be found, however.

On 20th October, a suitably refreshed and refurbished 'B' Squadron, with both G & Y patrols, reached Kufra. Teddy Mitford was replaced by Eric Wilson. The southerly oasis was about to be abandoned with the LRDG concentrating on Siwa. A fresh Allied offensive was in the offing. Siwa[51] is one of the most remote oases, around fifty miles long and a quarter of that in width. It has been inhabited for millennia and offers a rich archaeological heritage. Most LRDG were more attracted to the chance to bathe in cool waters, as Jim Patch recalls:

> Those of us who were privileged to visit the Siwa Oasis… used to gaze on the ruins of the temple of Jupiter-Ammon with only mild interest. My recollection is of some tumbledown walls with paintings on them which still retained a few vestiges of colour … but nearby was Cleopatra's pool, which was of much greater interest to us than the ruins of the temple. Returning from patrol,

> it was a joy to dive from the perimeter wall naked into its refreshing depths and enjoy the luxury of wallowing in all that water after weeks on the move without even enough water for washing.[52]

So much ferrying of agents had gone on that 'A' Squadron had been dubbed 'Libyan Taxis Limited'. Jake Easonsmith, patrolling from Siwa on the 14th of the month, had been tasked to recce the eastern flank of the Wadi Mra and the Mekili vicinity, investigating how conventional forces might be able to move, and also picking up Jock Haselden.

The latter was one of the legendary figures of the desert war, born in Egypt and fluent in several languages. At the outset he had been with the Libyan Arab Force before being transferred to Intelligence. Bill Kennedy Shaw describes him as *the outstanding personality of the dozen odd men who worked with the tribes in Cyrenaica behind the Axis lines. Untiring, strong, courageous, never without some new scheme for outwitting the enemy, yet with a slow and easy-going way of setting about a job which was far more successful with the Arabs than the usual European insistence on precision and punctuality which they neither like nor understand.* He and LRDG would see much of each other.

Locating Haselden on this mission proved tricky and he wasn't found till 19th October, though another three British escapees were also rescued. Jock Haselden and some of the LRDG, forming 'B' party, made straight for Siwa whilst Easonsmith with the remainder, 'A' detachment, took a look at an Axis laager at Ain-bu-Sfia. There, Easonsmith was moved to have some sport with enemy traffic.

On the 23rd he parked three trucks in dead ground near the track running from the Axis camp towards Mekili. After a swift recce on foot, he deployed two of these to some higher ground about three to four miles back, then took the remaining truck onto the track, intending to feign mechanical breakdown. Booby-trapped boxes of Italian rounds were placed back along the road. Obligingly, if rather more swiftly than had been intended, enemy traffic appeared, their approach screened by more dead ground.

The ambush party scrambled into position. Easonsmith boldly halted the first truck, but as he covered the astonished crew with his Thompson, one of them leapt from the cab and tackled him. The driver managed to grab Jake's SMG, but rather than turn it on its rightful owner ran off with it. He didn't get far; a lucky throw and a grenade stopped him. Meanwhile his officer passenger emptied his pistol at Easonsmith and, despite point blank range, missed every time. He also ran till a burst from one of the patrol's automatic weapons permanently curtailed his flight.

All Hell now broke loose. Great bursts of fire ripped through the desert air. The other two LRDG trucks appeared to pour rounds into the enemy whilst Easonsmith, like an industrial grim reaper, blasted enemy trucks with grenades. After a furious few moments, with the whole enemy camp alerted, it was time to clear out. Two prisoners had been netted, (one of whom was wounded and later died), and an undetermined number of others were dead or wounded. With only a single bullet hole in his radiator, Easonsmith's raiders sped off: as 'beat-ups' go, this was a lot more fun than road watch. The patrol returned to Siwa unscathed, although their topographical survey work had to be curtailed due to water shortage.[53]

Captain Ballantyne with T Patrol forayed from Siwa towards the final days of October. Their brief was more taxiing, then surveying the terrain around Jedabia and the escarpment between Benina and Antelat. The enemy made no attempts at interference and one of their salvage parties was captured. 'A' Squadron carried out one further patrol early in November with elements of R & T Patrols. Their hunting ground was south of Bir Hacheim and Bir-el-Gubi, which are relatively close to Tobruk, and the patrol was to ascertain levels of enemy activity and vehicle traffic. The detachment was to have split into two smaller patrols to cover each sector but mechanical troubles intervened so they continued together. They had some luck when they bumped a surprised enemy motorcycle patrol; all were captured.[54]

So far so good, but 'Crusader' was brewing, Auchinleck's long anticipated offensive, and another swing of the desert pendulum.

Notes

1 Kennedy Shaw, p. 42.
2 Laycock was a relation of Niven's wife.
3 IWM, p. 37.
4 Ibid.
5 Waugh used his experiences in Crete when writing his *Sword of Honour* trilogy.
6 The Lovat Scouts were the British Army's first sharpshooter or sniper unit, active in both world wars, finally stood down in Athens in 1947.
7 Bierman, J. and C. Smith, *Alamein, War without Hate* (London, 2002), p. 95.
8 John Edward 'Jock' Haselden MC, (1903–1942) Lieutenant-Colonel (acting) in Intelligence Corps, killed during Operation Agreement.
9 Bierman & Smith, p. 92.
10 Keyes won a posthumous VC for his role in Operation Flipper.
11 Bierman & Smith p. 97.
12 Robert Blair Mayne, after the war he returned to legal practice but did not settle in civilian life, he became an isolated figure, drinking and brawling, he died in a car crash, see 'Dramatis Personae'.
13 The Sacred Squadron or Sacred Band was a force comprised of émigré Greek officers and cadets under Colonel Tsigantes. Modern Greek Special Forces continue their tradition.
14 IWM, p. 196.
15 Sometimes referred to as the Special Identification or Intelligence Group ("SIG").
16 Lloyd Owen, p. 23.
17 Ibid., p. 54.
18 Moreman & Ruggeri, p. 24.
19 Ibid.
20 Ibid., p. 35.
21 Ibid., p. 34.
22 Morgan, pp. 98–99.
23 Kennedy Shaw, p. 90.
24 Wynter, p. 44.
25 Ibid., p. 45.
26 Kennedy Shaw, pp. 78–79.
27 Wynter, pp. 46–47.
28 Ibid.
29 Kennedy Shaw p. 81.
30 Wynter, p. 48.
31 Kennedy Shaw, p. 82.
32 Wynter, pp. 53–54.
33 Ibid., pp. 57–59.
34 Ibid., p. 59.
35 Moreman & Ruggeri, pp. 46–48.

36 Wynter, p. 61.
37 Ibid., p. 63.
38 Ibid.
39 Ibid., p. 64.
40 Ibid., p. 65.
41 Lloyd Owen, p. 52.
42 The Indian Long Range Squadron, formed part of LRDG during the critical stages of the desert war from October 1942–April 1943 (see Chapter 4).
43 Kennedy Shaw, p. 56.
44 Wynter, p. 69.
45 Ibid., p. 70.
46 Ibid., p. 75.
47 Ibid., p. 78.
48 Enoch Powell (1912–1998), a senior post-war Conservative politician, not immune from controversy.
49 Moreman & Ruggeri, p. 46.
50 Wynter, p. 50.
51 It actually features briefly as the LRDG base in *Ice Cold in Alex* and is famous for its traditional acceptance of same sex marriage.
52 Morgan, p. 86.
53 Wynter, pp. 83–84.
54 Ibid.

CHAPTER 4
'The Libyan Taxi Company Limited', 1941–1942

If you can soldier here without a worry
And eat your bread and cheese and M & V
If when the Stukas come, you never hurry
And bombs and shells and fleas don't worry thee

If you can laugh and sing when guns do rumble
Nor murmur when your tobacco don't last out
If you can eat your stew and never grumble
Yet keep a cheery smile when sergeants shout

If you can hear reveille call each morning
And rise and face the new day with a grin
If you can sleep with fleas about you crawling
And always tell your pal we're going to win.

If you can wait and never get tired of waiting
For mail that never seems to come
If you can face the desert heat each morning
And never let your thoughts stray back to home

If you can play your fiddle as good as Nero
And never swear or curse when things go wrong
Then, all I can say is you're a blinkin' hero
And, what is more, you'll be the only one!

—J. Campbell: *If*[1]

High Hopes

Operation 'Crusader' burst across the frontier on 18th November 1941 and sped forwards in a facsimile of dummy war. Opposition was minimal and no immediate counterpunch developed. Rommel was still fixated on the impudent garrison of Tobruk and dismissed the offensive as a probing raid. He himself had earlier instigated just such a reconnaissance in force, 'Midsummer Night's Dream', to glean what he might of Auchinleck's intentions. By evening 7th Armoured Brigade had reached Gabr Saleh, thrusting virtually unopposed. The Fox had been humbugged but, ironically, his very inertia had robbed General Cunningham of the decisive clash of armour his plan demanded.

Disconcerted, Cunningham proposed, on the second day, to split his armoured forces and seek out the foe. By now the Fox was alert and began to concentrate his own armour for a riposte. General 'Strafer' Gott,[2] at this point commanding 7th Armoured Division, expressed the view that the moment was now ripe for a break-out from Tobruk. This was contrary to the previous planned assertion that the Panzers must first be humbled. Nonetheless, Cunningham agreed and the move was planned for morning on 21st November. Meanwhile, armoured units were colliding piecemeal in the tanker's equivalent of a 'soldier's battle'. Not the precise, staff-college business of ordered formations but a swirling, dust-shrouded, grinding melee.

Despite the ferocity of these initial exchanges, the main armoured forces of both sides had yet to engage. Cunningham, nonetheless, appears to have considered that a major engagement had indeed occurred and was disposed to believe over-optimistic assessments of enemy losses. Not only were these wildly exaggerated, but DAK was still far more accomplished than its opponents at retrieving damaged machines from the field and restoring them to battle-worthy. Reassured, Cunningham gave the order for the Tobruk break-out, codenamed 'Pop'. This threw into sharp relief the need to hold the tactically significant ridge at Sidi Rezegh which lay between Gabr Saleh and the town. This otherwise unremarkable feature would now become a boiling cauldron.

Rommel was aware of the significance of Sidi Rezegh, a mere dozen miles from the beleaguered citadel. More and more Axis armour was fed in as the battle for the ridge intensified, drawing in much of Eighth Army's own tanks. The fighting was close and frightful; 7th Hussars were decimated whilst the dashing Brigadier 'Jock' Campbell performed prodigies of valour which earned him his well-merited VC. As tanks surged around the disputed higher ground, the ring of Axis forces besieging the port remained unbroken. Despite the fact that by evening on the 21st the break-out had been contained, Cunningham remained buoyant and Auchinleck was sending confident cables to London.

Though Rommel had been obliged to divide his available forces, he was far from defeated. Even as Churchill was drafting a victory address the Fox struck back on the 22nd, sending his Panzers in a flanking arc to strike at Sidi Rezegh from the west. This manoeuvre netted tactical gains, and various support units were overrun. Throughout the next day fighting raged unabated, a rough and savage collision of armoured leviathans, wheeling and blazing. Tanks were shot to pieces, others simply broke down; both sides suffered loss, and wrecks littered the scarred waste like primeval skeletons. The New Zealanders suffered grievous loss, though less than the South Africans. Overall Allies losses were significant; there was no victory in sight.

With that daring and tactical insight which would guarantee the endurance of his legend, Rommel planned a counterstroke of breathtaking audacity, one which sent shudders through his more cautious subordinates. He had resolved to draw off some of his forces from the furnace of Sidi Rezegh and strike towards Egypt. This was at the very moment Cunningham was suffering something of a personal crisis. On the 23rd, alarmed by his heavy losses, particularly in armour, he had broached the possibility of breaking off the action and retreating. This was not something the 'Auk' was prepared to countenance. By next day the C-in-C had decided to remove his Eighth Army commander and appoint Ritchie in his stead.

Now Rommel was leading his spearhead eastwards, leading very much from the front, the epitome of daring and gallantry, if not perhaps of prudence. Under his personal command he led the remnants of 15th Panzer and Ariete. The blow threatened to sever 30 Corps' line of retreat as it swept through rear echelons like the grim reaper. Axis

General Cruewell, his reservations dismissed, was ordered to send 21st Panzer to drive 13 Corps back onto the web of frontier minefields. For both sides this was to be the crisis.

Auchinleck, despite the seriousness of the situation, did not lose his nerve, and Rommel's sweeping gambit soon ran into difficulties. Ariete Armoured Division could not get past the South Africans, whilst 21st Panzer could make no headway against 4th Indian Division. Freyberg and the New Zealanders were meantime fighting hard for Tobruk. During the Crusader fighting one factor which told significantly in favour of the British was air superiority. The Desert Air Force was flying effective sorties against Axis ground forces, denying Rommel the comfort of 'flying artillery' which had shielded and aided previous operations.

On the 27th, union with the 70th Division was effected, the heroic garrison finally relieved. British armoured forces at Sidi Rezegh, despite their fearful pounding, were reorganising and still very much in the fight. Rommel's units by contrast were equally battered but now dispersed and vulnerable. At DAK Headquarters Colonel Westphal had already assumed responsibility for the recall of 21st Panzer, Rommel now being out of touch. On flying back that evening though, he tacitly approved and began drawing back 15th Panzer as well.

His priority now was to try and re-establish the ring around Tobruk. From the 28th November, there was more savage combat around El Duda, Belhammed and Sidi Rezegh. Ground was taken, lost and retaken; both sides sustained further, heavy losses. As November drew to a close, German armour was battering the remnant of the New Zealanders, unsupported by Allied tanks. Freyberg was pushed back, his division's casualties dreadful, Tobruk was again encircled. The battle was by now one of attrition, a fight in which the Allies were better placed, but Rommel was not yet ready to withdraw. On 2nd December he threw his battered formations back into the fight for a further five days of murderous intensity.

By 7th December the pace of attrition had forced Rommel to recognise the need for a withdrawal. Both sides continued to incur casualties but the Allies could replenish at a far faster rate. They had greater reserves, and this steady grinding down was not a fight DAK could win. Consequently, Rommel proposed to retire upon a fixed, defensive line running south from Gazala. The British, scenting victory, swooped after, hard upon the heels of the retreating Axis. By the 16th a further retirement became expedient and by 22nd December, as 1941 drew to a close, the Axis forces had fallen back as far as Beda Fomm and Antelat. Further withdrawals, first to Agedabia and finally El Agheila, followed, and though constantly harassed, the rearguard provided an effective screen. By now both sides were equally exhausted.

Nibbling at the Flanks

As these titanic struggles were breaking along the North African coastal battlefield, the deep desert, still shunned by regular forces, largely remained LRDG's private hunting ground. On 1st October the whole unit had been placed under the direct command of Eighth Army and its CO, General Cunningham. The role of Bagnold's buccaneers was defined as:

- Gaining intelligence as to enemy movements along main highways and to observe how Rommel reacted to Allied moves;
- To provide data on terrain, (suitability for movement of armoured vehicles etc);
- Biffing the enemy and beat ups generally, though offensive action should not prejudice intelligence gathering;
- Glean tactical information and relay this as quickly as possible, even at the risk of compromising wireless security.[3]

Siwa, from November, became LRDG's base of operations. This was much closer to the action, often uncomfortably so, being well within range of Axis bombers. These were more irritating than dangerous, but it was realised that patrols, typically comprised of one 15-cwt car and ten 30-cwts, were too large and unwieldy. They were already being split into two parties for operations. The lighter trucks were beginning to become something of an anachronism, exacerbated by frequent mechanical failures.

Now the existing patrol structure would be split into two, each with six 30-cwt vehicles. LRDG thus doubled its effective strength for a limited increase in manpower and resources, though much extra gear was, of course, needed. All patrols were now designated, say, G1 and G2, S1 and S2, etc. By the end of October, LRDG had been primarily concentrated at Siwa, keeping only a residual presence further south at Kufra. At Siwa: HQ 'A' Squadron with R1, R2, T1 and T2 Patrols. At Kufra: HQ 'B' Squadron with G1, G2, S1, S2, Y1 and Y2 Patrols. As the 'Crusader' offensive opened, the whole strength was moved up to Siwa.

Nearly all, that is: S1 and S2 were out on missions. The former, commanded by Holliman, was to beat up enemy traffic on the road from Hon to Misurata and, if the hunting there proved sparse, could have a crack at the coast road. When they reached their primary target zone, they initially had to corral some local workers before scoring their first success, taking out a heavy Italian lorry and crew. Having laid mines, they moved on towards the coast, destroying the captured truck en route.

Holliman selected a roadhouse halt as his next suitable target, but in the fog of war a friendly fire incident resulted in one of his troopers taking a round in the shoulder. His prisoners were duly brought back to Siwa and interrogated. Major Wilson, in his spymaster role, carried out the questioning, mixing threats with ample doses of restorative gin. This mix seemed to work and one of the captives, a pilot, blurted out that the 'jinking' manoeuvres all LRDG vehicles adopted when being strafed made them very difficult targets – useful information by any standard.[4]

S2 had a rather different assignment at this time, a classic exercise in disinformation. The patrol was to plant a fake Eighth Army map in the vicinity of Jalo (then held by the Italians), to suggest an imminent attack developing from an east-west axis, targeting the oasis. The incriminating evidence was cleverly, almost, hidden at a waterhole at

El Aseila. The ruse worked – when Brigadier Reid's force took Jalo, the dummy map had been pasted onto the overall scheme for the area. Bait taken![5]

As the high drama of 'Crusader' began to unfold, LRDG's role was clarified as primarily focusing on road watch plus supporting Brigadier Reid's mobile column, as the need should arise.[6] Reid commanded Force E, a mixed all-arms unit with some armoured cars in support. Jake Easonsmith also provided a taxi and guiding service for an SAS detachment under Stirling, *the first meeting between Stirling and the LRDG, and from it resulted the very successful combination of the two forces.*[7] Tony Hunter did the same for Hasledon and a team of his spooks. Road watch continued much as before, grinding, unglamorous, often dangerous and always vital. What was new was that the wearing of Arab headdress was discarded. The gear had proved generally satisfactory for patrol work but was always a dead giveaway in terms of disguise.[8] No Axis unit sported this type of casually exotic headwear!

Having safely guided Hasledon, Hunter resumed road watch northwest of Mekili, splitting his patrol into three teams of watchers. The weather was vile and the watch, besides being uncomfortable, yielded little intelligence. On 23rd November, Corporal Porter, who'd been one of those watching, went missing. Hunter went out to search for him with two troopers, Kendall and McIver. The trio ran into a score of Italians, beefed up with a 20-mm Breda. Hunter sent his own truck, the Bofors-carrier, back to alert the camp while his small group kept up the unequal fight. Lieutenant Freyberg wisely gathered in the patrol and led them clear of the area. When Dick Croucher, who'd been sent out to complete Hunter's original mission and collect Hasledon reached the RV, he found Hunter there; he'd managed to avoid capture.[9]

Easonsmith's mission with the SAS was to pick up Stirling's men after a parachute-borne raid on two aerodromes at Tmimi. This was very early days for the SAS and air drops were not destined to be fruitful. The men were very widely dispersed and when Jake Easonsmith brought in all he could find – returning to Siwa on 26th November – he could only account for 21 of the 55 troopers who'd set out. The attack had been a costly waste.

The varying fortunes of the main offensive brought about a switch of gears for LRDG. From 24th November they were ordered *to act with the utmost vigour offensively against any enemy targets or communications within reach;* game on for beat-ups. Despite their mastery of the many facets of travelling over desert terrain, even pros like David Lloyd Owen could still get caught out. The more cultivated nature of ground in Cyrenaica, closer to the coast, proved unexpectedly hazardous at times. Lloyd Owen mistook mudflats for fields, the trucks racing over like an LRDG derby until the gut-wrenching moment they nose-dived into soft, stinking slime: *Mickey was laughing so much when he saw the round little figure of Titch Cave hurled over the top of our truck that he himself was too slow to avoid the cause of it all.*[10] It took six hours in the very near proximity of the enemy to laboriously unload the bogged trucks and dig them free! After a very short while, it stopped being funny at all.

Prendergast let slip the dogs of war with gusto. Y1 & Y2 would concentrate on the Gazala-Derna-Mekili section, G1 & G2, would watch, wait and pounce along the Benghazi–Jedabia Road, while S2 & R2 were to keep an eye on the highway linking Marsus-Barce-Benghazi. Franks Simms with YI suffered a very poor beginning, their wireless truck being shot up by 'friendly-fire' from Desert Air Force, always a risk when operating so far behind enemy lines.[11]

This nasty near miss led LRDG to devise a form of Heath Robinson recognition panel, a plywood circle around eighteen inches in diameter, RAF roundel on one side Swastika on the other. The disc was attached to a five-foot pole and could be laid on the vehicle bonnet – right side up for whoever was prowling the skies above.[12] Aircraft were the enemy to be feared. Ground patrols could be outfought or outrun. Obviously, LRDG had tactics for avoiding hostile planes, but the desert is a bad place to hide at times. You can't outrun a Messerschmitt, and the trucks, laden with fuel and ammo, provided a nice, fat and satisfying target.

Vehicle identification was never entirely easy as both sides used captured transport. After the numerous retreats from France, Greece and Crete, the Axis had a fairly good store of Allied equipment. Lloyd Owen, patrolling in the cold light of a winter's dawn, *suddenly noticed that Brian Springfield – never at his most cheerful at that hour… was looking rather more alert than usual.* The watcher had spotted movement. Titch Cave lined up the handles of his Vickers. The vehicle was identified as a 15-cwt truck but was it theirs or ours? Titch was all for 'brassing-up', sure they must be hostile. Lloyd Owen was more curious, and besides the truck was useful plunder. The occupants were in fact Italians who threw up their hands when challenged. They were on their way to a spot of leave in Derna. The LRDG comics informed them that they wouldn't be going there after all but to Cairo instead; *the one who spoke the best English thought this a splendid idea, as he had, he said, always wanted to see Cairo!*[13]

After some empty-handed patrolling, Y1 got lucky on 2nd December, shooting up a transport park and accounting for more than a dozen vehicles. Although LRDG lost none killed or wounded in this action Lance-Corporal Carr went missing. Like others, he was determined not to surrender and though he didn't make the next RV, he headed north towards the coast, ending up there, a few miles northwest of Gazala. This area was already an LRDG target zone so he hoped to run into friends. Instead he found some Senussi who kept him safe for two weeks. As the ebb and flow of the main battle raged around, he was eventually picked up by Allied forces and got back to Siwa on 23rd December.[14]

David Lloyd Owen had brought up Y2 so the two patrols worked for a while in tandem, though after the beat up of the MT Park, there was little trade to be had. On 29th December Lloyd Owen had better luck, netting some prisoners, one of whom gave details of a nearby garrison outpost, located around seven miles east of the holy site at El Ezzeiat. After a short, sharp fight the fort surrendered, two men were killed and the place yielded seventeen prisoners and some kit.[15] After this it was back to road watch near Wadi Maalegh. Here Y2 attacked a petrol tanker and shot up a truck full of troops, two officers and seven enemy ORs' were accounted for. Despite the inevitable pursuit, Lloyd Owen avoided the posse and came safe back to Siwa on 3rd December.

In mid-November, G1 was dispatched to beat up any traffic around Bir-ben-Gania on the Trigh el Abd. Another enemy MT laager was duly shot up along with a tanker convoy next day. G2 was sent to operate in the vicinity of Maaten el Grara where, on 22nd November, the patrol came across a Fiat B.R.20 plane which had made a forced landing. The bomber was revving its motors, clearly had an engine stutter but at least one of its machine guns was manned. Timpson shot first. The aircraft was destroyed, some crew were killed and the survivors captured. John Olivey, destined to become one of LRDG's most energetic raiders, led both S2 & R2 on a patrol aimed at the highway between Benghazi and Barce. On 29th November they took on a number of enemy vehicles, knocking out a series of Axis transports and killing several of their occupants.[16]

These hit and run fights were swift and savage affairs. Surprise and superior firepower were the keys to survival. Even if the amount of traffic damaged or destroyed wasn't great in terms of volume, the enemy was forced to send up planes constantly in daylight, diverting these from offensive operations and consuming fuel. Convoys, even deep behind Axis lines, needed beefing up with extra protection. Everyone had to stay on the alert, with no such thing as a 'safe' zone or harbour.

LRDG raiders would erupt from the sheltering darkness, hose their targets in a storm of automatic fire and grenades, then roar off into the night unscathed. In modern terms this was a brand of asymmetric warfare where the two sides are unevenly matched, but the dash, energy and aggression of the smaller makes up for numerical deficiencies. As David Lloyd Owen confirms, the panic spread by raids was infinitely more damaging to the enemy than the losses inflicted:

The actual nuisance that Tony Hay and his men had caused was nothing to the alarming effect that it had on the enemy, who thought that he was the advanced guard of an enemy force striking towards Agedabia.

The Italians stopped all traffic on this stretch of road, and when convoys did start up again they were only allowed along it with an escort of armoured cars.[17]

Road watch and occasional beat ups were very much the order of the day throughout December 1941. With Jalo occupied by Allied forces, 'A' Squadron with several patrols and the mini artillery train of a single 25-pounder moved up early in the month, taking their orders from Brigadier Reid. Prendergast kept the remainder under his wing at Siwa. Their main role was to concentrate on the Benghazi to Jedabia, Barce to Benghazi, Tobruk–Derna roads and the Mekili area. G1 shot up some enemy traffic but Captain Hay was captured in a brush with the enemy on 16th December.[18] Several patrols were ranging during early December: G2 had to abandon operations when one of the Guardsmen developed appendicitis; Y1 and Y2 were out and Lloyd Owen, leading the latter, joined up with G1, and these combined patrols shot up an enemy convoy on the evening of 14th December.

Eighth Army was deploying larger columns of raiders, such as Reid's force, against specific enemy targets. This was edging towards the kind of operation Orde Wingate had suggested in 1940 – often unwieldy, too heavy for raiding and too light for an all-arms battle. Bruce Ballantyne took out T1 to guide another column, 'Marriott Force'. This was comprised principally of 22nd Guards Brigade, but there were no signs at the RV. It turned out the brigade had been swept up in the desperate fighting around Tobruk, which wasn't properly relieved till 8th December, and took a further fortnight to deploy southwards.[19] After some to-ing and fro-ing, due to the fast moving battle, Marriott Force did not begin its westward advance till 20th December. The target was Antelat. In best cavalry style, 11th Hussars would lead the charge with R1 & R2 patrols guarding both flanks.

Jake Easonsmith had taken R1 out of Siwa on 10th December. He was to join Marriott Force but found time for some hit and run strikes in generally pretty foul weather before catching up on the 16th. Both R1 & R2 were to cover the eastern flank of Marriott Force's axis of advance, establishing contact with 12th Lancers. These desert linkages could be tricky, with the possibility of friendly fire incidents, but happily there were none. Both patrols continued patrolling without incident whilst the Axis continued a rapid retreat. By 20th December Benghazi was captured and Rommel fell back on Jedabia.

Adventures with SAS

David Lloyd Owen had first met Stirling in the wake of the SAS' first disastrous 'parashot' raid: *What a man! Failure meant nothing more to him than to generate fierce determination to be successful next time.*[20] It was their leader's unbreakable enthusiasm that generated the 'can do' spirit which has led the SAS to become, in the seventy years since, the most respected and admired Special Forces in the world. At the outset, the respective roles of SAS/LRDG were not defined. There could even be conflict between pure intelligence gathering, which depends on being invisible, and sabotage, which stirs up the hornets' nest.

Stirling had realised, as he and Lloyd Owen sipped their mugs of tea in the aftermath of an early raid, that parachuting wasn't ideal. It was Lloyd Owen who had the idea of a joint effort between both groups, travelling overland to deliver the parashots to their target zone. LRDG would provide the taxi and navigation service; SAS could get on with blowing things up and killing Germans. This proved to be the ideal relationship and the birth of a Special Forces legend.[21]

Meanwhile, 'A' Squadron from Jalo, still under Brigadier Reid's orders, had undertaken further operations in tandem with the SAS. Their target was the airfields at Sirte while LRDG attacked the highway and Axis traffic. A lesser man than David Stirling might have been disheartened at his continuing bad luck. Both he and LRDG played their assigned roles superbly but there were no enemy aircraft to be had at Sirte. Paddy Mayne fared rather better. At Tamet his crew wrecked two dozen planes and shot up enemy positions: *the story was often told of how Paddy Mayne – who was an immensely powerful man and had been an Irish rugger international before the war – personally destroyed one aircraft with his own hands. He was always reported to have returned with the instrument panel, which he ripped out for a souvenir.*[22] All got away safely and were back in Jalo by 16th December.

Six days earlier, T2 patrol, commanded by Kiwi Lieutenant 'Bing' Morris, had motored out of Siwa intending to taxi a dozen SAS to El Agheila, looking for more aircraft to blow up. They were also tasked to beat up Mersa Brega, some 25 miles northeast, and shoot up whatever targets presented themselves along the coastal highway. Bad conditions, rough going and adverse weather threw up numerous hurdles, but the SAS were delivered to within striking distance of their target. Again, the birds, quite literally, had flown and the landing grounds were bare.

The raiders were not to be denied some trade, however, and on the evening of 16th/17th December brazenly drove along the main road towards Mersa Brega. At the stroke of midnight hey pulled into a large transport park, brimming with enemy vehicles. Battle was joined at no more than *25 to 30 paces.*[23] The firefight was furious and intense, the pale desert night ripped by blinding muzzle flashes and the tremendous din of long bursts of automatic fire. Despite all this huge sound and fury, the LRDG disengaged without loss, leaving around fifteen enemy dead and perhaps just over half a dozen vehicles totalled. Jock Lewes, who was leading the SAS detachment, chucked any number of time bombs into enemy trucks as the firefight was raging.

Lewes was a particularly inventive saboteur. He'd set out to devise an IED which would go off after an interval, but which would also be incendiary. He decided on the use of a time pencil, which worked on the notion of acid eating away at a wire. When this burnt through, a spring was released which caused the blast. This was immediately followed by a further explosion of flame. These proved very effective at destroying planes, habitually the SAS' primary target, and the time delay allowed the raiders to get well clear.[24]

For ten days, 13th–23rd December, John Olivey led S2 and the LRDG's artillery section on an operation from Jalo. This would be the first time an LRDG patrol could muster such heavy fire support. The gunner detachment, commanded by Lieutenant Paul 'Blitz' Eitzen, had originally come with a 4.5-inch howitzer but this had been gifted to Leclerc and the Free French. Gunner Bill Morrison and his chum Jim Patch volunteered to serve with LRDG – even though they weren't sure what the acronym stood for![25] 'Blitz' and one of the other volunteer artillerymen were South African and had the habit of lapsing into Afrikaans, disconcerting for the English. The gun they'd be using was a standard 25-pounder mounted in a Mack 10-tonner. Blitz had the use of a light 8-cwt car.

This was the LRDG artillery train, and their cumbersome truck proved unpopular with the Rhodesians. Macks were far from ideal for the desert, very heavy and much more so when acting as portee.[26] At one point they'd also had the use of a single light tank, totally unsuitable for patrol work as Lloyd Owen rather caustically observed.[27] Both the original howitzer and its 25-pounder successor remained truck-mounted. The force was ordered to scout an area east of El Agheila; to beat up the old fort at El Gtafia, shoot up whatever presented itself on the Jedabia-El Agheila road, and lastly, to recce the ground south and west of Jedabia.

The ramshackle post at Gtafia was surrounded and assaulted on 16th December. The 25-pounder soon proved its worth. Blitz, with Jim acting as his signaller, went forward to recce the target, leaving the portee hidden in dead ground. Contact was by field telephone. Blitz estimated the range and then gave the order to fire. Bill and the gun crew blasted the fort with fourteen rounds. The enemy fled and the place was thoroughly slighted.[28] Despite this resounding success, the artillery section was a relatively short-lived addition, as LRDG soon ran out of forts to bombard.

Another excursion with an SAS detachment followed four days later. This time the commandos were aiming for the airstrip at Jedabia. At last, here was a target with no shortage of trade, and thirty-seven aircraft were destroyed. No casualties had been sustained in either of these actions but two troopers, Corporal Ashby and Private Riggs, were killed in a 'blue on blue' incident at the Wadi el Faregh on 22nd December, strafed by RAF Blenheims, a bitter blow.[29]

Snapping at Rommel's Heels

Just before Christmas, on 21st December, Prendergast received fresh orders direct from the top. The various patrols detached with Reid and Marriott now reverted to Group HQ, and LRDG was instructed to step up offensive patrolling. The group was to report on terrain in Tripolitania (the western portion of Libya, Cyrenaica being the eastern), and conduct more road watch inland and on the coast, paying particular attention to the enemy's defences there. Eighth Army also wanted to know which posts were garrisoned by Germans as opposed to Italians.[30]

Evidence from captured enemy papers clearly showed the LRDG attacks were having an effect. They might snap like terriers but the magnified roar was leonine, as Axis officers believed their numbers to be far greater than in reality and were directing more and more resources to protect their logistics: *These early raids by Stirling's men, with the LRDG providing the method of transport, had an immense effect on Rommel's actions at a time when the Eighth Army was forging ahead. Already his Italian allies were none too certain of how much they wanted to be involved at all….*[31]

General Ritchie was convinced the enemy was exhausted and that, once he'd consolidated in Cyrenaica, he could advance into Tripolitania and finish the job. As events would prove, this was a trifle over-optimistic. However, this halcyon period did offer a chance to harness the aggression of Leclerc and his Free French, who were chomping at the bit. LRDG was tasked to take radio gear and weapons down to Zouar where the French had assembled a mobile column. This was small, a couple of infantry companies, some artillery pieces and a few obsolete planes. Leclerc's force would act under Eighth Army's orders and strike northwards, avoiding Vichy-held territories.

Leclerc was to move on 9th January 1942, but Rommel had other plans and by the 21st of the month was counter-attacking, rapidly re-taking Jedabia and Benghazi. Holliman with S1 took SAS parashots, as Kennedy Shaw described them at the time, for another crack at airstrips at Sirte and Wadi Tamet on 24th December. A very Merry

Christmas greeting from British Special forces saw another twenty-seven planes go up in flames at Wadi Tamet, but the raid on Sirte had to be abandoned when the attackers were rumbled by sentries. Nobody was hit or captured and the patrol skilfully evaded the pursuit.[32]

On Christmas day itself, no one was taking holidays that year, as Lieutenant Morris guided two more SAS teams, aiming to hit the landing grounds near 'Marble Arch'. Morris had fifteen men from LRDG and ten from SAS. The first group was taken to a point six miles from the aerodrome, the rest ferried closer to Nofilia. This second team, led by Jock Lewes, was collected from the dropping off point on 30th December. As the combined patrol drove nearer Marble Arch they were set upon by a lone Messerschmitt 110. This first strafing run inflicted no damage but more Axis planes followed. Stukas this time, and though the vehicles had been camouflaged, the enemy scored several hits and Jock Lewes was killed, a very great loss to the SAS. As the morning wore on, trucks were knocked out one by one. Morris managed to extricate one driveable vehicle and rally survivors, but nine LRDG and one SAS were left in the confusion.

This produced another LRDG epic as the men walked for 200 exhausting, cold and hungry miles to reach British lines; only the sole SAS trooper dropped out because his feet were in a terrible state. It took them eight days to cover the ground and they *heralded in 1942 with a mouthful of water each while they watched 'the RAF paying their respects to the Luftwaffe at what we thought was Marble Arch aerodrome as the flares were very bright.... At dawn the next day they saw some fires 'and we reasoned that where there was fire there was wogs and where there were wogs there was water and perhaps food.*[33] Whether men were wearing boots or the less substantial Chaplis, none of the available footwear stood up to the rigours of a desert march. Corporal Garvin's ad hoc solution was a slice of woollen greatcoat on one foot and a scrap of canvas cover from a Lewis gun on the other.

Lloyd Owen with Y2 was ranging over central Tripolitania in the dying days of 1941, while Timpson, leading G2, beat up the highway between Hon and Misurata. On 7th January, Jake Easonsmith took

R1 to waylay traffic on the Zella–Hon road. The ground the patrol traversed was made up of powdery limestone, or 'fesh-fesh', tricky at best and it proved impossible to conceal vehicle tracks. They were attacked by aircraft, followed by ground forces but managed successfully to avoid both and get back unscathed. Captain Frank Simms with Y1 had been temporarily attached to 13 Corps as guide and liaison, as Eighth Army was moving towards Antelat and Marble Arch. On a recce towards Marada, Simms was captured and Lloyd Owen took over. Rommel then trumped everybody by attacking at Msus.

On the surface, it appeared that the 'Crusader' battles had resulted in a significant victory for Eighth Army. This was largely illusory as the thinning of British dispositions left the gains in Cyrenaica, so dearly won, again at hazard. Auchinleck was proceeding to plan 'Acrobat' – a further attack upon the remaining Axis hold on Tripolitania. Strung out in winter quarters, the army had few fixed defences and penny packet garrisons, a doleful lack of concentration. 7th Armoured Division had been withdrawn for a much needed refit, and 1st Armoured, which lacked its fellow tankers' battlefield experience, was put in to plug the gap. Supply lines were tenuous and inadequate, plus there remained the problem of Malta. Eighth Army required the island fortress still in British hands to continue the fight, but to protect Malta it was necessary to maintain forward aerodromes in Cyrenaica.

Rommel had also noted these deficiencies, and a subtle shift in the balance of resources provided him with an opportunity, one which he, as arch-opportunist, was not about to ignore. On 12th January his senior intelligence officer, Major F.W. von Mellenthin, predicted that for the next fortnight the Axis forces would be slightly stronger than the British immediately opposed to them.

On 21st January, the Desert Fox threw two strong columns into an attack, one advancing along the coast road, the other swinging in a flanking arc, north of Wadi el Faregh. Caught off guard and dispersed, British units began to fall back. General Ritchie was, at this time, far to the rear in Cairo and disposed to regard these moves as nothing more than a raid or reconnaissance in force. He and Auchinleck did not detect the tremors of disquiet that commanders on the ground were experiencing. Early cables suggested the situation might be ripe for a strong riposte.

It has been said of military matters that 'too often the capacity to advance is identified with the desirability of advancing'. Never was this truer than in the Desert War, and the reality was that Rommel had seized and was maintaining the initiative. By the 24th the 'Auk' was sending signals in an altogether more sober tone. Rommel was still advancing, his own supply difficulties notwithstanding.

When one German officer had the nerve to point out that fuel stocks were critical he received the curt advice: *well go and get it from the British*. Within a day there were plans to evacuate Benghazi, producing a rather plaintive cry from Whitehall, *...why should they all be off so quickly?* Both Ritchie and Auchinleck flew to the front but the local commanders, their instincts more finely tuned, were preparing for withdrawal. 4th Indian Division was pulling out from Benghazi as 1st Armoured prepared to regroup near Mechili.

Swift as a terrier, Rommel, alerted by wireless intercepts, planned a double-headed thrust. One pincer swept along the coast road whilst the second, the Fox in the lead, pushed over higher ground to sweep around and come upon the port from the southeast. A dummy lunge toward Mechili was intended to fool Ritchie and succeeded. He dispatched his armour, leaving Benghazi exposed. Von Mellenthin, commenting on the effectiveness of the panzer tactics and the speed of the British withdrawals, observed scathingly: *the pursuit attained a speed of fifteen miles an hour and the British fled madly over the desert in one of the most extraordinary routs of the war.*

For LRDG the enemy's lightning advance meant abandoning Jalo and returning to Siwa. So swift was the movement that Captain Carr with an entire supply unit, fourteen men and seven vehicles, was captured in a job lot when he rolled into Msus. He had no radio and so couldn't be warned. As ever, LRDG was soon fighting back. On 17th January, Hunter had ferried another SAS team, led by Stirling himself, to raid Bouerat el Hsun. Despite a number of difficulties, mechanical problems and the attentions of enemy aircraft, the raid achieved its purpose and extended to more mayhem on the coast road. On the road home, they ran into an ambush but shot their way clear without loss.[34]

Constant patrolling and the relentless grind of desert travel had taken its toll on the trucks, and by the start of February a number of patrols had returned to Cairo for re-fitting where the worn out Fords were replaced by 30-cwt Chevrolets. New automatic weapons, including more .50 calibre Vickers, Vickers 'K' Lewis guns and the effective 22-mm Breda were issued. At the same time a further structural re-organisation took place. LRDG would now have its HQ, with a squadron of six patrols under hand, whilst a mobile or 'detachable' squadron of four patrols could be used as a flying column or columns as needed. An RAOC repair section plus signals team were attached to HQ. Eighth Army was now standing on the Gazala Line and Rommel had clawed back significant tracts of Cyrenaica. The Prime Minister was not amused.

For LRDG, this meant a shift back to road watch. Intelligence was vital. Rommel had caught Auchinleck completely unprepared, and the resulting rout or 'Msus Stakes' as labelled by the wags, was indeed something of an embarrassment. The Germans, at this stage, were still rather better than their opponents at recovering and repairing their damaged tanks and tucks. They proved equally proficient at recycling British abandoned stock. Many spare parts had been harvested from earlier retreats in France, Greece and Crete as well as the Desert.

When G2 under Timpson left Siwa on 9th February, Hasledon was with him. The patrol split into two teams for the road watch. Hasledon noticed how many enemy trucks were ours, recovered, repaired, re-branded and generally showing less wear than Axis equivalents. Most were heading east and the patrol managed to scoop up some British stragglers left behind in the race for safety. Quite a few others were on the move, seeking to regain Allied lines. On the whole, local Arabs were both loyal and helpful; however, any opportunity to plunder their Italian occupiers was always welcome![35]

Y2 recce'd ground northeast of Jedabia early in February but the featureless terrain made concealment tricky. They passed many abandoned British vehicles, most plundered by or being repaired by the Italians. On 25th February John Olivey took S2 back to watching the main Benghazi–Tripoli highway. This dreary routine went on for weeks, and numerous patrols were involved.

The favoured spot hadn't shifted from that chosen the year before, around thirty-five miles west of El Agheila and five miles east of Marble Arch: *Bill Kennedy Shaw recently sent me* [David Lloyd Owen] *the original sketch which he drew for the navigator of the first patrol to do this work. It records the position of the spot where the vehicles were concealed.… It also gives details of the best line of approach and the time of day that he recommends.*[36] As Lloyd Owen trenchantly observed, this was typical of the meticulous recording and briefing by LRDG. Their appearance from the still and all-encompassing dark might have been what frightened the enemy, but it was such intensive attention to detail that made these eruptions work.

As ever, the road drill didn't vary and there was no shortage of trade. As before, Axis vehicles were often being towed to economise on fuel consumption, and by now the watchers were expert at identifying truck and troop types. Holliman, returning from his refit in Cairo, was sent to watch the roads running east out of Barce. This mission ran into numerous problems, not least of which was a flash flood which engulfed several parked up trucks. Only two vehicles made the return journey to Siwa.[37] Dick Croucher also came back from Zouar, because Rommel's rapid recovery and counter-strokes had effectively neutralised Leclerc's plan to attack in the Fezzan.

As both sides paused to draw breath in early March, Eighth Army sent out yet another set of commandments, directed both towards LRDG and their SAS brethren:

- Beating up the enemy wherever the chance should arise;
- Specifically targeting airstrips and lines of communication ("L of C"), forcing the enemy to spread his resources; to destroy enemy vehicles and armour, supply dumps and repair shops;

- Gathering intelligence generally;
- LRDG to focus primarily on reconnaissance and intelligence gathering, and to continue providing a taxi service for the SAS.

David Stirling, though his SAS had a very close relationship with LRDG, did not always appreciate the need for reconnaissance over beat ups. For him, killing Germans was the priority. He was *naturally impatient with long-term reconnaissance missions, which might inhibit the spectacular results that might be his if only the LRDG's Road Watch wasn't in the way.*[38] The approach was different but the sentiments remained the same. Both units did good service. Blowing things up was spectacular and satisfying, but long-term intelligence gathering was vital – pedestrian by comparison but essential. Demolition would always be the optional extra.

GHQ's memorandum parcelled up the areas to be attacked by differing formations. In the forward zones this would be the regulars, with Middle East Commandos in an intermediate zone and LRDG/SAS operating further west.[39] Throughout March and April, as the giant brawl on the coast bubbled, LRDG were again in the field with SAS raiding parties. Olivey with S2, ferrying David Stirling, was to hit landing strips at Berca and Benina and target vessels in the harbour at Benghazi. TI, under Morris, was to take SAS to the Slonta area and pick up commandos who were already active there. Olivey would later sweep up that SAS team. Holliman and S1 were to taxi another gang of SAS saboteurs south of Barce and get them back to Siwa after their mission.

Holliman felt constrained to leave three trucks at Sidi Zamut, after he'd been warned enemy patrols were active. He took the team in with his remaining vehicles and dropped them without interference. Corporal Eastwood, in charge of the stay behind group, had moved to a new RV to avoid roving enemy aircraft. Holliman rejoined Eastwood on 21st March and the patrol was able to rescue two of the trucks lost to the flash flooding earlier. The SAS team was extracted after a successful foray. S2 with Stirling's troopers caught up with Holliman on the 28th. The raids on Berca, Benghazi and Benina had, as ever, met with mixed fortunes. Stirling again found no trade at the Benina airstrip. Mayne, who seemed to have the magic touch, smashed fifteen planes at Berca.[40]

The SAS leader was in demand so was to be brought back straightaway from the combined RV at Chedu bu Maun. This left the second SAS team under Lieutenant Dodds to be recovered, a task that now fell to Dick Croucher and R2. Croucher's patrol would also ferry in a commando team, commanded by a Major Glennie. It wasn't until 8th April that Dodds and his squad were picked up and, like the Pied Piper, the SAS had attracted a tail of stragglers, detritus from the fighting, including half a dozen RAF personnel. Ferrying this lot back meant Croucher had to make a second run to collect Glennie and his commandos. There were rumours of enemy activity about, gleaned mainly from local Arabs, but no actual contacts occurred during these taxi operations.[41]

Back on the Roads

Eighth Army had reason to be pleased with these hit and run missions, aside from destroying materiel, they forced the enemy to disperse scarce resources. However, on 23rd April, St. George's Day, LRDG was ordered to go back onto road watch. Of particular interest was the section of track between Mekili and Msus; the enemy was bringing much of his own warlike stores eastwards from Tripoli up to Benghazi.

Prendergast was placed in charge of both western zones with two squadrons from Middle East Commando now coming under his command, along with a miscellaneous collection of informers and agents. Anyone else operating on his extended turf would also report to him. Clearly, this much wider responsibility was a testament to his and LRDG's track record, but the absolute priority now was intelligence gathering rather than beat ups. Road watches were not to be compromised by attacking random targets of opportunity, however tempting.[42]

Middle East Commando re-organised their 'A' Squadron along SAS lines, splitting the men into three patrols, each equipped with new

Chevy 15-cwts. The commandos had a fairly circumscribed operational range but also formed another three offensive or sabotage sections for going in on foot and blowing things up. At the same time, (11th May), a pair of patrols from the Indian Long Range Squadron ("ILRS") was imported from Syria.

The ILRS only came fully under the wing of LRDG from October 1942 till the following spring and the advance into Tunisia. Captain Sam McCoy, a regular from the Indian Army, had the idea, approved by C-in-C Middle East, and the unit served as part of Ninth Army during 1941–1942. Its intended role was broadly similar to its North African equivalent but focused in the Iraq/Iran sector. Captain, then Major McCoy recruited from Indian Army units, primarily cavalry. In ethos and outlook it was very similar to LRDG and the unit integrated easily in the Western Desert.

Eric Wilson had been posted back to Blighty and Jake Easonsmith took over as 2I/C. Philip Arnold continued the unsung work of the 'heavies' by creating a whole series of escape dumps, essential when you need them. Despite this wider role, LRDG was 'blind' as both WACOs were temporarily *hors de combat* awaiting new engines. The RAF's disdain for the minor competition had not diminished. During the early spring it was back to Marble Arch and the roads. Despite the weight of enemy traffic and their past experiences of LRDG beat ups, there was little or no contact. Some back roads and tracks had been mined.

Lieutenant Crisp, on watch along the Mekili–Msus track during virtually all of May, picked up little traffic data but he did recover six RAF crewmen who'd crash-landed their Wellington bomber nearby. On 2nd May, Robin Gurdon taxied two intelligence officers to a location nearly 40 miles southeast of Benghazi. In the event, one of the IO's, Captain Melot, needed to be nearer the coast and the patrol motored another 15 miles northwest.

Alastair Timpson with G1 was allocated a section of highway between Marble Arch and Sirte. His mission was to seek and destroy enemy vehicles, not in the traditional shoot 'em up style, but by lobbing time bombs into passing traffic. This was easier ordered than accomplished. Chucking the devices into moving vehicles was very tricky. The bomber had to force or dupe his quarry into slowing down so that someone could throw the bomb into the open rear of the truck. This also had its hazards, for those riding in the back were liable to notice an explosive device arriving so suddenly in their horrified midst. The knack was to fake up a section of supposed road works, using 45-gallon drums with poles stretched over and between with suitably worded dummy warning notices put up.

A pile of road metal, handily dumped by the enemy, highlighted the ideal spot. On the night of 14th May, Timpson and his bombing party were lurking with intent. Their truck was well hidden back from the road, both machine-guns ready. Two more ambushers with small arms and grenades were in place nearby. The gravel was scattered over the road in a slovenly non-Teutonic, Italianate manner and five of the drums set up. It looked convincing enough, perhaps so much so that blasé drivers weren't inclined to take notice and simply drove around. All attempts proved abortive. Moving the obstructions further across the highway had no greater effect. Next idea was that an LRDG truck, lights doused, would follow Axis vehicles and then Sergeant Fraser, perched rather precariously on the bonnet, would lob bombs into the vehicle in front. That didn't work either.[43]

Abortive or not, such impudence was unlikely to go unpunished. Next afternoon, in the dull sheen of midday heat, the LRDG sentry saw an enemy vehicle approaching at about 200 yards. Probably the Italians had spotted the patrol's radio antenna. They began shooting with rifles and automatic weapons. This was foolish and wasteful as the raider's trucks were well camouflaged, and a sharp little skirmish kicked off. Enemy fire soon slackened and the patrol managed to get all their vehicles out of the Wadi. Had these attackers been German then it might have been very different. As it was, the Italians' enthusiasm for continuing soon ebbed. One trooper, Guardsman Matthews, was killed in the action.[44] Undeterred, the patrol beat up a roadhouse on the night of 22nd/23rd May before returning to Siwa on the 28th.

At the beginning of the second week in May, John Olivey with S2 was taxiing commandos to and from the foothills of the Jebel-el-Akhdar. The hope had been that these could take on some of the chore of road watch but they hadn't built up the necessary skills base. By now LRDG were past masters, so the experiment was abandoned. As a substitute, 'Popski' and his brigands were detailed to undertake road watch in this vicinity. In the middle of the month Robin Gurdon, leading G2, ferried in the indefatigable Stirling for another crack at Benghazi. As a secondary objective, they were to mine the Benghazi–Barce railway line. En route, they encountered Nick Wilder and T2 who warned that the Axis had planted agents amongst hitherto friendly Arabs, and their route was varied accordingly.

In the wee small hours of 22nd May, Corporal Wilson successfully mined the tracks in two places. Despite the care and ingenuity of the sabotage squad, the mine failed to explode (more probably it was detected[45]). As usual, they fared better than Stirling, who'd spent two busy if fruitless days in Benghazi. The Italians never suspected who was in their midst but their shipping stayed safe, for the moment at least. Nick Wilder had been looking for road traffic to bomb. His idea had been similar to Timpson's and worked no better. Their attempt at impromptu road works was treated with the same casual disdain by Axis drivers, though one vehicle was shot up and bombed.

Lloyd Owen was briefed to ferry a team of spooks up to Tarhuna, some forty miles southeast of Tripoli. Once the shepherding duty was completed, he was given free rein to beat up a large MT depot nearby. So far all good, but the inaccuracy of the maps meant the distance was far greater than imagined, a total trip of some 2,000 miles and operating further west than any previous patrol. Lloyd Owen wasn't overly enthusiastic about his passengers, the senior member being *an Italian civilian prisoner who professed to be anti-fascist;* to whom he took *an instant dislike.*[46] His suspicions proved entirely justified, the Italian was indeed shifty, and Lloyd Owen decided he should be 'banged-up' for the rest of the war. To dodgy Italians was added the problem of dodgy tyres, a duff batch which meant the patrol never got as far as Tripoli.

The 'Gazala' Gallop'

Rommel's offensive and the Battle of Gazala, dubbed 'the Gazala Gallop' by Eighth Army, can be divided into three phases: (1) Rommel launches his flank attack, 26th–29th May, attempting to overrun British defences from behind; (2) fighting in the 'Cauldron' as Rommel tries to re-supply and consolidate his forces; and (3) the reduction of Bir Hacheim, and the pounding of British armour 11th–13th June, followed by withdrawal from the Gazala line. A fourth and final phase of this battle was the subsequent storming of Tobruk.

By 14th June, Ritchie was seeking permission to draw off, fall back to the frontier and save his forces from encirclement. Rommel was master of the central battlefield. This would imply the temporary abandonment of the Tobruk garrison, which would again be isolated. Auchinleck was not yet ready to throw in the towel, however, insisting that further counter-attacks be launched to deny the approaches to Tobruk. As C-in-C he had to answer to the Prime Minister who was already querying his intentions.

Withdrawal in the face on an aggressive enemy is never a smooth business and the retreat of Eighth Army inevitably produced a semblance of rout. Rommel would not relinquish pressure and struck toward the airfield at Gambut. The rump of 4th Armoured sallied out but was again badly mauled; control of events had passed irrevocably beyond Ritchie's grip. For Rommel, there was now the matter of his unfinished business with the defenders of Tobruk.

As early as January 1942, the joint Middle East commanders, Auchinleck, Cunningham and Tedder, had agreed that Tobruk, if isolated, should not once again be defended. Militarily, this was eminently sensible but the place had become imbued with a great deal of political capital at a time when British arms had endured such a series of dismal defeats in Norway, France, Greece and Crete with such sharp reverses in the Western Desert.

By 17th June, Rommel had secured Gambut airfield and beaten off the remnant of British armour. Tobruk was again invested. Two days later there was still some ill-founded optimism that the perimeter could be held on the basis or in the pious hope that Axis forces would settle down for a lengthy siege. However, the situation now within the ring was very different from before. Hitherto strong defences had been denuded and pillaged to meet the exigencies of the now defunct Gazala Line, and the garrison was badly placed to resist a sustained attack.

Rommel, scenting this weakness, unleashed the *Luftwaffe,* which began blasting the fortress on 20th June as the precursor to a determined attack from the southeast. By 7:45 the anti-tank ditch, equivalent to a medieval moat, had been breached and the perimeter was collapsing. There had been talk of a breakout should this occur, but in reality no escape route was viable. Auchinleck's report to London, late on the 20th, sounded a note of impending catastrophe, and then Tobruk fell. 35,000 Allied soldiers passed into captivity, and 2,000 tons of fuel and as many vehicles fell into Axis hands. It was a disastrous defeat. The debacles in Greece and Crete combined had not witnessed such fearful loss.

As the storm broke over Eighth Army, new orders came to LRDG:

- Road watch on the Mekili-Msus section was to continue;
- Beat ups were to be planned for the area around Lamluda (some 28 miles west of Derna, a key junction for several tracks);
- A taxi service to be provided for Bertie Buck's irregular irregulars and a detachment of Free French who were about to have a crack at Martuba airfield;
- The commandos were detailed to beat up the two parallel roads running through the Jebel el Akhdar. LRDG would do the ferrying but should keep out of any fighting;
- Two patrols were to guide Stirling for another attack on the aerodromes at Berca, Benina and Barce (if the raid went ahead);
- Road watch on the main Tripoli highway should be maintained;
- At least one patrol was to be held in reserve and be ready to recce desert terrain in Cyrenaica.[47]

One of the more depressing features of road watch at this time was the large number of Allied POWs being marched west. Indian (1) Patrol was sent out from Siwa on 30th May to ferry spooks toward Benghazi and to collect Captain Melot as they returned. On his instruction, they might mine the Barce–Benghazi line. They achieved all of these objectives. The railway was indeed mined and, despite some pursuit, they got clear without loss, back at Siwa by 9th June. The commandos were less fortunate, losing most of their transport to enemy air attacks.

Nick Wilder fared rather better. He'd led both T1 and T2 out on 4th June to beat up the road section from Jedabia to Benghazi. He divided his force into two assault groups, targeting specific areas. On the night of 7th/8th June, T1 'brassed-up' an enemy convoy, wrecking numerous vehicles and leaving as many as thirty Axis dead in their wake.[48] On the 9th the combined patrols got ready to attack an enemy bunker but the assault was postponed and they had to be content with beating up an enemy patrol in a short, sharp firefight, killing several and taking a number of prisoners.

It fell to Robin Gurdon with G2 to taxi Stirling, Mayne and several SAS detachments, including a Free French team into the Benina–Barce sector. LRDG had eight patrols working this same zone, and G1 would be relatively close and able to provide back-up if needed. The enemy was getting smarter, tracks were now regularly mined, and several vehicles were damaged. Aircraft were constantly on the prowl. Despite difficulties, Stirling and his raiders were dropped off near Regima, as planned, on the evening of 11th June. The SAS were recovered two and three days later, intact except for one man who'd been mislaid.

On the 16th they moved again – the French would hit Berca and the British would go back into Benghazi. Stirling not only had Fitzroy Maclean with him but also Randolph Churchill. Bill Kennedy later wished, writing in May 1943, that the episode could be read out to Il Duce, letting him know that the British Prime Minister's son spent thirty-six hours lurking undetected in the capital of Cyrenaica![49]

Nobody seems to have told the RAF, who carried out a big beat up of their own on the Berca airstrips on the night of the 12th/13th, compromising the French SAS raid. Despite this, the French wrecked eleven planes and killed fifteen of the enemy. Stirling inflicted some damage at Benina. At Benghazi in the witching hours of 16th/17th June, Stirling did yet more damage. None of these raids would materially affect the course of the main battle, which overall went disastrously badly for the Allies, but, as ever, the pinpricks could amount to a serious bleed, as the enemy had to divert personnel and resources to repairing the damage and beefing up security.

Holliman with S1 took another Free French SAS team to Barce on 8th June. Little could be achieved as the enemy had significantly boosted their defences and increased their vigilance. Frustrating as this was, it reflected the success of the earlier raids. These troops, now enduring the tedium of guarding airfields, might otherwise have been deployed in the main battle. LRDG/SAS were still punching way above their combined weight.

Alastair Guild with R1 was also ordered to transport yet another Free French SAS unit, fourteen troopers under Lieutenant Jordan plus Captain 'Bertie' Buck and another fourteen of his SIG German Jews from Palestine, dressed as DAK. Buck commanded both commando units. His targets were the airfields at Martuba and Derna. At the outset Buck's raiders did very well, knocking out a score of Axis planes. It seems likely one of the SIG was an Abwehr plant, however, and he betrayed them all. In the melee which followed, all of the Free French were killed or captured, though Lieutenant Jordan subsequently contrived to escape. LRDG successfully extracted the survivors.[50]

Lieutenant G.W. Nangle and Indian (2) Patrol spent a tedious and enervating week on the Jalo–Jedabia track but found no trade. Meanwhile, Timpson with G1 had teamed up with Dick Croucher and R2, for a joint assignment to watch the road from Afrag to El Carmusa, some twenty miles southwest of Derna. Again, the track was bare of any trade. Timpson next decided to have a look at the coast road, since locals had advised of several enemy camps.

The patrols selected a suitable tactical vantage about three miles south of the main highway near Sidi Scisher Ruhai. On the night of 18th/19th June, both units moved into offensive positions. At first, all went well when a pair of Italian tank transporters were stopped and their crews taken prisoner. So far so good, but radio contact between the two patrol groups had been lost and, with confusion rampant, both began firing at each other! Despite their combined weight of firepower, nobody was hit. They were all back at Siwa by 22nd June.[51]

Lieutenant Crisp with T2 was in the field from 19th to 25th June. His job was to pick up an RAF survivor who'd been recovered by Popski's guerrillas in the Jebel Akhdar. He was also to insert a dozen volunteers from the Libyan Arab Force led by a Captain Grandguillot into the area as an escape and evasion team, assisting other flyers who'd come down there. On the day he returned, there were momentous changes taking place within Eighth Army HQ.

Mersa Matruh

On that same day, General Auchinleck, accompanied by Brigadier Eric Dorman-Smith, arrived from Cairo at Maaten Baggush, Ritchie's Eighth Army HQ. It was not a social call. The army commander was curtly relieved of his post and Auchinleck, as C-in-C, assumed direct tactical control of Eighth Army. Dorman-Smith – 'Chink' – was to act as an unofficial chief of staff. On the flight from Cairo the two had discussed the current, dire position, concluding that the only course open was for a further tactical withdrawal to the El Alamein line a hundred and fifty miles east of Mersa Matruh, where the army was attempting a stand. Wavell had previously identified the small port as the absolute 'last ditch' position for defence of the Delta. Otherwise enemy aircraft could strike at vital installations and civilian targets there.

Despite the scale of the recent reverses, Eighth Army HQ persisted in a degree of upbeat assessments whose optimistic tone rested on the belief that Rommel, for the moment, was spent and could not maintain his offensive. Bastico, with Kesselring, reminded their impetuous paladin that it was time to draw breath whilst the agreed strategy for Operation '*Herkules*', the reduction of Malta, was effected. Bastico, who like Rommel, had now attained his field marshal's baton, demanded a halt. The Desert Fox, who modestly ascribed his successes solely to the valour of his troops, persisted in arguing that to ease pressure at this juncture would toss away a hard-earned opportunity. On 24th June Rommel received the green light, just as well perhaps as his forward units had already been advancing for the last two days!

The Fox, his hunter's instincts attuned, was poised to deliver what he believed to be the killing blow. In the circumstances, it is difficult to see what other course remained for Auchinleck, other than to take direct command. Ritchie was floundering and Eighth Army was in a most parlous state. Brooke maintained his confidence in the 'Auk' and Churchill, who could be as magnanimous as he could be bullying, lent his hearty approval. In choosing Dorman-Smith as chief of staff, he found a subordinate of considerable intellectual capacity and strategic insight, but one who, like himself, was not able to fully mesh with the army commanders themselves. These were frequently both confused and demoralised by orders they received but did not fully understand. Auchinleck commanded the army's resources but he did not control its soul, without which the sinews could not flex properly.

'Chink', whose views on his fellow officers tended to be unflattering, was made to 'writhe' when he learnt of Ritchie's dispositions for the defence of Matruh. It was as if Eighth Army had learnt absolutely nothing from previous mistakes. 'Strafer' Gott with 13 Corps was to hold the perimeter around the port, with hastily dug and inadequate defences – inviting a repeat of Tobruk. 20 Corps was deployed a score of miles to the south astride an escarpment; Freyberg with his New Zealanders was posted 'in the middle of nowhere'. Remnants of 1st Armoured Division were lurking far to the south while the yawning gap between the two corps was patrolled by a brace of relatively weak mobile columns.

Auchinleck was painfully aware of the political capital invested in the 'last ditch' position at Matruh. Britain's faltering credibility would slide yet further and there was the inevitable knock-on effect on civilian morale in the Delta, where anti-colonial sentiment was already hopeful of an Axis victory. He had thus decided to make a stand at Matruh whilst allowing his army the necessary flexibility to fall back toward the El Alamein position, perhaps the worst of both worlds as it implied any withdrawal would literally be under the enemy guns.

This obvious difficulty would be compounded by the fact the principal Corps positions were so far apart. Battle was joined on 27th June. 'Pike' was the code for retreat and both British Corps were to converge on Minqar Omar which lay some 30 miles east. Gott had already acted but his disengagement soon ran into difficulties. Though 1st Armoured withdrew smoothly, the New Zealanders ran into opposition. Freyberg had been wounded and Brigadier Inglis took over to find the division boxed in around Minqar Quaim.

The Kiwis reacted vigorously, broke through the ring, inflicting loss upon the enemy. In Matruh, General Holmes was completely out of touch and was even planning a counter-attack. This came to nothing and by 28th June his corps was isolated and encircled. Holmes then planned for breakout: Both 50th and 10th Indian divisions would begin to move after 21.00 hrs and hasten south for 30 miles before swinging eastwards into the vicinity of Fuka.

British formations, thrown into brigade groups and moving in columns, endured a dangerous passage. Axis forces were already at Fuka where 21st Panzer had overrun the remnant of 29th Indian Brigade and a series of sharp, confused actions ensued. 10th Indian Division, in particular, suffered considerable casualties. Thus the decision to stand at Matruh had precipitated a further debacle and the *Panzerarmee* seemed unstoppable. In accordance with the notion of diminishing power of the offensive, Rommel should have run out of steam. The rule applied doubly in the desert where supply difficulties imposed such severe constraints, but DAK had, in part been sustained by captured materiel in Tobruk, and more garnered in the wake of Eighth Army's precipitate and frequently headlong retreats.

Prior to Rommel's offensive supplies had been stockpiled for 'Acrobat' – the onward Allied rush into Tripolitania. Now, the hard-pressed rear echelon units of the RAOC and RASC struggled to salvage or destroy their precious stores in the confusion of defeat.

Prodigies of deliverance were indeed effected but such was the scale and extent of the build-up that much still fell into Axis hands. If the Axis were doing well on the ground, however, their grasp of the skies was crumbling. Squadrons of Kesselring's planes were being fed into the endless mincer of the Eastern Front whilst sorties from Malta were exacting an increasing toll. The pendulum had not yet swung for the final time.

Farewell to Siwa

Rommel's seemingly unstoppable run of successes spelt the end for LRDG at Siwa. It was no longer a secure FOB, so 'A' Squadron went back to Kufra and the rest withdrew into the Nile Valley. Aside from being demoralising, these moves complicated patrol operations. From the Nile, LRDG teams had to either pass through the lines at El Alamein or negotiate the horrors of the Qattara Depression. The road watch along the coast highway was being conducted some eight hundred miles west of Cairo and six hundred northwest of Kufra. Cooperation with Middle East Commandos also came to an end in July.

Matruh had been another reverse for Allied arms, yet despite this setback, Auchinleck had kept the army in being. This, as he and Dorman-Smith had identified, was the prime objective. Only by preserving mobile field forces could the British position in the Middle East be saved. He had now gone beyond Wavell's 'worst case' and was considering how best to defend the Delta itself should he be pushed that far.

Meanwhile there was the ground south of El Alamein, a strip of desert some 38 miles in extent that lay between salt marsh and sea to the north and the impassable Qattara Depression, where no tank could tread. Here was ground that favoured a defensive battle, to be fought by an army markedly inferior in armour and less mobile than its opponent, one that needed time to rebuild and replenish.

For the most part this ground is featureless, till one reaches the rock-strewn hills that flank the waste of marsh and dune announcing the depression. Even these are no more than 700 feet above sea level but much nearer the sea are the twin eminences, rounded hillocks or 'tells' of which Tel el Eisa and Tel el Makh Khad would prove significant. The terrain is everywhere barren; loose, deepening sand alternating with unyielding rock which emerges in the narrow lateral ridges Miteirya, Ruweisat and Alam el Halfa.

These insignificant features would assume considerable importance in the fighting to come, and blood would be poured out in torrents to secure them. Once taken, such features were heartbreakingly difficult to fortify, horribly exposed. In places the ground dipped into shallow depressions ('deirs'), natural saucers. That Auchinleck and Dorman-Smith should focus on the potential here was nothing revelatory, as the Alamein position had been identified as a natural defence line for the Delta some years beforehand.

Efforts at constructing a line of fortifications had been begun in the early days but operational priorities had relegated the endeavour. Initially, the plan had been for the creation of three heavily defended localities at El Alamein and the coast, at Bab el Qattara (Qaret el Abd) and at Naqb Abu Dweis. By the coast some positions were completed, wired and mined, in the centre there was rather less completed, and in the south very little. Water supplies were, however, on hand along the axis of the intended front.

Rommel, on 30th June, was poised for the attack. His men were utterly weary and suffering from the customary shortage of supply. He did not pause but moved straight into the offensive. His limited reconnaissance was soon to be found wanting for he had failed to appreciate the strength of the South Africans dug in around El Alamein. His plan was that both 90th Light Division and DAK would charge the gap north of Deir el Abyad. Whilst the Light Division would seek to replicate its earlier success in interdicting the coast road and thus isolating the Alamein garrison, DAK would sprint south to swing around behind 13 Corps. As ever the Italian formations were given a subordinate role, one division assaulting Alamein from the west, another behind 90th Light and the remainder trailing the panzers.

Matters did not go according to plan. Foul conditions delayed the progress of German armour, and 90th Light bumped the Alamein defences and suffered under the intense weight of fire the South Africans brought down upon them. DAK found Deir el Shein unexpectedly held by 18th Infantry Brigade and a fierce battle erupted. Newly arrived and inexperienced, 18th Brigade had struggled to dig into the stony surface and had limited support.

Nonetheless, the brigade fought hard against lengthening odds and with a crumbling perimeter, their few 'I' tanks and guns disabled. Despite a very gallant stand, the survivors were forced to surrender by evening on 1st July. The loss of the brigade was yet another blow, and an intervention by 1st Armoured Division was so long delayed as to be too late. DAK had won another tactical victory, but at the cost of a badly disrupted timetable.

90th Light, having extricated itself from initial contact, sought to resume its headlong dash, but intense fire from South African positions descended like a deluge and stopped any advance dead in its tracks. The Desert Air Force was living up to its role as the main striking arm, and the Axis sprint was grinding to a halt. DAK had suffered significant reported losses in available tank strength, and its supply columns had been bombed incessantly. By 2nd July Rommel was still making no progress and resolved to throw his armour behind the assault on the coast road.

Auchinleck had quickly appreciated that Allied outposts were exposed, and moved to concentrate his forces. Both sides attacked during the afternoon of 2nd July. In the north General Pienaar's South Africans again resisted the Axis strike, aided by mobile elements drawn from 10th Indian Division. 90th Light was, once more, harassed by the incessant attentions of Desert Air Force and could make no headway. To the south and west, just beyond Ruweisat Ridge, British and German armour were heavily embroiled. At the end of a hard day's fighting, neither side could claim victory, but the Axis offensive had not progressed.

During the hours of darkness air attacks continued till battle was rejoined on the morning of the 3rd. There was yet more heavy fighting south of Ruweisat Ridge. In the south, Freyberg's New Zealanders scored a signal success when they overran the artillery component of Ariete Division, netting a fine haul of prisoners and captured guns. 5th New Zealand Brigade was in action against the Brescia division at El Mreir. By now the Axis formations were severely ground down. Rommel reported his own divisions could only muster 1,000 or 1,200 men apiece, and incessant aerial bombardment was playing havoc with already overstretched supply lines. Skirmishing continued throughout 4th July but the main German effort was, for the moment, spent. It had been a failure.

The pendulum was poised for a decisive swing.

Notes

1 Included by kind courtesy of the Fusiliers Museum of Northumberland.
2 Gott, Lieutenant-General William, Henry, Ewart CB, CBE, DSO & Bar, MC 1897–1942 ('Strafer'). Having served with distinction in the KRRC with the BEF 'Strafer' Gott, (so-named in WWI after *Gott strafe England*), was stationed in Egypt in 1939 commanding 1st Battalion KRRC. A series of rapid promotions followed for this blunt, soldierly figure who, had he not died in an air crash would have commanded Eighth Army and not Montgomery.
3 Wynter, p. 87.
4 Ibid., p. 91.
5 Ibid., p. 92.
6 Ibid., p. 93.
7 Lloyd Owen, p. 57.
8 Wynter, p. 94.
9 Ibid., p. 97.
10 Lloyd Owen, p. 63.
11 Ibid., p. 58.
12 Ibid.
13 Ibid., p. 65.
14 Wynter, p. 103.
15 Lloyd Owen, pp. 65–66.
16 Wynter, pp. 105–106.
17 Lloyd Owen, p. 68.
18 Wynter, p. 109.
19 Ibid., p. 111.
20 Lloyd Owen, p. 61.
21 Ibid.

22 Ibid., p. 71.
23 Wynter, p. 117.
24 Lloyd Owen, p. 72.
25 Morgan, p. 42.
26 Ibid., p. 43.
27 Lloyd Owen, p. 75.
28 Morgan, p. 43.
29 Wynter, p. 118.
30 Ibid., p. 119.
31 Lloyd Owen, p. 75.
32 Wynter, p. 122.
33 Lloyd Owen, p. 77.
34 Wynter, pp. 126–127.
35 Ibid., p. 130.
36 Lloyd Owen, p. 85.
37 Wynter, p. 132.
38 Lloyd Owen, p. 89.
39 Wynter, p. 135.
40 Ibid., p. 136.
41 Ibid., p. 139.
42 Ibid., p. 140.
43 Ibid., p. 143.
44 Ibid., p. 144.
45 Ibid., p. 146.
46 Lloyd Owen, p. 93.
47 Wynter, pp. 147–148.
48 Ibid., p. 151.
49 Lloyd Owen, p. 95.
50 Wynter, pp. 153–154.
51 Ibid., pp. 154–155.

CHAPTER 5
Sting of the Scorpion, 1942

What did I see in the desert today,
In the cold pale light of the dawn?
I saw the Honeys creaking out,
Their brave bright pennants torn;
And heads were high against the sky,
And faces were grim and drawn.

—L. Challoner, *Desert Victory* 1943

When the Allied advance in the winter of 1942 carried them far to the west, further than they'd been before, they would approach past Agheila that great soaring folly of Il Duce's new and short-lived empire, the *Arco Philaenorum.* This impressive if pointless piece of architecture, as previously mentioned, our fellows dubbed 'Marble Arch'.

Bill Kennedy Shaw recalls how, filtering in the great haze of desert heat, the sea to one side, bare stripped desert inland, the arch appears as a speck, a pimple, as incongruous as any mirage, yet one that looms larger and more substantial as you get closer. Not far away, only a couple of hundred yards or so to the southwest, stands a far more ancient altar, a memorial to classical rivalry between Carthage and its neighbouring city, Cyrene. Conflict, in North Africa has a very long pedigree.[1] By the time of the final Allied breakthrough and the last great swing of the North African pendulum, the men of LRDG were very familiar with this particular grandiose landmark.

Alam Halfa

Auchinleck, though much concerned with the state of Eighth Army, could never ignore other threats which loomed over his wide satrapy. An Axis breakthrough in the north would be calamitous, threatening Iran, Iraq and Syria, all volatile in themselves. As the Soviets were not in the habit of sharing plans it was difficult to ascertain if the northern front could be secured.

The increasing demands of campaigning in the Far East, where one disaster followed another, also drained resources. Auchinleck simply did not have sufficient troops to fight in the desert whilst creating a viable defence to the north. The question was: which constituted the greater imperative, to hold Egypt or the Persian oilfields? By 12th July Churchill cabled that as it was impossible to do both, defeat of Axis forces in Cyrenaica must remain the absolute priority. Despite the considerable gains German offensives in southern Russia appeared to be achieving, it was unlikely that a complete breakthrough could be anticipated before the onset of winter halted operations. The question, however, remained: could Auchinleck, increasingly perceived as a spent force, deliver the long hoped for victory?

Both he and Dorman-Smith were painfully aware Eighth Army was not placed to deliver a decisive blow. Though Rommel had been halted, this was only a check and not a reverse. Allied efforts to assume the offensive in July had been, at best, disappointing. There were significant gaps in Eighth Army's tactical competence and these would have to be resolved.

Dorman-Smith was confident that a renewed Axis offensive could be successfully countered and that a 'modern defensive battle' could be waged in the El Alamein sector. Rommel did not have sufficient infantry reserves for a blow to the north, therefore he would be obliged to attempt another wide, flanking move from the south. At this time, Auchinleck wished to formally appoint Brigadier Freddie de Guingand as chief of staff, freeing Dorman-Smith to return to his preferred job in the Delta.

Auchinleck, when penning his own further appreciation a day later than the first, took all of his subordinates' thinking into account. He examined the prospects for an offensive, in the north, centre and south. Each was fraught with difficulty but he echoed General Ramsden in viewing the vicinity of Miteirya Ridge as most promising. A break-in here could corral the Axis forces in the north and expose those in the south. In essence, the plan for the forthcoming offensive comprised the following elements:

- A major blow in the north;
- Diversionary activity and phoney preparations to the south;
- Disruption of enemy supply and communications;
- To create a defended zone behind the main El Alamein line to defeat any Axis thrust from the south;
- To ensure armoured forces were fullly prepared to exploit any breakthrough(s).

This was to prove Auchinleck's legacy. Far from being washed-up he had, with his subordinates, produced the blueprint for final victory in the Western Desert, even though full credit has traditionally gone to his successor. No sooner was this appreciation committed to paper than Eighth Army staff, under de Guingand's able control, began working up detailed plans. This would be the true 'tight' battle, planned in detail and intensively trained for. Previous operations had failed but the lessons derived from those mistakes would lay the groundwork for final success. It should be noted that Rommel, for all his brilliance, did not appear to learn from past errors. This defect would cost him dear and ensure his eventual defeat.

Hand in hand with the need for intense preparation and training, was recognition that key operations, particularly mine clearing, should be standardised. In consequence a clear doctrine for gapping and clearing mines emerged. This emphasised the need for intense artillery bombardment to smother the enemy gun line, followed by a creeping barrage and the establishment of forward positions, enabling sappers to approach their task. Full fire support could thus be directed to cover the dangerous work of the mine clearance teams. As soon as possible the lead elements of the armour should advance to test the gap, supported by anti-tank guns. Behind this vanguard the main body with infantry support would then move forward, broadening the gap as required.

The Prime Minister wanted a new broom; a general who was imbued with an innate flair for difficult diplomacy. Churchill expected his new C-in-C to lead the onslaught against the Axis personally, and proposed to hive off the 'northern' Iraq/Iran sector, leaving the C-in-C Middle East better placed to concentrate his energies in the Western Desert. Dorman-Smith and others who Churchill saw as tainted with the Auk's brush were to be cleared out.

Churchill had been impressed by Gott, but random fate relegated him to one of history's tantalising 'what ifs'. On 7th August his plane was ambushed by fighters from JG 27 and he was killed. Not all in Eighth Army mourned his sudden taking off. Bernard Montgomery thus gained Eighth Army as Alan Brooke preferred, but ironically by default. Auchinleck, having been summarily removed was offered the truncated northern command, more of an insult than a compromise, and understandably declined. Alexander, in taking over his new command, was blessedly free of the peripheral entanglements that had bedevilled his predecessors.

He reinstated McCreery whom Auchinleck had dismissed, and this proved a most judicious appointment. It is hard not to feel that the historical record has been unfair to Auchinleck. Much of what was subsequently achieved was due to his and Dorman-Smith's solid preparation. He had, above all, kept Eighth Army in being. Without this, neither Alexander nor Montgomery could have succeeded in their designated roles. Of course 'Monty', it has to be said, was not one to share the limelight.

Monty was nevertheless very much the new broom. Unlike his predecessor he was definitely part of the UK military establishment and knew which officers he wanted – invariably men who he already knew. He was not shy over getting rid of those who did not fit the bill. Alexander had made it plain that there would be no further retreats and that established divisional formations would stay as they were. Both of these pronouncements produced collective sighs of relief. Morale was not low but it was obfuscated by uncertainty.

As matters improved for Eighth Army the position overall of *Panzerarmee Afrika* was deteriorating. Rommel continued to suffer supply difficulties. Axis shipping was suffering heavily from the attentions of British planes and warships; the air route from Crete, whilst less risky, was cumbersome. Most supplies, once unloaded at Tobruk, had to be brought forward by road, and the port received unending attention from British night-bombers, roughly fifty aircraft every twenty-four hours. Axis intelligence forecast the arrival of a massive Allied convoy due at Suez in early September. If Rommel was to attack it had to be soon before the disparity became crushing. The full moon was due on 26th August. Clearly this was the moment to strike.

Alam Halfa was, as both sides saw, the key. If Rommel could get safely past, his planned offensive stood a very good chance of achieving success. If he could not, if the Allies remained in possession, then his position would become untenable. The ridge completely dominated his lines of communication. Though Rommel might have judged his opponent overly cautious, the British attacks in July had clearly indicated that Eighth Army was not yet fully ready for the offensive role.

Much additional training and preparation was needed. Time, despite any urgings he might receive from Whitehall, was on Montgomery's side: *Although it was clear to General Montgomery that Rommel had shot his bolt, he resisted the temptation to start a general counter-attack. He judged the 8th Army to be unready, and going off at half-cock would only make it harder to prepare for the decisive blow he had in mind.*

In assessing the results of the Battle of Alam Halfa, the O.H. defines the effect on morale as being of greater importance than the material gains which were indeed insignificant: *To the Axis the battle seemed to put an end to their hopes of reaching the Delta. To the British it appeared as a clear-cut victory in which Rommel had been defeated at his own game.* This must substantively be correct, for Eighth Army had won no new ground nor destroyed the *Panzerarmee Afrika,* but it had fought Rommel to a standstill and obliged him to withdraw.

A Raiding We Will Go

With Siwa now abandoned, LRDG remained under the orders of Eighth Army, a state of affairs which persisted till after the major raids in September. At the end of that month, command reverted to GHQ Middle East. From the end of June, LRDG 'A' Squadron HQ was back in the Faiyum district of Cairo along with T1. Y2 with GI and G2 were 'up the road' by Alexandria and the rest fairly dispersed mainly on road watch. During these summer months the humdrum of surveillance was enlivened by yet more raiding with SAS, particularly Stirling and 'L' Detachment. The desert buccaneers were getting a reputation and were now equipped with jeeps of their own – the iconic image. The partnership flourished though with LRDG still regarded as the master navigators.[2]

It has to be stressed that the psychological value of the Special Forces worked on two levels: demoralising the Axis while boosting Eighth Army. The constant allure and glamour attaching to Special Forces is largely a post WWII phenomenon, but even in the dark, terrible days of the Western Front, T.E. Lawrence and his brilliant, asymmetric war in Arabia fired the imagination. Lawrence's exploits harked back to Doughty, Burton and the elite company of 19th-century gentlemen-adventurers, who filled in many of the vast blank spaces left on contemporary maps of Africa and Arabia.

R1 was watching near the coast road in late June–early July, and it's interesting to note that Alastair Gould was reporting the Italians were getting more proficient at camouflaging their MT. Clearly they'd twigged we had 'eyes' on their convoys.[3] Comms were proving tricky at the time and troopers were plagued by desert sores and prone to 'cafard'. T2 set out from Kufra on 12th July, initially as watchers, but orders were changed to favour aggressive action. They successfully shot up a small convoy travelling twenty miles northwest of Marble Arch on 22nd July.

For 'A' Squadron patrols operating westwards out of Faiyum, there was the complication of the front lines, the dense militarised zone stretching south from El Alamein. Nonetheless, at the start of July, both Y2 and G1 passed through. By 6th July both patrols plus an SAS team from Stirling's 'L' Detachment were at Qaret Tartura, some eighty miles south of Mersa Matruh on the rim of the Qattara Depression. They'd be operating along the coastal route some fifty–sixty miles west of Allied lines. Y2 spent some unprofitable time on road watch, then some more productive demolitions with SAS, attacking airstrips around Fuka. A number of enemy aircraft were accounted for and the combined force got back safely despite air attack and the loss of several vehicles.[4]

Alastair Timpson with G1, hosting two SAS teams, was seeking targets east of Sidi Barrani. This proved unprofitable as the enemy, disobligingly, provided no aircraft to blow up. Some 3,000 gallons of fuel which the Axis had stashed nearby were gratefully accepted and pressed into service; however, looking for somebody to shoot up on the roads proved fruitless. Meanwhile Robin Gurdon in charge of G2 and accompanied by Stirling in person, drove out of Alexandria on 3rd July. Three days later they rendezvoused with the other two patrols at Qaret Tartura. The SAS would hit the aerodromes at El Daba; G2 would beat up the roads around Fuka.

During the witching hours on 8th July, Gurdon laid waste an MT park, tanker convoy and enemy camp in quick succession – swift surgical strikes, creating havoc and accomplished without loss. With the raiders re-united, a lying-up place was selected and the men stayed low throughput 10th July. Next day, Robin Gurdon guided a Free French SAS team, led by Lieutenant Martin, to attack an airstrip near Fuka. On the 12th their run of luck ended abruptly when they were strafed by Italian planes. Gurdon had tried the old trick of waving to the pilots but this lot weren't taken in and opened up. As his truck wouldn't start, Gurdon made a dash for the next vehicle but he and his driver, Guardsman Murray, were both hit. Despite the severity of his wounds, Gurdon urged his men to continue but the patrol elected to rush the wounded men back. Murray survived but Gurdon died next day, an extremely brave and skilful officer – a very palpable loss to the close-knit brotherhood of LRDG.[5]

Stirling didn't ever give up or let up. He was all about taking the fight to the enemy and killing them. Next to step out with SAS was Nick Wilder leading T1: getting through the lines proved impossible so they drove down through the Depression to RV with Stirling on 12th July. After an unproductive spell of mundane road watch, they reverted to more profitable action amongst enemy planes in the vicinity of the Mersa Matruh–Qara Road. This was on the night of 26th July and much sport was had – fully three dozen Axis planes were wrecked. Enemy aircraft were quick to seek revenge but at least one was shot down and a follow-up attack by truck-mounted infantry seen off after a running fight.

Stirling wasn't the only Special Forces celebrity being taxied at this point. Both 'Popski' and a party from the Inter-service Liaison department ("ISLD") were ferried to and from the Benghazi area. The Group's supply section was kept busy in its unsung labour, without which neither LRDG nor SAS could have functioned behind the lines. Stirling, in mid-July, was summoned to Cairo and received fresh orders both for himself and Prendergast.

They were to set up an FOB at Qara on the northwest shoulder of the Depression as a lair for further raiding. This time their prime targets were to be enemy logistics, fuel, supplies and workshops. More specific missions would be comprised of forming a block on the coast road at Sollum, which would have to be held for forty-eight hours till the raiders were relieved by Royal Marines. Halfaya ('Hellfire') Pass was also to be barricaded. The Allies had suffered here during the ill-fated 'Brevity' and 'Battleaxe' episodes. Further action against the coast road southeast of Mersa Matruh was in contemplation. GHQ Middle East didn't much like any of these ideas. Qara was felt to be insecure and the projected attacks too difficult to coordinate. In the light of what was to follow in September, this was sage advice.

Meanwhile for LRDG, it was very much a case of business as usual. Lloyd Owen attempted road watch between Bardia and Tobruk but the ground was bare of any cover and this proved abortive. Bill Kennedy Shaw took Y2 and G2 Patrols to Qara to seek local intelligence and establish contact with the inhabitants. There was more cloak and dagger work, as several ISLD personnel were to be ferried in and dropped off, cash for Popski as bribes and agents to taxi back. These various tasks were accomplished without mishap or interference from the enemy. Lieutenant Talbot took another group of spooks, Captain Grandguillot and a team from the LAF, to Bir Gahau, and this mission too passed without incident.[6]

Alastair Guild was yet another on taxi duty. With R1 he drove out of Kufra on 29th August. His assignment was even more taxing as he had to ferry an officer and three soldiers of the ISLD up to Tarhuna, a mere forty miles southeast of Tripoli. This was, in part uncharted territory so Guild mapped as he motored. Most patrols at this time were constantly plagued by duff tyres. These gave out constantly, a major headache when operating at long distances from re-supply.

A week earlier, Brigadier George Davy had summoned a conference at GHQ aimed at establishing the best means of coordinating the activities of all the disparate bodies operating in the desert. This included not just LRDG and SAS but ISLD & LAF. Brigadier Davy proposed that a GHQ staff officer should be detailed as coordinator or, alternatively, a single controller should be appointed. Prendergast wasn't particularly keen on either notion but he did accept that having a designated planning officer within GHQ might be sensible.

Finally it was agreed that LRDG would keep up reconnaissance, intelligence gathering and taxi services much as before. SAS, also much as before, would deal with sabotage and avoid reconnaissance.[7] LRDG lost Gus Holliman at this time; he went back to his original home with RTR. Ken Lazarus took over command of S1. Lieutenant Sweeting now led G2 after Gurdon's death. Dick Croucher would run the office setup in Cairo. Another lost sheep, the lesser WACO, returned after a full and lengthy refit. It promised to be a very busy autumn.

Operation Agreement

There's a principle in Special Forces Operations – 'K.I.S.S.' or *keep it simple stupid.* This is a very sound concept. The greater the complexity of covert missions the wider the scope for evil consequences to intervene.

And so to 'Operation Agreement', a bold and brilliant idea on paper but doomed to failure almost from the start. Of all the layers of participation, only LRDG achieved their allotted tasks with a mix of steadiness and élan.

The idea of further exacerbating Rommel's weak supply position by more spoiling raids was solid enough in theory. The joint Commanders in Chief were mainly enthusiastic, though Air Marshal Tedder less so, as he wouldn't be able to provide fighter cover. For once Montgomery, who as Eighth Army commander was not directly involved, agreed with Tedder, an unusual occurrence in itself as there was no love lost between them.[8]

Tobruk would be the main objective. SAS, guided in the usual way by LRDG, would cross the desert from Kufra, get through the defence cordon, and seize and hold the inlet of Mersa Sciausc which lies east of the main harbour. This detachment, Force 'B', would be joined by an amphibious group, Force 'C', brought from the Delta in fast MTB's. This combined unit would then fight its way westwards, taking out coastal defences. Meanwhile Force 'A', a seaborne battle group of marines, would be landed north and west of the port at Mersa Mreira from the destroyers HMS *Sikh* and HMS *Zulu*. They would seal off the tongue of land separating the cove from the main harbour and penetrate into the town itself.[9]

Bombing raids would cover the noise of the landings, soften up the target and fully occupy the enemy's attention. The plan was predicated on the basis that opposition would be provided by Italian and not German defenders. This was clearly important, as the former would be as sure to surrender as the latter could be relied upon to doggedly fight. Once the harbour guns had been silenced, the MTB's would play havoc with enemy vessels in the eastern portion of the port whilst the two destroyers would land sappers to undertake selective demolition of facilities. Job done, the ships would take off the regulars whilst the raiders drove off westwards seeking yet more mayhem.[10]

Whilst Tobruk was being biffed, a second raid would target Benghazi. This group, dubbed Force 'X', would be comprised of Stirling himself leading L Detachment of 1st SAS, supported by two LRDG patrols (S1

& S2), with a further detachment of Royal Marines. Their objectives were substantial – to block the inner harbour, sink ships and blast port installations. Mission accomplished, Force 'X' would retire only as far as Jalo and launch more raids over an intense, three-week period.[11]

Another LRDG patrol would guide a unit of the SDF to Jalo Oasis (then in enemy hands) on the night of 15th/16th September. The RAF would bomb Benghazi as well as Tobruk; planes would sow a harvest of dummy parashots over Siwa, which would be ostensibly threatened by a dummy feint mounted by SDF. LRDG would also beat up Barce, purely their affair and destined to become the stuff of desert lore.

Force 'B' left Cairo on 22nd August on a truly epic mission. The journey to Tobruk covered some 1,700 miles, much of it through enemy territory. After a halt at Kufra, they struck north for the coast on 5th September. Haselden's plan was a brilliant bluff. Bertie Buck with a handful of his SIG stormtroopers, fluent in German (for most it was their native language), uniformed, armed and equipped as DAK, provided the 'guards' – the rest posing as POWs. Their trucks carried Axis markings and the whole party comprised eighty-three officers and men.[12] By the 13th of the month, having dodged around Jalo, they were on the target.

Continuing their charade, the 'POWs' were driven through an Italian checkpoint without a second glance. Safely, or as safely as it was likely to become, the raiders were inside the enemy's defensive ring. The SIG's changed into British uniform, though none could have been in any doubt as to their eventual fate if captured. As being both German and Jewish, they were doubly damned. As bombs began to fall – the RAF would be overhead from 22.25–03.30 hours – they seized their first objective, the inlet at Mersa Sciausc. Force 'C' had become somewhat dispersed during their approach and were fired on as they entered the creek. Only a single machine-gun detachment was successfully landed.

Force 'A' had meantime run into serious difficulties. Attempting to get the parties ashore from 03.00, the swell had prevented pathfinders from marking the landing cove, and the assault-craft themselves, backstairs children of improvisation, functioned badly if at all. After two hours, less than a single company of marines was ashore, and two miles or so too far west. They never got into the town; the German defenders – and Boche they were, not Italians – responded with customary vigour and blocked the approaches.[13] Looking for salvageable landing craft to put more troops onto the beach, the two destroyers steamed within a mile of the coast. Both ships now had to endure a well directed barrage from the coastal batteries.[14]

Sikh was the first to suffer a palpable hit, her steering gear wrecked. Though *Zulu* took her under tow, this was soon severed and both ships suffered extensive damage. Finally *Zulu* had to make a run for it. *Sikh* was scuttled. The surviving marines and sailors were all taken prisoner. Force 'B', though they'd knocked out the coastal guns by the inlet, came increasingly under pressure from mounting odds. Haselden was amongst the casualties.

It got worse. Axis planes relentlessly stalked *Zulu*. HMS *Coventry*, an anti-aircraft cruiser coming up in support, was herself bombed and sunk. This sacrifice failed to save the destroyer, which also went down. Five of the assorted small boats were sent to the bottom and another left abandoned at Mersa Sciausc. Eight Allied aircraft were shot down. In total, some 280 naval personnel, 300 marines and 160 infantry & support troops were killed, wounded or captured. The raid achieved nothing of significance.[15]

It was no better at Benghazi. Possibly, it was the air raid but the defenders were fully alert and at their guns. Stirling and Force 'X' met stiff resistance at the first roadblock, long before the town. There was no point in going on. Force 'Z' received a similarly warm reception from a well prepared garrison at Jalo and abandoned their brief siege on 19th September. The demonstrations towards Siwa aroused no interest or reaction.[16] It was failure all round, except at Barce. Here LRDG conjured a very different story.

The Barce Raid

'Operation Caravan' was, from the outset, purely an LRDG affair. Jake Easonsmith led a force of two Patrols, T1 (Nick Wilder) and G1 (Alastair Timpson). Some support personnel including, providentially,

Dick Lawson the MO, were along from 'B' Squadron's HQ detachment. 'Popski' and two Senussi drawn from the LAF provided the intelligence cell. There were a total of forty-seven raiders in twelve trucks and five jeeps. They had some heavyweight company from a brace of Mack 10-tonners as far as Ain Dalla. The group drove out of Faiyum on 1st September, with their target 1,150 miles away in Gebel Akhdar. Dick Lawson, as MO, was in demand from the start. As they traversed the Egyptian Sand Sea, Timpson was injured as his vehicle careered over a razorback dune, the old perennial hazard. Another trooper was paralysed. Both were evacuated by air from Big Cairn.[17]

Easonsmith made up for lost time, dashing over the firmer *serir.* It wasn't until 10th September that they debouched from the western rim of the next belt of sand sea. The dunes end abruptly there, *as if tidied up by a giant's broom.*[18] The raiders crossed the ancient camel road from Jalo to Siwa, the timeless desert highway which had witnessed its fair share of invaders come and go over the centuries. After another 200 miles of changing terrain, moving from the stripped and scorched to the border of vegetation, spare and clinging to begin with, then thickening into a form of rough savannah. The two Arab irregulars were dropped off a few miles short of Barce to contact locals and bring back up-to-date intelligence.

On 13th September, fifteen miles south of their objective, the patrols halted. Here, Easonsmith gave a detailed briefing and the men prepared for action: guns cleaned, ammo and vehicles checked. Under cover of the velvet, late summer darkness, balmy and alive with insect noise, they drove boldly towards their target. At one police post, a single native copper came out to challenge them and found himself an LRDG volunteer. Hamed, as he was called, would spend several months of cheerful servitude before being got safe home.[19] As Hamed was being pressed into service there was movement from inside the roadside blockhouse. Only one Italian officer came out to investigate and was promptly shot. The rest of the gendarmerie left via the rear door. In the excitement two trucks banged into each other and both had to be dumped.

When the patrols, still combined, got as close as the village of Sidi Selim, Dick Lawson was left there with T Patrol's radio truck as rearguard and rally point. As the rest of the vehicles struck the main highway to Benghazi and breasted an escarpment five miles out of Barce, they encountered a pair of Italian light tanks. Easonsmith drove towards them unhesitatingly; no one was expecting raiders this far west. The tank crews received a most unexpected surprise when the LRDG opened up on them at point blank range. They caused no further trouble.[20]

Just outside of town, at the principal crossroads, Easonsmith divided his forces. Nick Wilder, with T1, would attend to the airfield while Sergeant Dennis, leading the Guards after Timpson's evacuation, would beat up the downtown zone and barracks. Wilder drove around the outskirts till he reached the aerodrome. Shooting up those light tanks earlier did not seem to have alerted anyone, and the raiders drove through the gates unopposed. Belatedly, the garrison woke up and several came running out. This became their final deployment.[21]

As the Italians sprawled in the dust, tracer set a nearby petrol tanker ablaze, the most perfect illumination. Grenades were chucked into the airfield's canteen, and the attackers, down to four 30-cwts and a lone jeep, hosed enemy aircraft in a storm of bullets. Those which survived the hail of incendiary rounds were each awarded an IED. Thirty-seven planes were attacked and at least a score of these were complete write-offs. By now, the surviving Italians had woken up and were blazing away at everything and nothing. Despite this enthusiasm the patrol came through without a single scratch.[22]

Behind them, the airfield was wrecked and ablaze. Down the long straight to the station at the far end of town, Wilder's trucks charged headlong. Two more light tanks barred the far end, their shot whistling up the road, happily firing too high. Wilder rammed the first tank with sufficient force to push this into the other. The Chevy was a write off but after a bunch of grenades had been deftly rolled beneath both armoured vehicles, so were they.

Wilder and his crew, unharmed, jumped onto the jeep. The over-laden Willys roared towards the station, Wilder on the Vickers firing bursts of tracer. Blinded by white light from the rounds, the jeep's driver struck the kerb and the vehicle did a somersault, spilling its stunned passengers. Wilder was pinned and knocked unconscious. The following truck righted the jeep, which was still a runner, collected Wilder and drove on. Trooper Craw and his truck became separated at some point in the melee and lost.[23]

Sergeant Dennis and the Guards were keeping up trade at the other end of town. As their trucks rolled past the hospital, two sentries challenged from the darkness: *Dennis rolled a four-second grenade between them and turned them from sentries into patients.*[24] Next it was the barracks' turn; two more sentries were disposed of, then the trucks drove around the site, bombing buildings, shooting up trenches and generally anything that moved. Dennis only finished the attack when he'd run clean out of bullets after playing dodgems with another pair of light tanks in the hospital grounds. Trooper 'Jock' Findlay's truck was mislaid sometime during this mad career.

As it later turned out, Findlay had missed the road out of town and had picked up a vengeful posse of Italians who chased his lone vehicle across the plain as dawn was breaking. Ahead of them, the escarpment rose dizzyingly, far too steep for any two-wheel drive vehicle, so they abandoned the truck and set it on fire. After a day of dodging their pursuers, Findlay found himself alone. He walked eastwards for three days before being picked up by friendly Bedouin. He wasn't recovered until October: *There he stood, surrounded by goats and sheep, a tall, bearded figure in Arab gear with a big, beaming smile on his face. 'What took you so long?' he said.*[25]

Jake Easonsmith was on his own where the patrols had split, as ever determined not to let others have all the fun. It probably isn't a commander's job to get too close to the action but the temptation was overwhelming. He first attacked some small bungalow type units which might have been officers' quarters. Next he took on a further pair of light tanks before terrorizing a central piazza, scattering grenades amongst startled Italians. Next one up was an MT park containing a dozen vehicles; none of these would be going anywhere soon. By 04.00 hours both raiding parties were back at Sidi Selim; ten of the original twelve vehicles had come through, three jeeps and seven trucks in total. All they had to do now was to sweep up the two vehicles left earlier at Sidi Raui and be on their way.

For once the Italian complement there proved capable of aggressive action, setting up a neat ambush in a narrow defile south of Sidi Selim. All hell suddenly broke loose. Three men were wounded and Dick Lawson's car temporarily immobilised with a shot out tyre. Calmly, Sergeant Dennis backed up to shield the stricken vehicle with his own while the wheel was changed. This accomplished, everyone got clear and the two busted trucks were recovered under tow. Clearly it wasn't possible to drag both of these all the way back so they had to be fixed and got going. This meant another halt and the posse caught up. Jake Easonsmith kept the Italians and their local Arab levies busily occupied in a bold flanking attack with only his own jeep until the column got moving again.

It was all going rather well, too well in fact. Luck finally deserted them when G Patrol's wireless truck broke down in, inevitably, a totally exposed location. Frantic efforts to get the vehicle under any kind of cover took just that bit too long and the fighters found them. Carrying out a beat up after a concealed approach march was one thing; getting away with it quite another. Stung by losses and humiliation, the enemy's vengeance came roaring out of a shining sky. From late morning till sundown, the patrols were attacked relentlessly. By the time darkness brought relief, only a single truck and two jeeps remained serviceable. These would have to ferry thirty-three men back to Kufra. Worse, there were now several wounded. Nick Wilder had been hit in both legs and trooper Parker in the stomach. Dick Lawson performed prodigies, working unconcerned and incessantly during the strafing.

Given the fury and duration of the bombardment, it could have been much worse. It did get rather worse just as darkness was falling. Jake Easonsmith had wisely unloaded all of the precious water and rations, dispersing them around. It seemed safe to load all of these onto one of the two surviving Chevys, but just as this essential cargo was being stacked, the fighters came back for a final pass and hit the lot.[26] This was both galling and serious, but Easonsmith had foreseen this dire possibility and had earlier created an emergency dump located some sixty miles southeast of Barce at Bir Gerrari.

As dusk fell on 14th September, the party set off. Dick Lawson had one jeep and one 30-cwt, and with his group he took the six wounded men, plus driver, fitter and navigator. They had 700 miles to cover. Two marching detachments moved off at the same time, only a single jeep between them carrying supplies, or such as they still possessed. The ground was hard and unyielding. Lawson's jeep gave out, the gas tank holed by a random round during the beat up. Next, the second jeep stalled; its sump fractured, though this was repairable. One man became lost in the darkness, probably having succumbed to exhaustion. He could not be found. They kept walking, dodging aerial sweeps. At last some good luck arrived as they came across a Bedouin encampment and bought some food and milk. More good fortune on the 16th – they discovered blessed water.

Next day, as dawn broke, they heard vehicle engines with a reassuringly friendly beat. Easonsmith fired off several flares but to no avail. Barely an hour later, as they trailed on disconsolately, they stumbled upon John Olivey and his patrol – salvation! When they reached the stash at Bir Gerrari, Lawson had already passed through and deposited a note. This still left the second walking group unaccounted for. With Olivey's Rhodesians, Easonsmith combed the area for the missing men; they'd been sighted by local Arabs. By the evening of 19th September the eight missing troopers were finally located, though two injured men, who'd been left behind, could not be traced.[27] When the combined groups reached LG 125, they discovered Ken Lazarus with two of Dennis' guardsmen who'd been left behind in the fracas; the wounded men had been taken off by the RAF.

Two days later they had traversed the sand sea, and then on to Howard's Cairn where Arnold with the supply section was waiting. By the 25th all were back at Kufra. The LRDG beat up of Barce was the only one of these September raids to succeed. The Axis had lost perhaps thirty planes and as many dead. That the raiders could strike so far behind the lines was a significant dent in Axis morale and a comparable boost to the Allies. LRDG had suffered none killed, half a dozen wounded, ten POWs and lost fourteen vehicles. One MC, two DSOs and three MMs were awarded;[28] all in all, a very impressive undertaking.

With so many vehicles trashed, LRDG had to accept a quantity of re-conditioned 30-cwts from RAOC. These came with bland assurances if no specific guarantees. Six of the Mack ten-tonners were swapped for ten Ford three-tonners; these admittedly performed better than the heavier vehicles over soft ground. David Lloyd Owen was temporarily invalided out after being injured during an Axis air raid on Kufra. Captain Spicer acted as his replacement. Meanwhile the 'Big Push' was brewing, the battle that would be, as Churchill memorably remarked, *an end to the beginning.* For the Axis, El Alamein would also be the beginning of the end.

Notes

1 Kennedy Shaw, p. 207.
2 Wynter, p. 157.
3 Ibid., p. 158.
4 Ibid., p. 160.
5 Lloyd Owen, p. 102.
6 Wynter, p. 164.
7 Ibid., p. 165.
8 O.H., vol. IV, p. 20.
9 Ibid.
10 Force 'A'–11th Royal Marines, detachments from RA, RE, R. Sigs., RAMC; Force 'B'–D Squadron 1st SAS Regt., plus RS, RE, & R. Sigs., support; Force 'C'–D Coy 1st A&SH, detachments of RNF, RA, RE, R. Sigs., RAMC (O.H, p. 21).
11 Ibid., p. 21.
12 Ibid.
13 Ibid., p. 22.
14 Ibid.
15 Ibid., pp. 22–23.
16 Ibid., p. 23.
17 Moreman, pp. 49–50.

18 Kennedy Shaw, p. 200.
19 Ibid.
20 Ibid., p. 201.
21 Ibid.
22 Ibid., p. 202.
23 Ibid.
24 Ibid.
25 Morgan, p. 74.
26 Kennedy Shaw, p. 205.
27 Ibid., p. 206.
28 Ibid.

Chapter 6
Out of Africa, 1942–1943

Hail, soldier, huddled in the rain,
Hail, soldier, squelching through the mud,
Hail, soldier, sick of dirt and pain,
The sight of death, the smell of blood,
New mean, new weapons bear the brunt;
New slogans gild the ancient game:
The infantry are still in front,
And mud and dust are much the same.
Hail, humble footman, poised to fly
Across the west, or any, Wall!
Proud, plodding, peerless P.B.I. –
The foulest, finest, job of all

—A.P. Herbert: *The Poor Bloody Infantry*

By early autumn 1942 Rommel, if depleted, was by no means impotent. The Fox knew that the hounds, at some stage, must be unleashed and he prepared to defend his ground. Defence in depth was a concept the German Army understood well and one which it had perfected during the Great War. Moreover, the Allied build-up gave the Axis time to strengthen their already formidable defences. The front was defined by coastline to the north and impassable desert to the south.

El Alamein

This line could not be outflanked; therefore it must be breached in a grinding battle of attrition. Rommel had provided a double mesh of mines all along the front. The belts were, at intervals, linked to form boxes. The defenders' role in any sector was simple: to hold the line for long enough to allow the armour time to come up. Part of his difficulties lay in that he had insufficient German troops to form the static garrison, and he had proven doubts over some, if not the majority, of Italians. To stiffen the collective spine of his allies, Rommel mixed units along the line, down to battalion level, so that every Italian formation had intervening German troops to act as a brace.

His armour he kept to the rear, 15th Panzer in the north, 21st to the south. Littorio Armoured division was attached to the former and Ariete deployed before the latter, thus splitting Italian XX Corps. Both 90th Light and Trieste Motorised Division were left in the north, westwards along the coastline. From the Mediterranean shore to Miteirya Ridge, the 164th Light and Trento Divisions held the line. Southwards, as far as Deir el Shein and Ruweisat Ridge, was the responsibility of Bologna Division. Southwards again, Brescia was deployed around Bab el Qattara. These two Italian formations were stiffened by dispersed battalions of *Fallschirmjager* drawn from Ramcke's Brigade. Down to Qaret el Himeimat, Italian paratroopers from Folgore and infantry of Pavia Division manned the front.

General Brian Horrocks, in the southern sector with 13 Corps, would 'break into the enemy positions and operate with 7th Armoured Division with a view to drawing enemy armour in that direction. This would make it easier for 10 Corps to get out into the open in the north' The Desert Rats were not to get drawn into a mauling or engage in attritional 'dogfights'. They were to husband their strength for pursuit once the breakout was achieved. Monty allows himself full credit for the idea of delivering the main blow in the north and avoiding the tried tactic of the flanking attack from the south: 'I planned to attack neither on my left flank nor on my right flank, but somewhere right of centre; having broken in, I could then direct my forces to the right or to the left as seemed most profitable'.

Leese was to put four divisions into the attack. Nearest the coast Morshead's 9th Australian would have the extreme right, breaking in eastwards from Tel el Eisa. Next, Wimberley's 51st Highland division, charged with assaulting towards Kidney Ridge. Then Freyberg's 2nd New Zealand Division would strike towards the western extremity of Miteiriya Ridge with, on the far left, Pienaar and 1st South African Division attacking the centre.

The front stretched for four and a half miles with a depth, on the right, of five and a quarter, shrinking to two and three-quarter miles on the left. Horrocks was to launch his offensive, diversions aside, on a narrower front with Harding's 7th Armoured and Hughes' 44th Divisions striking out south of Ruweisat Ridge. In the main this was to convince the Axis that the main blow was indeed falling in the south, and to fix 21st Panzer's full attention here. Secondary objectives included attacks on Himeimat and Taqa Plateau, but these were not to be pressed home in the face of strong opposition.

An intense artillery barrage, the most potent since 1918, would begin the fight at 21.40 hrs on 23rd October. The guns would deluge German artillery with a weight of counter-battery fire before moving to plaster the forward defences. A rolling barrage would cosset the attacking infantry battalions, proceeding in 'lifts'. With a sufficiency of anti-tank guns in theatre, the whole weight of field artillery could be brought to bear under a centralised fire plan. Early in October, Desert Air Force had taken advantage of wet weather to biff the *Luftwaffe* whilst much of its strength was grounded. The Axis aerodromes at Daba and Fuka were targeted and some thirty aircraft destroyed.

On the 18th of the month, with just five days to go till the launch of 'Lightfoot', bombing raids began in earnest. Tobruk was further damaged. Next day Daba was bombed again together with troop concentrations, and road and rail traffic along the coast. Sidi Barrani, Tobruk, Daba and Fuka fields were repeatedly hit. During the night of 21st/22nd October Allied bombers ranged over installations on Crete. The overall strategy was for Desert Air Force to win hegemony in the air, then switch to close operational support. The bombers would fly in support of the opening bombardment, seeking out those guns still able to reply. Wellingtons, suitably equipped, would jam enemy radio signals, thus leaving the Axis 'blind' during those critical opening hours.

Montgomery subsequently divided the fighting at El Alamein into three distinct phases.

- First, the break in, which he defined as a struggle for tactical advantage. He felt that this was successful, though the record might tend to question.
- Second, the crumbling or dogfight phase, aimed at 'crippling the enemy's strength'. This did succeed; a nasty, vicious attrition that told heavily in favour of the Allies. This was as much due to the fact Rommel squandered his precious resources in set piece counter-attacks in unfavourable conditions. Allied success was mainly due to Axis inability to learn from past mistakes and a propensity to fling men and vehicles into a maelstrom where the Allies held vital trumps in air and artillery superiority.
- Finally, the break-out which Monty saw as successful as it was aimed at the weakest link in the crumbling Axis chain, the juncture between Italian and German units. Rommel had taken the gamble of drawing his remaining strength into the northern sector where he was misled into thinking the final blow would be directed.

For Rommel, the scale of this defeat was enormous. Assessments differ, but the Axis lost something in the order of 30,000 prisoners, two thirds Italian, and perhaps as many as 20,000 dead and wounded. Most of his Italian formations had been decimated, and such transport as could be found was reserved for German survivors. Out of nearly 250 tanks DAK could barely field three dozen after the fight, and though the Italians had more runners these were inferior and no match for Shermans. Well might the marching soldiers have lamented, those who would never see Rome or Naples, Milan or Bologna again.

Despite the failure of the major September raids, the indefatigable Stirling saw his fiefdom swell to become a full SAS regiment with him as Lieutenant-Colonel. A further re-ordering of roles was laid down by GHQ on 22nd September. All reconnaissance and intelligence gathering remained LRDG's responsibility, but when it came to raids, the 'turf' was divided into short distance (SAS) and long (LRDG). The dividing line between these respective kingdoms was drawn north-south through Jedabia.[1] However, the speed of the Allied advance following the Axis collapse at El Alamein forestalled any significant raiding activity.

Monty wrote that he was determined to have done with 'that sort of thing', the constant swings of the desert pendulum. Egypt would be made absolutely secure for the duration of the war. In the wake of the Alamein fighting, he defined his continuing objectives:

(a) To capture the Agheila position, and hold securely the approaches to it from the west.
(b) To locate a corps strong in armour in the Jebel about Mekili, trained to operate southwards against any enemy force that managed to break through the Agheila position and make towards Egypt.
(c) To get the A.O.C. to establish the Desert Air Force on the Martuba group of airfields, and to the south of Benghazi.

For LRDG, this heady period as the pendulum entered its final decisive swing was largely spent in the same old way – road watch. Watching the coast highway to Tripoli continued from 30th October to 22nd December. Victory might be in sight at long last but maintaining watch on this sector was both difficult and dangerous. It was during this period that S2, whilst patrolling around El Agheila, discovered a hitherto unknown east/west passage through the Harudi Hills. This would prove rather valuable.[2]

As the Axis attempted to disengage from the shambles of Alamein, vehicle traffic heading westwards increased exponentially. By early November over 3,500 vehicles a day were piling past Marble Arch.[3] On 13th November Indian (3) Patrol, was able to confirm that the enemy had abandoned both Siwa and Jarabub. The pendulum was swinging inexorably westwards again. G2, on road watch near Tripoli early in November, was able to confirm that far more traffic was headed west than east and a third of vehicles were still comprised of plundered Allied stock. The enemy hadn't lost the will to fight. R1 was strafed by Italian fighters near Wadi Tamet on 18th November. The planes were eventually seen off but not before Captain Pilkington and Lance-Corporal O'Malley were both killed, Private Fogden was shot through both legs.[4] Y2 was also bounced on the same day but sustained no casualties.

Jalo Oasis was the next target. Ken Lazarus with S1 and Lieutenant Crammond with T2 went up to investigate on 13th November. Local Bedouins confirmed that the Italians still kept a toehold. Lazarus went on to beat up an Italian convoy travelling on the Marada–El Agheila road. T2 was able to enter Jalo unopposed on the 22nd, neatly capturing the last two defenders and a whole cornucopia of assorted booty. The Tripoli road watch was doubled up at this time as the Axis flight continued. Despite the ingenuity and stealth of the watchers, the watched knew they were being observed, and they had sown mines liberally and increased their own counter-patrolling. T1 lost one of its vehicles to a mine in November.

Alastair Timpson with GI found his patrol up against armoured cars. Dodging around the opposition to reach the coast he ran into another detachment and had to fight his way out. Four out of seven LRDG trucks were lost in this scrap with superior enemy firepower and their crews were captured.[5] Rommel wasn't ready to throw the towel in just yet. In spite of these losses Timpson forged on to the coast road and resumed the watch recently vacated by G2. Their circumstances were much reduced; only two officers and eight troopers still standing, two of their three remaining vehicles were in states of disrepair, and fuel and food were running short.

These tribulations and the need to laager well back, thirty miles back in fact, added fresh hazards. Annoyingly, the enemy at various times insisted on pitching his own camps all around, and at least one watch party was captured as they blundered into the wrong group of tents.[6] Alastair Timpson had a close shave while he and the other observer, Guardsman Welsh, suddenly found the Germans setting up all round, having *macaroni and goulash for lunch*. Bluffing their way out failed to convince an alert sentry and they were constrained to take smartly to their heels. Both Timpson and Welsh had a strenuous time and became separated. The Guardsman had to walk for a score of miles before being picked up, having thrice been shot at from the enemy's camps.

Road watch was clearly more high risk than ever, but the need for intelligence stayed critical so the job went on. Ken Lazarus with S1 and Captain Cantley with Indian (1) Patrol took over from the Guards. They pushed further west than before and reached the shore on 11th December. Again their work was hampered by intense enemy activity, stirred up by the SAS who were poking the hornet's nest in their usual inimitable manner. Indian (1) Patrol was diverted to ease the plight of Timpson's survivors who were by now desperately short of everything. Ron Tinker, leading S2, was next into the fray, taking over the watch on 20th December. Two days later they were discovered and another running battle with Axis armoured cars erupted. At the end of the brawl six men were found to be missing. As December 1942 drew to a close, and the main battle line moved forward to El Agheila, road watch was finally abandoned.

A few weeks earlier, on 8th November, a joint Anglo-American fleet had made several landings on the coast of French North Africa – the long-heralded liberation of Vichy provinces had begun. The Allies came ashore at Algiers, Oran and Casablanca. If Eisenhower, as C-in-C, was expecting a rapturous welcome he was sadly deluded. The French in fact resisted, treating the landings more as a hostile invasion than liberation. Memories of the sinking of French ships and the fight for Syria rankled.

Even the presence of the Americans, who might have been expected to be less tainted than the British, did not prevent stiff fighting. Admiral Darlan, who commanded all Vichy forces, was a rabid Anglophobe and had to be bribed with residual power as 'supreme civil authority'. This angered supporters of De Gaulle and the Free French who regarded the Admiral with loathing. Compromises were needed as speed was of the essence. The Axis had to be caught and crushed between a swift advance from the west and Montgomery closing in from the east.

Despite the mounting odds, Axis reinforcements were arriving in Tunisia and an active defence was underway. The country was mountainous, and winter rains barely a month away. General Anderson, commanding British First Army, made good progress, despite renewed activity from the *Luftwaffe.* Rommel continued to fall back, ignoring all and any pleas to make a stand. By the end of November Anderson's forces appeared to be closing in upon Tunis, but deteriorating weather imposed its own check.

Anderson's planned swoop down from the hills was met with determined resistance, the formidable Tigers (*PzKw VI*) making their first appearance. Fighting hard and utilising interior lines, the German defenders could not be budged, Allied losses were mounting steadily and Axis forces were able to mount a series of sharp, local counter-attacks. Then the rains began to fall in earnest, turning ground into quagmire, bogging men and vehicles in a viscous sea of impotent misery. Tunis was not about to fall, and Eisenhower wisely decided to suspend further major operations.

Back to the Fezzan

Operations planned by the Free French striking up from Chad had been overtaken by Rommel's earlier and spectacular advances. By November 1942, with the Axis fully in reverse gear, the timing once again became propitious. Leclerc would strike out towards distant Tripoli, marching first on Uigh el Kebir then advancing towards Umm el Araheb and Sebha. On 15th November, GHQ issued orders for LRDG to facilitate this offensive. Five patrols were to be allocated to strike enemy logistics, and beat ups were back on the agenda. As Eighth Army continued its relentless spurt west, LRDG HQ would be moved either to Zella or Hon.[7]

It wasn't possible to provide Leclerc's forces with air cover, so several patrols were ordered to seek and destroy enemy aircraft on the ground.

Y1, Indian (4) Patrol and R2 all attempted beat ups, but their quarry, in each instance, proved elusive. Beat ups of Axis convoys were also on the 'to-do' list; Y2 was sent to raid roads passing through the Harudi Hills. Despite filthy weather, they planted mines and, on 29th December shot up a small Italian convoy.[8]

For Leclerc and the French, this was the stuff of history. After the humiliation of defeat and the collaborationist contortions of despised Vichy, they were really fighting back. Cooperation with LRDG was already established, and Lieutenant Henry with S2 was the first patrol to link up. The French were due to hit Uigh el Kebir by 14th December but the relative inexperience of their drivers slowed progress and they didn't in fact arrive till after a week later. Gatrun was their next target, Henry's patrol driving forward with the vanguard.

The oasis was well defended and the attackers came under fire from a range of assorted guns. After a hurried council of war, Lieutenant Henry suggested LRDG should skirt the northern flank to draw out any mobile detachments and lure them under the French seventy-fives, venerable Great War pieces but still extremely effective. LRDG found themselves under sustained air attack as they came out into open ground and a very lively battle with Italian planes ensued. Honours went to S2, who accounted for one aircraft for sure, possibly a brace.

Henry was then detailed to motor up towards Magedul Oasis, provoking more fury from the skies. The main Free French column also came under aerial attack and the W/T truck became a casualty, despite the best endeavours of Sergeant Jackson and Signaller du Toit who manned the machine-gun and gave a very good account of themselves, even though both were wounded.[9]

By 28th December they were a few miles short of Umm el Araneb where they took on both more Italian planes and one of their Auto-Saharan companies on the ground. Both were seen off with loss, thanks in no small part to those French seventy-fives. After a further bombardment, the garrison at the oasis struck their colours on 4th January 1943. Gatrun, bypassed during the French advance, surrendered two days later. The advance became a triumphal march as the Italians withdrew from their now hopelessly isolated garrisons; by 12th January the Axis had abandoned Hon. Four days later LRDG HQ was fast on their heels and took over the oasis.

At the start of December, LRDG had been tasked with another mammoth enterprise: the outflanking of Rommel's defensive line at El Agheila. R1 was to guide the 2nd New Zealand Division, the patrol to be led by Captain Browne. His job was to move the Kiwis around the Axis' right flank. The Allies marched on 14th December with cavalry to the fore. Swinging out in a desert arc, the attackers emerged some twenty miles south west of Marble Arch. Despite being caught wrong-footed, the Axis forces retreated clear of the trap.

On 19th December Captain Browne received fresh orders – to recce the terrain westwards to Wadi Zem Zem[10] and ascertain if the going was suitable for armour. On the 22nd, however, Browne was injured as his vehicle struck a mine, and Captain le Rou was mortally wounded. Lieutenant MacLauchlan then took over command, and the patrol moved out on Christmas Day, aiming to recce Bu Njem.

On the 28th McLauchlan received information that the ground he was intending to cover was free of enemy. Not quite true as it turned out. The patrol was motoring along the road between Bu Njem and Gheddahia when they ran into a skilful ambush. Spread out, the LRDG column found themselves being overtaken by several armoured cars. They took these to be a detachment from the King's Dragoon Guards whom they'd encountered earlier. They weren't.

As the lead vehicle pulled alongside MacLauchlan's, the driver levelled a rifle and advised the LRDG they were now prisoners. MacLauchlan ordered his driver to step on the gas and a movie-style chase ensued, the jeep jinking wildly to avoid the enemy's 20-mm cannon. Those in the W/T truck were less nimble and went into the bag. Despite the best efforts of the Dragoon Guards, the Italians weren't caught.[11] Nick Wilder meanwhile took T1 to beat up traffic on the road between Hon and Sebha. The same weather as had hampered Y2 also plagued Wilder, but the combined patrols did manage some successful shooting up of convoys, destroying vehicles and taking some prisoners.

The Final Pursuit

On 21st December, Eighth Army issued LRDG with a fresh range of instructions:

- Topographical reconnaissance was the number one priority. This was to extend past Tripoli to Gabes and an inland route first to Homs and then west through the Gebel Nefusa.
- Sabotage in partnership with 1st Special Demolitions Squadron. This apocryphal sounding unit represented a re-branding of Popski's banditti which came under LRDG control on 10th December. Popski's favoured tactic was to blandly insert his trucks into an unsuspecting convoy, then when a suitable avenue of escape presented itself, open up with all guns; crude perhaps but certainly very effective.
- Taxiing services for ISLD (an escape network for Allied POWs).
- Further liaison with the Free French.[12]

The scent of victory in North Africa could plainly be detected but there was no rest for LRDG. The pace of the Allied advance westwards and the significance of the 'Torch' landings in November 1942 began to move the campaign from Libya into Tunisia, a very different environment, far more mountainous. At the end of 1942, Y1, G2 and Indian (2) & (4) Patrols were all active. In January 1943, Indian (2) Patrol staged a beat up some ninety miles south of Esc-Sciuref, a regular drive by, shooting up a column of thirty trucks herded by armoured cars.

Charging 'line ahead' in best Nelsonian style, they inflicted some damage before breaking off. Theirs was an eventful patrol as another fire-fight with a small Italian group, motoring under French colours, occurred on 11th January.[13] Hunter with Y2 and Nick Wilder leading T1 were both probing across the Tunisian border in January. The going was frequently tough, and a series of escarpments proved very tricky.

On 6th January, Ken Lazarus led S1 out of Zella to recce an area further to the northwest; this effectively marked the southern fringes of Tunisia, almost as far as Gabes. On the 15th the patrol was jumped by an Axis convoy near Zem Zem. Ken Lazarus had been scouting ahead and saw that the enemy possessed both AFV's and well-armed field cars. Several of the LRDG trucks got bogged and their crews captured; only the W/T truck got clear. Meanwhile Indian (1) Patrol was with the Free French, still battering triumphantly northwards.[14]

Ron Tinker with T2 left Hon on 16th January. His brief was to escort a section of the heavy mob that was creating a dump along the line of the Esc-Sciuref–Mizda road; to ferry some demolishers to RV with Popski, and at the same time map the terrain. This proved quite an eventful patrol, as Tinker collected, like the Pied Piper, a motley collection of various stragglers, including Free French parashots and two SAS. Getting all of these back to safety proved difficult and time consuming.

All were, however, successfully rescued. Quite what role LRDG might have in the coming battle for Tunisia hadn't been decided, so Jake Easonsmith visited Allied HQ in Algiers during the course of January. Despite the considerable successes won by LRDG, there was no particular appetite for their deployment in northern Tunisia, a very different type of terrain.[15] Easonsmith's ideas, eminently sensible, were for LRDG to work along the Allies' southern flank which was relatively exposed.

In late January, R2 went to re-join the Free French, catching up with Leclerc at Mizda. They were to carry out further reconnaissance but the job went to an armoured car detachment. From 21st January, Captain Rand with Indian (3) Patrol was sent out to map the 'Erg Oriental', the southernmost region of Tunisia extending into Northern Algeria. They were seeking a safe passage for an all-arms conventional force. They recce'd with R1 whom they'd picked up on the first day. Initially the terrain was passable but they soon encountered a nasty belt of dunes which proved hard going for the two-wheeled drive trucks. They were soon joined by Nick Wilder with T1. Rand later found the wreckage of S1's earlier disaster. The captain was subsequently de-briefed by General Freyberg. The recce had been crucial as it might enable Allied Forces to slip past the southern flank of the 'Mareth' Line.[16]

A month or so beforehand, in December 1942, the DMI (Director of Military Intelligence) at GHQ had written of LRDG's achievement that:

> LRDG Road watch provides the only trained road traffic observers. Not only is the standard of accuracy and observation extremely high, but the patrols are familiar with the most recent illustrations of enemy vehicles and weapons…. From the point of view of military intelligence the risks and casualties which the patrols have accepted and are accepting have been more than justified.[17]

On 25th January, Allied forces occupied Tripoli, that decisive goal which had proved so elusive for the last two years. Shortly afterwards, on 15th February 1943, Eighth Army moved against Rommel's positions at Beurat. Hopelessly outnumbered and outgunned, the *Panzerarmee* could only continue with a further withdrawal. Rommel thus retired behind the relative security of the Mareth Line (pre-war French fortifications in southern Tunisia constructed to guard against an Italian offensive from Libya), which afforded him a respite and the opportunity of striking a fresh blow in the west. As ever, the Desert Fox chose an ambitious and risky strategy whilst his fellow officers, Sixt von Arnim, commanding 5th *Panzerarmee* in North Tunisia and, equally predictably, Kesselring favoured a less perilous course.

The result was an inevitable compromise. The Germans made initial gains. The Americans, facing these battle-hardened desert veterans, were caught off-guard and suffered losses, but the offensive soon began to run out of steam. Von Arnim had severe doubts and these translated into lukewarm support. Rommel's assault on the Kasserine Pass, spectacular and rapid, ran into a thin screen of Allied guns and stalled. With resources depleted and the Allies recovering, the attack was abandoned.

Rommel was next ordered to launch a blow in the east, despite his misgivings, exacerbated by failing health. This attack, hurled at Eighth Army positions at Medenine in early March, ran into a well prepared and concealed gun line; both tanks and infantry were badly shot up as they struggled to come to grips. Rommel's last attack was a total failure. Very soon after, the Desert Fox took his final leave of North Africa, placed on mandatory sick leave. Despite heavy losses incurred at Medenine, von Arnim felt he could continue to hold the Mareth Line, still formidable and with both flanks secure. The line was, however, less solid than the Germans might have hoped.

Montgomery had definite ideas about the role of LRDG. The Mareth Line was a major obstacle and battering through would be costly. What he required was a detailed recce of an area of 'No-Man's-Land' ahead of Eighth Army's left flank and the right wing of Alexander's group in Algeria and Tunisia. This was roughly bounded by the coast to the north with its western face skimming along the rim of the Erg Oriental. The prime objective was to map the terrain and identify a viable route for outflanking the Mareth Line.

Lieutenant Henry with S2 set off from Hon on 25th January. They were to carry out reconnaissance while also delivering Captain Grandguillot and a party of spooks up to Tozeur. The patrol was bringing up spares for T2 and Popski. The recce was initially frustrated by the dune belt lining the eastern edge of the Erg. Patrols were fast learning that local Arabs couldn't be trusted; T2's woes had probably arisen after they'd been spotted and 'grassed-up' by Bedouins. Having finally got across the soft humps of dunes they did pick up a couple of survivors from the wreck of T2. These dunes were hard on vehicles and fuel consumption soared – the 30-cwts were only getting about three miles per gallon.[18]

On 5th February, Henry went in to Tozeur with his jeeps to seek fuel where he met up with Ron Tinker and the survivors of his patrol. Sergeant Calder-Potts with the rump of S2 had come across a first class potential airstrip, one already earmarked by the French. By the 9th the patrol was concentrated at Tozeur, though minus the W/T truck which had struck a mine; two men were wounded. After another three days of reconnaissance, they delivered Captain Grandguillot and his miscellaneous group to their RV. Fresh orders awaited them – the recce work was to be discontinued and Henry should report as soon as possible for de-briefing. Moving east along the northerly fringe of the Erg, they were warned by a French irregular of an Italian Camel Corps company close by. This meant another fuel-draining detour over the dunes.

On the 20th they sighted a convoy which they took to be French, and encountered a camel detachment which they assumed to be of equally Gallic provenance. Lieutenant Henry motored forward in his jeep to speak to one of the cameleers who came down from a small knoll on which the rest were stationed. It soon became horribly obvious that these were enemy, or seemed to be, as they opened up on the exposed jeep. Henry was badly hit and his driver, Private Rezin, killed outright. As the LRDG returned fire, half the guns jammed; they were clogged with fine sand, but the 20-mm Breda cleared the enemy from the knoll. It was only afterwards they learnt that this was a tragic 'blue on blue' incident and the supposed 'enemy' were indeed French. Lieutenant Henry had been hospitalised but died of his wounds.[19] This was, in no small part, a consequence of the loss of wireless comms with the W/T truck.

Guy Prendergast had quartered the overall area allocated by Eighth Army. Three of the Indian patrols (2), (3) & (4) went out in January and early February, specifically to get an idea about the ground in the Jebel Tebaga sector. As ever, the question was could an all-arms force safely pass across. In fact, the patrols concluded the terrain was unfavourable, but there was good going over a more level belt to the south and this was bare of any enemy presence.

Captain Spicer took Y2 from Hon at the end of January. He was to search for a possible route over the escarpment which rises from Tripolitania, northeast of El Genein towards the Dehibat region. Any such passage to the right of the Mareth Line would offer scope for an outflanking manoeuvre by Eighth Army. Spicer was also to check out which enemy outposts were still manned. A 'tanker' accompanied the patrol to judge the going for heavy armour. On the march, the patrol encountered Ken Lazarus with R2. Next day Spicer forged on alone, reaching the location of what was to become known as 'Wilder's Gap'. This area was to prove to be of considerable interest. By 21st February, both Spicer and Lazarus were being de-briefed by General Freyberg, at that point based some fifteen miles south of Tripoli. The Gap could take any vehicle and was around three miles wide.

Ken Lazarus was ordered to make a more thorough reconnaissance and to set up a further fuel reserve at Wilder's Dump. He pushed west and north, finding that there was a continuously viable route, wide enough and firm enough for heavy vehicles and armour, the only chokepoints being wadi crossings. On 3rd February, Lieutenant Bruce leading 'G' Patrol, and with an officer from 7th Armoured attached, recce'd the salt marsh south from the Shott Djerid.

His findings were not encouraging. The difficult, unforgiving ground took a toll of specialist desert-worthy LRDG vehicles; more conventional and heaver traffic would get nowhere.[20] The earlier maps proved useless and the natives very far from friendly – two troopers were wounded in a skirmish with them. The French garrisons they encountered were much more welcoming, extending to a brace of puppies donated by the Foreign Legion at Fort Flatters!

It would be Ron Tinker who'd lead the Kiwis around the right flank of the Mareth Line. On 9th March his detachment joined up with HQ NZ Division, then at Medenine. On the 12th the Kiwis moved up towards Wilder's gap where they halted. Tinker and his patrol then recce'd both north and northwest. The LRDG now marked out a potential line of advance as far as the Jebel Tebaga, an extended range of hills running east to west from Gabes to the Shott Djerid.

By the 19th of March, the NZ Division had pushed on to the Wadi el Aredj, and next day, they'd moved up to within thirty odd miles of Gabes. By now the Kiwis were meeting scattered opposition and didn't take Gabes till the 29th. Monty had begun battering the Mareth Line on 20th March and it proved as formidable as anticipated. Fearing they were about to be outflanked, the Germans slipped westwards on the night of 27th/28th.

As March gave way to April and the intense desert spring, LRDG moved back from Hon to Alexandria – 'Alex', the fabled city of antiquity. Lieutenant J.M. Sutherland had recently taken over command of R2 and suffered the misfortune of losing one truck to a mine *1,000 miles east of the area of active operations*. This loss, happily bloodless, proved to be the last one sustained in Africa, and as Guy Prendergast drily observed, *a fitting curtain to the Desert activities of the unit.*[21] Monty, not one to offer praise unless it was earned, wrote to him on 2nd April noting: *Without your careful and reliable reports the launching of the left hook by the NZ Division would have been a leap in the dark; with the information they produced the operations could be planned with some certainly, and as you know, went off without a hitch.*[22]

As ever, the Fox had lived to fight another day, but the end was now in sight. Relentlessly, the Allies tightened the vice. General Patton, with the US 2nd Corps, displayed his customary bullish energy. Von Arnim was threatened with encirclement. The Italian General Messe commanded a strongly posted Axis line which was to be assaulted using both First and Eighth Armies. Montgomery was to punch though at Gabes Gap to break out onto the coastal plain where his superior armour would deploy to best advantage. Ghurkhas led the assault in a classic night attack to secure vital high ground, but 51st Division ran into heavy fire, losing many casualties and the Germans again avoided encirclement. Finally, Indian soldiers from Eighth Army shook hands with Americans from Patton's 2nd Corps. By 10th April Sfax had fallen, Sousse two days later.

Despite these expanding triumphs, Alexander had decided the final blow must fall further north and thus be delivered by First Army, though Eighth Army was to assault the remaining Axis bastion at Enfidaville. This was essentially a sideshow. In part this was due to recognition that the Enfidaville position was an extremely strong one. Nonetheless, the orders were subsequently modified, perhaps in consequence of matters in the north proving more strenuous than anticipated. Several army commanders had grave doubts over the attack on the Enfidaville defences, fearing the price paid in casualties would be exorbitant. Montgomery, as ever, was aggressive and fully confident.

In the third week of April, fighting in this sector reached an intensity and fury easily the equal of the worst which had gone before. Men scrambled, fought and died on scarred and rock-strewn slopes, pounded by artillery and small arms, a soldier's battle of rifle and bayonet. As this attack stalled, similar difficulties were experienced in the north, where Axis formations bitterly contested each foot of mountainous ground. Montgomery, not to be denied a victor's crown, renewed his attack on 25th April. Both sides fought with great skill and valour, losses again were high with every inch of ground contested. The result was a temporary stalemate.

On 6th May, Alexander planned a final, overwhelming blow in the north. Von Arnim knew that the plight of his exhausted survivors, some 135,000 Germans and nearer 200,000 Italians, was desperate. Despite the odds, Axis defenders continued to fight long and hard as the onslaught began. After intensive bombardment and a successful break-in, dusk found the leading British units some fifteen miles from Tunis.

Out of Africa

On 12th May 1943, General von Armin and General Messe each formally surrendered their commands. At 14.15 hrs on the 13th Churchill finally received the telegram from Alexander he had waited so long to read: *Sir, it is my duty to report that the Tunisian campaign is over. All enemy resistance has ceased. We are masters of the North African shores.* The War in the Desert was indeed over but the bones of some 220,000 British and Imperial soldiers would remain. Final victory was still a long way distant in the spring of 1943, but the era of continuous defeat was over and the men of Eighth Army became the stuff of legend, perhaps none more so than the men of the LRDG.

It wasn't all grim of course. Shooting gazelles not only honed marksman's skills but could reap an unexpected cash dividend. Bill Johnson, who served with the Rhodesians, shot and butchered stags – then *we would dig a shallow slit trench, soak the sand with petrol, place over a well-polished sand tray and set fire to the petrol* – a desert barbecue. Bill's comrades complained about the smell from the uncured hides which he stashed in his truck. In Cairo, however, *we found a handbag factory and, after lots of bartering, I finished up with £150.00 in cash, a sheikh's ransom.*[23]

John Olivey with S1 nearly earned notoriety when they came close to shooting Harry Secombe. The future goon and TV star was serving as a dispatch rider in June 1942 and became lost. The Rhodesians, hearing the beat of the bike engine, decided he must be Boche and prepared the appropriate introduction. Thankfully, Bill Johnson recognised the distinctive note of a BSA or Matchless, and the patrol held its fire. Rider and posterity were spared – *here today, goon tomorrow.*[24]

Born in the desert, LRDG was a specific and very individual response to a clearly perceived tactical problem. The Group's bespoke nature endowed its patrols with their unique status. All of LRDG's tactics, command and control structures, vehicles, weapons, comms, training, et al were tailored to the needs of their environment. In the desert, LRDG had no equal. Its creators were men who had already traversed the great vastness of the empty sands. They knew their trade and their mission. The final Axis collapse and surrender in North Africa changed everything. Did the victorious Allies need a Long Range Desert Group when there were no more open deserts to fight over?

All involved passionately hoped that they did; if not for desert warfare then for fighting in forests and mountains. Prendergast, Easonsmith and Lloyd Owen all saw how LRDG tradecraft could be adapted to clandestine intelligence gathering in Europe. Right across the Axis' sprawling, oppressed empire, resistance movements had sprung up. These had been very low key and small scale to begin with, but as the Allies' successes multiplied, as the myth of German invincibility was dented and fractured, they grew.

If LRDG was to respond then new tricks would have to be learnt: parachuting, fighting in snow and ice, working with disparate and often unreliable partisans. For the moment, victory brought release, leave and pay arrears, and the dizzying fleshpots of fabled Alexandria: *Guns, equipment and vehicles had to be cleaned and overhauled, clothes to be mended and replaced and time found to enjoy good meals taken off plates on a table and beer drunk from a glass.*[25]

Guy Prendergast spent his time constructively in defining a new role for the Group. This was to be a variation on the familiar theme. LRDG would re-organise, forming smaller, ever more specialist patrols, capable of subsisting for significant periods behind enemy lines. Prendergast remained as C/O with Jake Easonsmith as 2I/C. Alastair Guild would command one Kiwi Squadron of six patrols, Lloyd Owen the other with an equal number of UK and Rhodesian squads.

Their new role would demand a different kind of stamina, and although jeeps would be retained there'd be far more marching than motoring.[26] Egypt was no longer a fit training ground, so Lloyd Owen took his squadron to Lebanon and the high mountains. Here, at the aptly named Cedars Training School run by James Riddell, a noted Olympic skier, they'd learn the art of mountaineering. Happily the unit's MO, Griffith Pugh, was also an enthusiastic rock-climber.[27]

This was an altogether different landscape. Their billets were in a ski resort six thousand feet up, with peaks towering jaggedly above. In the bowl of a vast natural amphitheatre stood some magnificent ancient cedars which lent both beauty and timelessness to the scene. In some ways, this sudden relocation almost had a holiday air. Almost but not quite, for the training was arduous and long; some very tough tabbing with seventy pound packs, and freezing nights on the exposed snowfields, lashed by relentless, ice-laden winds. They worked with obstinate and unlovable mules, and struggled with the intricacies of unfamiliar Greek and German. Old skills were honed and new equipment tested, sometimes rejected. Lloyd Owen had a very long shopping list and GHQ was by no means quick to oblige. Spring passed into summer as they toiled on the slopes.

Rumours of fresh wars abounded and nobody wanted to miss out. What would be essential would be the ability to jump. Stirling's early efforts with his parashots in the desert had proved totally unsuccessful. But in Europe, using vehicles for insertion would not be an option. The Sand Sea was being swapped for a real one, the Mediterranean. Teams would go in via small boat or parachute. Most troopers were fully up for this, and only six out of 130 demurred[28] – after all parachute wings brought in an extra 2s a day in pay!

Training would take place at Ramat David in Palestine. There appeared to be no great degree of urgency and Lloyd Owen was given a month's leave. He intended, providentially as it turned out, to begin his R & R by watching the men's first attempts at jumping. No sooner had he arrived at Ramat David than Jake Easonsmith announced the whole squadron was under orders for a rapid deployment from Haifa at noon the next day. Half the teams were here in Palestine with little or no kit, the rest were back at the Cedars, some distance away. The signals establishment were all still in Cairo. A frantic night of telephoning, cajoling, bellowing and some alcoholic stimulants followed. By dawn, some semblance of order had been achieved, no mean feat.

Lloyd Owen had no current idea where the squadron was headed or why the sudden flap. The fateful signal from Lieutenant-General Anderson actually read: *Most secret and officer only....* LRDG's *most likely role will be to move into Kos and Samos, if the situation permits, to stiffen resistance of the Italian garrisons and local guerrillas to German control of the islands. You may however be ordered to operate in Rhodes.*[29] For Lloyd Owen and the LRDG, this vague and rather vapid instruction would be their introduction to the Dodecanese campaign of autumn 1943. They would, every man, soon have cause to wish it had never been sent.

Notes

1 Wynter, pp. 176–177.
2 Ibid., p. 177.
3 Ibid.
4 Ibid., p. 179.
5 Ibid., p. 181.
6 Ibid., p. 182.
7 Ibid., pp. 184–185.
8 Ibid., pp. 187–188.
9 Ibid., p. 186.
10 A place which features in one of wartime poet Keith Douglas' works: *Alamein to Zem Zem* edited by Desmond Graham (Oxford, OUP 1979).
11 Wynter, p. 190.
12 Ibid., pp. 191–192.
13 Ibid., p. 194.
14 Ibid., p. 196.
15 Ibid., p. 198.
16 Ibid.
17 Ibid., p. 201.

18 Ibid., p. 205.
19 Ibid., p. 206.
20 Ibid., p. 209.
21 Ibid., p. 211.
22 Ibid., p. 212.
23 Morgan, p. 94.
24 Ibid., p. 96.
25 Lloyd Owen, p. 122.
26 Ibid., p. 126.
27 Pugh later accompanied the successful post war climb on Everest.
28 Lloyd Owen, p. 128.
29 Ibid., p. 129.

CHAPTER 7
The Wine-Dark Sea, 1943

'Greater love hath no man',
We turned our eyes away
To where the sunshine on the hills
Claimed glory for the day.

'Than this that he should give',
Our thoughts cast far away
To red-gold hair, soft creamy skin
And sunlight in the bay.

'Should give for his friend his life',
Our memories floated wide
And wandered in some distant vale
To the lapping of the tide.

'Amen', the chaplain's voice soft fell
We bowed our heads to pray,
'Oh God, it cannot be, this price
So soon be ours to pay'.

—Lieutenant E. Yates: *Parade Service on Deck*

I believe it will be found that the Italian and Balkan Peninsulas are militarily and politically linked and that really it is one theatre which we have to deal with. It may not be possible to conduct a successful Italian campaign ignoring what happens in the Aegean. The Germans evidently attach the utmost importance to the Eastern sphere. What I ask for is the capture of Rhodes and the other islands of the Dodecanese.

—Churchill (to Roosevelt)[1]

Context

The Dodecanese campaign, one of Churchill's less brilliant ideas, came about through the PM's obsession with peripheral strategies. Britain had plenty of experience with such. From the time of the Seven Years War (1756–1763), the dominance of the Royal Navy enabled England to strike at the soft underbelly of her continental foes, France and Spain, prising away their far flung outposts; taking from their empires to add to its own. Churchill did not much care for the idea of a cross-Channel invasion, fearing it would be too costly. Instead nibbling at the margins, death by many cuts, appeared less risky. It wasn't, as although the doomed campaign spawned, it is said, Alistair Maclean's best-selling novel *The Guns of Navarone*, the rest is all bad.

In 1912, that group of the Southern Sporades, called the Dodecanese, a necklace of fourteen islands that lie off the Turkish coast, came not to Greece but to Italy. Later, Il Duce was very pleased with his Aegean mini-empire. Rhodes has always been strategically vital, one of the very largest of all in that luminous sea of beautiful islands. Its classical traces abound. The place was 'duffed up' by Caesar's assassin Cassius in the time of the late Roman Republic, and the Knights of St. John made it their great fortress and church after the final fall of the Christian kingdoms in the Levant. They held out there for two centuries, defying the rising Ottoman power, a thorn in the Sultan's side. Twice the Turks laid siege in 1480 and again, finally successfully, in 1522. The knights, with their colours flying, marched out from the ruins with full honours. Malta would be their new home and scene of their greatest, epic battle with the Sublime Porte.

Fascists tend to like tales of knightly valour, it appeals to their warped version of a crusader ethic. Mussolini rebuilt the citadel of Rhodes town for the glory of his re-born Roman empire and to the undying gratitude of a modern tourist industry. Rhodes became a must-enjoy fascist holiday destination. Northwards lies Cos and north again, Leros; all of these islands were strategically important in the long wars between Cross and Crescent, near to the Turkish mainland, sheltered anchorages with repair yards on Symi and Leros.

Cos has always attracted entranced visitors from the days of Asclepius; Leros less so:

> Leros is a gloomy shut-in sort of place, with deep fjords full of lustreless water, black as obsidian and as cold as a polar bear's kiss. Leros means dirty or grubby in Greek, and the inhabitants of the island are regarded as something out-of-the-ordinary by the other little Dodecanese islands. They are supposed to be surly, secretive, and double-dealing and, in my limited experience, I found this to be so.[2]

Churchill's plan was that with the fall of Axis North Africa and the collapse of Mussolini's regime, a swift occupation of the Dodecanese might entice Turkey to commit on the Allied side. He envisaged a warm water route to Russia through the Dardanelles, an area the PM might have been wary of, given past experience. This one would prove no better, if at least less bloody. Nonetheless, at the Casablanca Conference in January 1943, Churchill received the thumbs up, and planning commenced at the end of January 1943.

Operation Accolade

The concept involved direct amphibious assaults on Rhodes and Karpathos, landing three divisions plus armour. Crete, of evil memory, was originally included in the plan but the strength of the German presence was rightly judged to be too great. Besides, the largest of the Greek islands was bottling up a substantial garrison, virtually a free POW camp. As with any such operation, control of the skies was essential and this was the prime difficultly. Allied planes from Cyprus and the Middle East would be at a disadvantage while the fighters of *X Fliegerkorps* were an awful lot closer. Besides, much Allied strength would be tied up in the forthcoming invasion of Sicily.

Eisenhower was not impressed and remained sceptical. When, on 9th October with all going horribly wrong, General 'Jumbo' Wilson[3] had to go cap in hand to the Americans at La Marsa in Tunisia to beg for aid, he came back empty handed. Even Ike's British advisors, Tedder, Cunningham and Alexander, wished to distance themselves from Churchill's perceived folly. Alanbrooke[4] caustically commented: *Another day of Rhodes madness. He* [the PM] *is in a very dangerous condition, most unbalanced, and God knows how we will finish this war if he goes on.*[5]

What made the idea more attractive during the summer of 1943 was the collapse of the Italians and their falling out with their erstwhile German allies. Italy threw in the towel on 8th September but plans for a mini version of *Accolade* had already been scuppered by the Americans' continued refusal to provide air support. The surrender did open up possibilities. Italian garrisons appeared inclined to swap sides, a prospect the Germans viewed with alarm and they rushed forces onto the islands to discourage mass-defections.

Rhodes, strategically, was the key. Both sides knew this and Boche Army Group E had committed a full division, *Sturm-Division Rhodos*, to its defence. On 8th September, an outlying Italian garrison on Kastelorizo surrendered to the Allies. George Jellicoe of the SBS was dropped in by parachute onto Rhodes. His mission was to persuade Admiral Campioni and his 40,000 soldiers to defect. Meanwhile, General Kleeman wasn't taking any chances and he moved rapidly to disarm his former allies. By 11th September the Italians had been disarmed and neutralised.

Despite this failure, Wilson pressed ahead with plans to occupy Cos, Samos and Leros. The Royal Navy was largely unchallenged at sea and two fighter squadrons were moved to Cos. It was hoped these smaller islands could form a base for an invasion of Rhodes. Enter the LRDG; they were to provide 130 troopers to support the planned landing. From 10th–17th September a full brigade of infantry (234th under Major General F.G.R. Brittorous) with SBS detachments, the Greek Sacred Band and a company of Paras secured Cos, Kalymnos, Samos, Leros, Symi and Astypalaia. The Germans responded by consolidating their grip on the islands they'd already secured and laid plans to recapture the rest.

The Achilles' heel was the RAF aerodrome on Cos. General Muller, commanding 22nd Infantry Division tasked with ejecting the Allies, ordered bombing raids which began on 18th September. By the end of the month, the *Luftwaffe* had over 350 operational aircraft committed. By 3rd October the thin Allied forces on Cos, mainly from 1st battalion

DLI and some 3,500 Italians, were fighting for their lives. It was a disaster; the island fell and nearly 1,500 British went into the bag.

The surviving Italians also capitulated, though their commander and over a hundred officers were shot. Changing sides was never a popular move. With Cos gone and its vital airfield lost, the campaign was doomed. Wilson plaintively cabled an exculpatory message to Churchill, saying he apparently had, *no intelligence at our disposal which would have led us to foresee that the enemy would be able to collect and launch at such short notice an expedition of the magnitude which made the assault on Cos.*[6]

Operation Typhoon

Muller's planned invasion of Leros got off to a bad start. He had trumped the British very effectively with Operation *Polar Bear* against Cos, but the Royal Navy took a hand in sinking, literally, his projected move against Leros. A supply convoy headed for Cos was sent to the bottom, along with personnel and landing craft. The general was forced to assemble a new invasion flotilla, ships and boats scattered amongst the islands under camouflage. Though the navy kept up a relentless pressure, shelling ports and installations, Muller was, by 12th November, fully ready. His composite force or *kampfgruppe* was comprised of infantry, paras, an Axis SBS-type group and Brandenburgers – the *Abwehr's* Special Forces. The bulk of the Allied garrison on Leros was formed by roughly the 3,000 infantry of 234th Brigade and 8,500 Italians.

Prior to the attack, the Allies had been heavily bombed and Muller's forces landed on both the east and west sides. Paratroops were dropped on the central high ground of Mount Rachi. British counterattacks failed to eliminate the beachheads and the navy could not prevent further German reinforcements coming ashore. The defenders' positions were cut in two and within four days, on 16th November, the survivors surrendered. Another 3,200 British troops marched into captivity. The remaining footholds were evacuated, and the rump of Italian garrisons surrendered. By the latter part of November it was all over.

It would be difficult to suggest anything good that, from the Allied perspective, came out of the campaign. The Germans had air superiority virtually throughout, and their plans were both well laid and well executed. General Henry Wilson was not amongst the casualties. He kept his job as C-in-C Middle East Forces and, in January 1944 succeeded Eisenhower as Supreme Allied Commander in the Mediterranean. LRDG, on the other hand, lost more men in the Dodecanese than during the whole of the desert war. This was the last full campaign where the British were defeated and the Germans victorious.[7]

Enter the LRDG

As noted in the preceding chapter, David Lloyd Owen received orders on 11th September to take a full squadron to the small island of 'Castellorosso' (this is Castelorizo, a tiny island south of Rhodes that almost touches Turkey), and be ready to deploy at six hours notice. The orders, from Lieutenant-General Anderson, read: *Most likely role will be to move into Cos and Samos, if the situation permits, to stiffen resistance of the Italian garrisons and local guerrillas to German control of the islands. You may however be ordered to operate in Rhodes.* As Lloyd Owen himself comments, *Thus began, in a tragically vague way, the Aegean campaign of September, October and November 1943. It was tragically vague throughout.*[8]

There was little time for speculation. Men, vehicles, kit and supplies had to be pulled together on Haifa docks for sailing that evening. The ramshackle orders contrasted sharply with the months of re-training and detailed instruction they'd been through. At least they set off in fine Henty-esque style, sliding through clear blue, late summer waters in a Greek sloop. Her patriot crew were elated that, after the years of oppression, they were sailing for home waters under their own flag. Two more sloops, one British and one under French colours, joined their little international flotilla. Spirits were further buoyed by the enthusiasm which the locals showed as, on 13th September, they cruised into Castelorizo.

Their base, once stores and gear were ferried ashore, seemed idyllic; classic white painted cottages surrounding the harbour, a scene from Durrell's *Greek Islands.* There was, however, still a war to be fought and what the hundred men of Lloyd Owen's squadron were to be doing about that remained as vague as before. The small town was delightful and the Greeks, who had little to share, hospitable. The troopers found it rather bizarre to be so close to their former enemies, and Lloyd Owen decided not to pass on an order that Italian officers were to be saluted. The idyll was short-lived as orders were received to move north to Leros. The message did not provide any inkling as to how the ground lay, whether the Italians were friendly, or even how the squadron should get there. All three sloops had returned to base.

They did, hopefully, have the use of a fast Italian boat and a single seaplane. They also had George Jellicoe, who had abandoned his abortive mission to Rhodes. As David Lloyd Owen points out, this initial and telling failure to seize Rhodes should have been the signal to abandon the entire scheme for the Dodecanese. Possession of the 'Island of Roses' with its airfields was crucial. Lloyd Owen sensibly decided to send his W/O ahead in the seaplane to recce Leros and report whilst the rest struggled to get there as best they could. The aircraft's Italian crew proved very unenthusiastic and contrived to collide with a Short Sunderland whilst taxiing. This mishap could have served as a metaphor for the whole mess.

The LRDG doesn't give up. Lloyd Owen, with Stormonth-Darling, commandeered the Italian motor boat and its unwilling crew, crammed her to the gunwales with men and kit, and set off for a night dash over the Aegean. If we had not been fighting the Germans, this would have been high adventure, a fast, sleek raider sliding through the fabled sea at night, still balmy at that time of year, their passage lit by towering fires on Rhodes, like beacons from Troy, courtesy of the RAF. Lumbering transports crammed with paras bound for Cos waddled overhead.

In the wee small hours the mighty roar of the boat's twin engines subsided as she cruised towards the dark harbour of Leros. A kerfuffle and some wild shooting broke out as the vessel's crew negotiated to have the boom lifted, but finally she nosed gracefully into the deep harbour to a formal welcome from Admiral Mascarpa and his entire staff, parading resplendent as though to receive royalty.

LRDG, in terms of numbers, fell rather short of the two full divisions the Admiral was hoping for. Lloyd Owen and a score of his brigands inspired alarm rather than confidence. He hastily and with fine bravado announced he was the mere tip of the vanguard of a mighty force that was to follow. It was impossible to work out if the Italian believed him; he didn't really believe himself.[9] He did at least receive an invitation to lunch the following day.

This was not entirely a success. Lloyd Owen, very much attired as the warrior for the working day, found his glittering, perfumed hosts, their table groaning whilst others starved, increasingly repugnant. The Admiral's hospitality might be impressive; his plans for defending the island were not: *Even with my limited knowledge of military tactics I could see that the whole defence scheme was futile. There was no depth in the defence, and no provision had been made for a reserve to counter-attack any enemy that might land.*[10]

Lloyd Owen took charge. Transport to supply the coastal battery sites was inadequate and lines of defence needed to be dug both north and south to seal off the landing beaches. The centre of the island, ideal for parachutists, would also have to be fortified. The Italians were truculent. Whilst they agreed to the plan, they proved snail-like in its execution. LRDG found tools, organised the 5,000-strong garrison into working parties and, stark horror, obliged the immaculate officers to strip their laundered sleeves and work alongside their men. For the Italian officer corps this was tantamount to social engineering. Happily, the element of choice was removed.

This type of impromptu defence, *Seven Samurai* style, wasn't really the designated role of LRDG. Some days later a trio of British destroyers delivered the whole of 234th Brigade and disgorged men and kit onto the harbour. Communications were so poor Lloyd Owen had no idea these reinforcements were due. Defence now became the regulars' responsibility. Other welcome additions were Jake Easonsmith and his Kiwis, followed by Guy Prendergast. LRDG, plus SBS detachments, were now on Leros in force but there was no gainful employment for any of them on the island. It was now a regular bastion in a regular war.

However, occupying the neighbouring island of Calymnos might prove more profitable:

> Calymnos and Leros are almost Siamese twins, but there could not be two more contrasting places. Calymnos is big, blowsy and razor shaven, yet open to the sea and sky and all their humours … you are in the island of sponges now, and it is on this hazardous trade that the reputation of Calymnos depends … the hills are shaven and smooth as a turtle's back and the bare rock with its fur of hill 'garrigue' [scrub] has the slightly bluish terracotta tinge of volcanic rock.[11]

Transport would be provided by the rather grandly named Levant Schooner Flotilla ('LSF'). This was in fact comprised of five armed caiques commanded by Commander Adrian Seligman, a celebrated yachtsman who'd circumnavigated the globe in a windjammer before the war. The boats, typically crewed by five or six sailors, were armed with a mix of machine guns and 20-mm cannon. The whole purpose of the LSF was to facilitate the infiltration and extraction of commando raiders. Like LRDG, their kit had a certain Heath Robinson quality; the vessels were often powered by marinised Matilda tank engines with comms salvaged from Curtiss P-40 fighters! These were just the breed of buccaneers whose bravado would appeal to the Prime Minister.

By 25th September, LRDG was set up on Calymnos where they could better deploy their intelligence gathering skills. The picture was depressing. It was obvious Axis air raids were pounding Cos and Leros, grinding Allied airfields to dust. The RAF, as ever, put up a good fight but the odds were always impossible: *I never saw more than two of our fighters in the air at once, yet these tackled any numbers the Germans chose to send over. We picked up a few pilots out of the sea, and watched others go down in flames.*[12]

At least one Axis flier was dragged from the Aegean into a small boat LRDG had rowed out to save him. No sooner was he aboard than a German flying-boat pounced and swooped to land next to the startled rescuers, relieving them of their captive – a very short incarceration![13] Cairo remained immured in Nero-like calm; messages were received intimating that no seaborne enemy action against the garrison on Cos was anticipated. Such action may not have been anticipated, but it arrived at full blast, the very next day![14]

Easonsmith and Lloyd Owen awoke in the early dawn to witness a strong squadron of ships moving on Cos. If any lingering doubts remained as to whether these were hostile, the flashes from their gun muzzles soon dispelled any uncertainty. Cos was doomed. The port of Calymnos faces directly towards Cos so withdrawal might be tricky. No matter, Cairo sent another message commanding LRDG to immediately counter-attack and recover Cos, *one of the most brainless and preposterous orders that I ever heard.*[15] Apparently Churchill had instructed Wilson at GHQ Middle East to 'play high; improvise and dare'. Stirring stuff but how a mere three hundred men without any heavy weapons and only a flotilla of caiques were to recover Cos when a brigade of infantry had failed to hold the place wasn't specified.

Later, a more realistic communiqué ordered a retreat to Leros. On the evening of 4th October, all personnel and stores were loaded onto the LSF caiques and the diminutive fleet stole way into the autumn darkness to arrive and unload safely on Leros. They came in like thieves in the night, unheralded and unwelcomed. The only people to pay them due attention turned out to be the ever vigilant *Luftwaffe.* Soon the bowl of the ancient harbour was lit by furious light, the clatter of AA guns and the deadly whine of Axis bombs. The bay became an inferno of noise, explosions, the crash of fallen masonry, dust, death, chaos. Miraculously everyone survived.[16]

Ungainly and outmoded, the JU87 'Stuka' was a fearful instrument of torment if you happened to be pretty much defenceless beneath the tortured, wailing scream of its dive. Lloyd Owen and Easonsmith set up the LRDG's automatic weapons to take on the dive bombers but, without any air cover, this was a one sided fight. As the Axis predators swooped again, they hit a ship in the harbour, a great coiling stack of black its obituary. During a lull, the survivors scrambled out of the trap of the bay and into the hills. Casualties had been remarkably light considering the fury of the aerial tempest – *I remember seeing David Sutherland of the SBS covered in blood.*[17]

In the centre of the beleaguered island, the ground was held by a battalion of Royal Irish Rangers. LRDG became their eyes and ears. Patrols went down to each of the Italian shore batteries. This boosted their shaky morale and also deterred any who might think of swapping sides again. Theirs became a miserable, hunted existence. Axis planes controlled the skies and accounted for most of the Allied ships. LRDG lived in caves, kept constant watch and endured life under siege. This was all a very far cry from their previous existence as desert raiders. *Rare as fairies* had been the taunt in the last disastrous Greek campaign of 1941, and the RAF came in for a lot of stick. The navy was much in evidence, still carrying the fight to the enemy, pounding the harbours at Cos and Calymnos by night.

Some patrols were active in the outlying islands. Ken Lazarus on Stampalia, Dudley Folland on Giaros, others on Kithnos and Simi. At least in these tiny listening stations the patrols could achieve what LRDG was intended to do: watch, listen and count. They could also bite. A stiffening of LRDG on Simi, backed by a company or so of Italians, saw off a German beach landing, giving the attackers a very bloody nose. Inevitably, swarms of Stukas came over to exact retribution.[18]

This wasn't the only aggressive action. As the Axis had now garrisoned Calymnos, a Greek-born officer, Lieutenant Pavlides volunteered to row over and recce. Three nights after this successful beginning Stan Eastwood and two of his Rhodesian troopers went across. Their foray proved more adventurous. Onshore, they bumped a German patrol and Eastwood with one of the men was captured.

Lance Corporal Whitehead escaped and swam for it, evading capture and landing elsewhere on the island coast. Taken in by a friendly shepherd, he was able to get a message back to Leros by another swimmer. Receipt of his message was to be acknowledged by a particular firing of some of the big guns. Whitehead was brought off five days later. Eastwood and his other trooper also gave their captors the slip, though they then had to go the long way round through Turkey to get back.[19]

Belatedly, Cairo was listening to the sage counsels of experts like George Jellicoe who was lobbying to have all Special Forces brought under some form of centralised command function. The new creation styled 'Raiding Forces' was to be commanded by a Colonel Turnbull, a regular without experience of behind-the-lines operations. On 18th October, Guy Prendergast, to his surprise was suddenly elevated to 2I/C of this new outfit and magicked back to GHQ. Jake Easonsmith became leader of LRDG with Lloyd Owen as his deputy.

Both men were already close friends:

> I never knew his equal. He had a guile which was almost uncanny in his ability to foresee how the enemy would react. He was always thinking ahead and asking himself what he would do if the enemy adopted a certain line of action. Thus he was always prepared, and I never knew him to be caught on the wrong foot.[20]

These were perhaps the best of Britain's civilian soldiers – men who had never necessarily thought of a career in arms yet answered the call and rose to the challenge. Leros would test them to the limit and the toll would be dreadfully high. Easonsmith's first executive task was to send a fifty-strong raiding force to recapture the tiny island of Levita which the Axis had stormed. In fact Levita had been taken by prisoners pulled out of the carnage of the Axis supply convoy the Navy had decimated early in October. Forty or so of these had been en route to captivity aboard His Majesty's very small ship *Hedgehog.* The vessel's engine broke down and the skipper put into Levita where his prisoners took over the ship by coup de main. The small Italian force on the island hadn't interfered.

Easonsmith saw this raid as completely pointless. Lloyd Owen agreed but their brigadier did not. In the expanses of the desert with so much room to manoeuvre, interference from 'top brass' had been minimal. Conversely, in the shrunken theatre of the Dodecanese, the 'bull' closed in like a net. It was impossible to avoid. Levita had to be re-taken as it seemed like a good idea at the time, and such cheek from the Germans could not pass unnoticed.

The Battle of Leros

John Olivey with Dick Lawson the MO would lead the operation against Levita. He would have forty-five troopers, and the tiny expedition weighed anchor at 19.30 hours on 23rd October. The plan was for a classic pincer, one party landing at the southwest tip of the island and another at the northwest. This party, all Kiwis, experienced heavy contact, and the watchers on Leros, queasy with worry, watched packs of JU87s & 88s swarming all next day. As Jake Easonsmith returned with the launches to collect the raiders, he found only Olivey, Lawson and half a dozen others. Of the rest there was no sign. Olivey had experienced very heavy fighting and had been obliged to break through the ring to escape.[21]

It was a costly fiasco. The small German garrison of escapees had been heavily reinforced, the raiders were hopelessly outgunned, and the cost was very high. This pointless, unnecessary little raid had cost LRDG more in losses than they'd incurred during three years fighting Rommel. There was some comfort in that when Brigadier Davy, Director of Military Operations in Cairo, came for an inspection, *very wet and rather oily after having had his destroyer sunk beneath him on the way*, he grasped the futility of LRDG's deployment and, in consequence the GOC Aegean was, in Great War slang, promptly *stellenbosched.*[22]

It was obvious to those immured on bony Leros that the game, in this case, was up. Turkey wasn't interested and the Axis controlled the skies. Evacuation seemed the only sensible course. Morale was low as each creeping autumn dawn the brigade stood to arms awaiting the inevitable onslaught. RIR was still holding the central massif, Mereviglia; King's Own the south with the Buffs to the north. The defenders had the existing coastal guns, a single battery of 25-pounders and a dozen Bofors'. Lloyd Owen was spared the last act of this very British Greek tragedy when Jake Easonsmith sent him back to Cairo to acquaint those in the fairy tale castle what was actually happening. It is entirely possible Easonsmith wanted to ensure his old friend survived what was coming, and so would be the rock around which the unit could be rebuilt.

With a soldier's comradely instinct, Lloyd Owen knew he would not be seeing Jake again. He boarded an Italian submarine for a five-day passage first to Haifa then on to Cairo. He arrived in this oasis of surreal, cosmopolitan hedonism just as, on 12th November, the final act on Leros commenced. Landing craft came in with the dawn, attempting beaches in the south and middle of the island. They took hits but battered on, gaining a foothold. Stukas came down like prehistoric winged predators, no sign of the RAF. Mid-afternoon and JU52s, fat bellied with their heavily armed human cargo, came in at 500 feet and dropped parachutists in the centre of the defences.

LRDG patrols were thrown in to stem the rot, to engage the formidable *Fallschirmjager.* Alan Redfern, a very popular and experienced officer, became an early casualty. The enemy was checked, held but not repulsed. Nobody had any illusions about the outcome. A further flotilla of transports was lying offshore, whatever small ships the defenders had were long sunk and, that night, enemy reinforcements were ferried onto the beachheads. The defenders fought hard. The parachutists were contained and losses were inflicted. John Olivey was holding the six-inch gun battery at Clidi on the northern flank of Leros. The Italians, for the most part, had cleared off but Olivey blasted the attackers over open sights till they were virtually on top of the position before spiking the gun and withdrawing. He still wasn't done. That afternoon, leading a detachment from the Buffs, he retook the position despite being wounded.[23]

Still no sign of the RAF, and the grinding attrition continued. On 15th November, the Germans could deploy 450 planes, constantly bombing and strafing. On the following day the Axis attempted to take the high ground in the centre, and the *Luftwaffe* threw in every type of plane imaginable, antiques included; all were safe as there was none of ours to intercept them. For David Lloyd Owen this was a terrible day. Tim Heywood called to give him the news he'd dreaded. Jake Easonsmith had been killed. Typically, he'd insisted on leading a patrol into the village of Meriviglia, crawling with Germans. He was shot by a sniper.[24]

Jake's death was more than a personal tragedy for his friends. LRDG had lost one of its most respected and inspirational leaders. Perhaps it is more galling to lose so valued a comrade in a doomed operation, a pointless and unnecessary sacrifice. It was also the beginning of the end on Leros. Meriviglia was lost, the depressing stench of burnt papers wafting over the confused battlefield. By the 17th, the Axis had sent in yet more reinforcements. What remained of the garrison mustered in the south but there was no real prospect for further resistance. LRDG W/O Sergeant Hughes was the last to transmit, at 18.35 hours that day, confirming that silence had indeed now fallen and Leros was gone.[25]

John Olivey, despite wounds and exhaustion, was still in the ring. His Rhodesians had formed an ad hoc perimeter on the high ground at Clidi, and kept on fighting. He'd had to abandon the battery but wasn't going to let the enemy grab ammunition stocks. As he carefully probed one of the casemates, he found two astonished Germans already in possession. The dispute was short lived: *they didn't have long to think about things because I had to shoot them.*[26] Olivey and his troopers fought on for another thirteen hours till he passed out from injury and utter exhaustion and was captured. For his outstanding bravery, he earned a bar to his MC; Sergeant Coventry, his steadfast NCO, won a DCM.

The LRDG contingent on Leros had numbered 123. Not all went into the bag; their remarkable talent for escaping meant 70 odd got clear away in the ensuing weeks. It was still a body blow. Lloyd Owen had foreseen just how bad the outcome on Leros might be and had pressed GHQ to set contingency evacuation plans in motion. There was no arguing with the logic of this. He pressed for a signal he'd drafted to the garrison commander to be sent whilst there was still time. He'd planned to send small boats to the neighbouring islands nightly to pick up survivors. This would have saved many men, but the message wasn't sent till the fight was nearly over and comms were gone.[27]

Lloyd Owen writes that he felt great bitterness as a consequence, and rightly so. Though nearly a thousand men were rescued, the total could have been far higher and the defeat made less palpable. As ever, LRDG members proved infinitely resourceful. Ashley Greenwood had escaped to the Turkish mainland. Pausing only to disguise himself as a suitably disreputable peasant type, he returned to help others. One of the beneficiaries of this telling individual initiative was W/O Peter Mold, who made it safely to Turkey by 2nd December.

With Jake Easonsmith killed, Guy Prendergast returned to the unit to pick up the reins of command, and his dynamism saved many. A large proportion of those infantrymen left behind were too exhausted to think of escape. Prendergast got his survivors out through Bodrum in Turkey. Amazingly, another irrepressible escapee was John Olivey. Despite having done far more than 'his bit', he gave his captors the slip in Athens and managed to get word to Lloyd Owen at the end of January 1944. He was successfully ex-filtrated.

One of the more epic stories is that of Gunner Patch and Trooper Hill. They'd been captured on 24th October during the abortive raid on Levita. They were sent by flying boat to Piraeus, then on to Athens, and then with minimal rations they were bundled into cattle trucks for the long haul to Germany. By 5th November they'd chugged as far as the Yugoslav border but they'd spent the long hours productively by removing the wire from the truck windows. They and two Kiwis removed themselves from the train and spent a freezing week in the bare highlands till they stumbled into partisans. These were Chetniks[28] and, though they were in a bad way themselves, they soon became indispensible paramedics to the disorganised partisans. Hunger and sickness stalked the pair relentlessly but they had no intention of giving up. The winter weather was vile, food scarce or non existent; Christmas was toasted in local Raki. They were a very long way from home.

Their ordeal continued through a grim Balkan winter. Food was always much on their minds, along with sickness, the appalling cold and the fugitive hunter/gatherer lives they led in the high mountains. It wasn't until 10th February that they made wireless contact with a British liaison officer. Overall, their present hosts were a pretty dismal crew, with little or no active interest in the war – *all drunkards, always at loggerheads and sometimes coming to blows….*[29] It was a nasty little war, inconclusive brushes with Bulgar patrols, *informers shot and mutilated.*

Their precious wireless had to be abandoned in a hurried scramble for safety and they didn't get another until early May.

Despite the unprepossessing nature of their Chetnik comrades, the LRDG men attempted to wean them from the path of indifference or collaboration into a more fruitful alliance with Tito's partisans. These were, in terms of politics, very much of the left but also vastly more proactive in the business of killing Germans. Under their patient mentoring, the band swelled to around three hundred. It wasn't until 1st September 1944, the fifth anniversary of Hitler's invasion of Poland, that they could join forces with a British mission. They would not return to the fold until February 1945.

Six years later, while working at the War Office during the war in Korea, Lloyd Owen heard from Trooper Hill, saying that both he and Gunner Patch were ready to sign up to the colours again. Their story embodies the very spirit of courage, resourcefulness and indomitable will that was the soul of LRDG. Little else that was good could have come from the debacle in the Dodecanese. Bizarrely, Churchill had sent a message to GHQ in October: *Efforts must be made to withdraw the Long Range Desert Group… this would be much better than their being taken prisoners of war.* It deepens the tragedy that no one was listening.[30]

Counting the Cost

It was time to consult the oracle. LRDG's losses in the abortive campaign had been so high it raised the question of whether the unit could be rebuilt at all. Lloyd Owen was now de facto commander, as Guy Prendergast had not yet returned from temporary exile in Turkey. The only great fount of LRDG wisdom to hand was the founding father himself, Ralph Bagnold. As ever, the great man was courteous, listening to the younger officer's passionate entreaty that LRDG still had a role to play and could be fully resuscitated. Lloyd Owen saw, rightly, that the flowering of resistance forces throughout Greece, Italy and the Balkans offered plenty scope. He reckoned he needed to find and train enough new volunteers to fill the empty boots and that this had to be accomplished within a span of six months, a big ask all round.

What he was in fact proposing in terms of attaching LRDG patrols ('teams' as they'd now be called), to guerrilla bands would, in contemporary terms, be defined as generating the 'force multiplier' effect. This in practice implies that highly trained, well equipped specialists infiltrated to mentor and direct insurgent forces can significantly boost the effectiveness of those irregulars to a degree far beyond their own small number. Few modern Special Forces commentators would disagree. The employment of UK and US operators in Afghanistan in late 2001 to bolster the Northern Alliance forces, combined with effective use of air strength, defeated the superior Taliban army, previously unstoppable, in a matter of weeks.

Bagnold, having deliberated, uttered his Olympian pronouncement – *I think you should try to keep the unit in being.*[31] This was the holy covenant and Lloyd Owen went forth, the fire in his loins that had been dampened now re-kindled. The history of the LRDG did not end with the fall of Leros. It tells us much about the high calibre of both men. Brigadier Muir Turnbull did not demur, and Lloyd Owen was confirmed as CO. LRDG was back in business.

Guy Prendergast duly returned and resumed his role as 2I/C to Turnbull. Inconveniently, the New Zealand government now wanted its troopers back. This was a blow, naturally, as the Kiwis had been magnificent throughout. Freyberg, as ever, would listen, but his hands were tied. The Home Government, understandably, was concerned at the high level of losses on Leros – given they hadn't been consulted in the first place. Besides, casualties from the desperate slog up the Italian Peninsula had to be made up.

Good fortune now intervened. The Rhodesians had always been first class, and more of them could make up for the loss of the Kiwis. Sir Ernest Lucas Guest, Rhodesia's Air Minister, paid a visit to his own lads who were serving with LRDG. He was impressed with them and Lloyd Owen with him. This new relationship bore fruit and more Rhodesians arrived. The minister remained an ally till the end of the war.

Recovery was swift. Stormonth-Darling, who'd managed to extract himself from the Aegean whirlpool, would command the UK squadron. This was one of two; each would be comprised of eight patrols with one officer and ten troopers. Moir Stormonth-Darling had been immured on Mykonos, surrounded by Axis, but had got back through Turkey. Like Lloyd Owen, he was a Wykehamist and the two men were firm friends, an ideal choice for squadron commander.

Ken Lazarus would lead the Rhodesians; another excellent candidate, he'd proven himself many times and was an expert cartographer. He too had seen service in the dismal Aegean, supporting the Italian garrison on Stampalia. At the first sight of *Fallschirmjager* the defenders fled. Grabbing a boat, he and four troopers pulled for the Turkish Coast, then took a caique to Cyprus and finally returned via Haifa.

> Ken was a rather quiet, dour man who took a bit of time to get to know well but he had great courage, a fine heart and a true love of his fellow men. Moir was much more of an extrovert, with an infectious laugh, a splendid sense of duty and a slow, deliberate and thorough mind. He was worshipped by his men, for they trusted him implicitly, and they always knew that he would support them.[32]

The rejuvenated unit was to be housed in the Arab village of Azzib, north of Haifa on the Syrian border. The place had little inherent charm; *an Arab village of no outstanding note, smelling as strongly as most Arab villages, and its houses were just as squalid.*[33]

Camp was an unedifying mix of old Nissen huts with the rest under canvas. The workload was formidable. LRDG was almost being rebuilt from scratch and the Kiwis departed on 29th December – their farewell was fairly lively. With the New Year came new skills: parachuting at Ramat David twinned with small boat sailing (George Jellicoe's SBS provided the instructors). Mountain warfare was practised from the Cedars. The skills list seemed endless: improved orienteering and map-reading, use and handling of explosives, recognising enemy aircraft, loading of transport from jeeps to mules. Recruits also had a crash course in the byzantine maze of Balkan history and topography, the latter being slightly less twisted. Tim Heywood was drilling signallers, and the new MO, Michael Parsons, who'd replaced Dick Lawson (captured in the Dodecanese disaster), taught first aid.

Training was augmented by free-ranging exercises where patrols lived out in the open. These forays intensified after the unit moved to Syria, close to ancient Baalbek. Those two ageing WACO planes amazingly were still flying (if, at times, only just) and kept giving good service, ferrying men and kit from Cairo, over the stark expanse of Sinai to Beirut. Meanwhile Guy Prendergast, in his role as deputy chief of Raiding Forces, had been discussing, in very high places, how the restored raiders might best be employed.

In late February, Lloyd Owen was instructed to fly to Italy and attend upon Alexander himself. Reality proved less stimulating. When he flew into Bari nobody had heard of him. He borrowed a car to drive the fifty miles to catch up with the SAS, as he'd been instructed, before they left for Blighty. Virtually all had gone, and those who remained denied all knowledge! Lloyd Owen's attempt to fly across Italy from Bari to Caserta was met by obfuscation. Again he had to beg the loan of a car and drive.

Unwashed, unfed and very tired, he arrived in the early hours. He did have an ally to hand in the person of Brigadier Hugh Mainwaring, who knew LRDG well from their days in the desert. This got him through the door of General Harding, Alexander's chief of staff. Harding too was a friend and he was amenable to the idea of LRDG being deployed in Italy under his control. Lloyd Owen wanted a look at this new front line, to gauge the ground over which patrols would be operating. Most told him it was impossible to get across Axis lines, the country too broken, too mountainous.

This was, of course, precisely the type of terrain they'd trained for, and he remained undaunted. Another close ally, Bernard Bruce who'd commanded G Patrol, was with Eighth Army tactical HQ and proved very helpful. Lloyd Owen then wrote an encouraging note to Guy Prendergast: *Everyone was inclined to tell me that the mountains were dangerous and difficult to move over but I hope that fact will be an ally to our patrols, who are trained for it. On the whole, I think the country is ideal for our kind of work.*[34]

Tim Heywood became the pathfinder, scouting for a permanent base in Italy. As ever, he did a good job and LRDG moved to Rodi on the Gargano Peninsula. The place was chosen had the advantage of reasonable proximity to the airfield complex at Foggia whilst sufficiently off the beaten track to maintain secrecy. *Rodi itself was a pretty little Italian town with narrow, cobbled winding streets, and it was a little cleaner than many similar places. The people were typical of the rather indolent and backward southern Italian. They did not like the British much….*[35]

Meanwhile, there were many ideas and projects for LRDG, veering between the barely realistic and plain daft. None amounted to anything concrete. Lloyd Owen had sagely adopted the operational principle that he would never commit men to an enterprise unless their extraction route was sound. Oddly, when he did call for volunteers to attempt a near suicidal raid on the Brenner Pass railway tunnel, a mission that offered little hope of ex-filtration, nearly everyone volunteered at once![36] Happily, this plan foundered in its conceptual phase and was quietly buried without mourners.

Disruption of enemy communications became the favoured path. A dozen patrols would be committed fighting alongside additional UK and US units. Railways would be hit first, then roads. Three main railway routes were to be targeted: first, Parma to Spezia; second, Bologna to Pistoia; and last, Faenza to Florence. Intelligence on each sector was provided by Allied agents already in place. A great deal of planning activity followed; Stormonth-Darling, with Dick Croucher as IO, spent weeks in careful preparation. As usual, Lloyd Owen was concerned that the patrols, which amounted to some 75 percent of unit strength, should be sure of their reception in the target zone and that their exit routes were feasible. Both LRDG officers became worried over the first problem, the need to ensure a friendly reception. They proposed that three pathfinder patrols go in ahead of the main body to ensure everything was as it should be.

In the event, the whole scheme was abandoned due to a lack of air transport. For LRDG this was particularly frustrating, for surely this major logistical impediment should have been obvious from the start. Lloyd Owen bluntly demanded to know if there were in fact *any* sensible proposals in the offing. There weren't, so he suggested that a full squadron should be placed with Force 266,[37] responsible for coordinating all of the many teams active in the Balkans providing aid to the partisans.

Here, at last, a stroke of good fortune: LRDG found another ally in Tom Pearson, a Rifleman and now GSO1 to Force 266. After all the messing about, here at last was a kindred spirit and a realist. Ken Lazarus and his Rhodesians went on loan to Pearson on the sole proviso they'd be returned if an urgent need arose on the Italian Peninsula. By 7th May, Lazarus was setting up in Bari, which was to be his and his troopers' base for the rest of the war. The Greek officer Pavlides, who'd proved himself so ably in the Dodecanese, went as his IO.

It was time to get back into the war.

Notes

1 Quoted in Ball, S., *The Bitter Sea* (Harper Collins, 2009), p. 248.
2 Durrell, L., *The Greek Islands* (Faber & Faber 1978), pp. 153–154.
3 Field Marshal Henry Maitland Wilson (1881–1964) – a Boer War veteran, Wilson saw much action in the Great War. After being involved with the success of Operation *Compass* in 1940, he'd led Ninth Army in Palestine and Syria during 1941 then was appointed to command in Persia and Iraq, becoming C-in-C of Middle East Command from February 1943.
4 Field Marshal Alan Francis Brook, 1st Viscount Alanbrooke (1883–1963), was CIGS, promoted to Field Marshal in 1944.
5 Ball, p. 248.
6 Ibid.
7 The Jews of the Dodecanese, who'd escaped relatively lightly under the Italians, became yet more victims of the Nazis. Few of Rhodes' ancient 2,000-strong Jewish community survived.
8 Lloyd Owen, p. 129.
9 Ibid., p. 133.
10 Ibid.
11 Durrell, pp. 153–154.
12 Lloyd Owen, p. 135.
13 Ibid.
14 Ibid.

15 Ibid.
16 Ibid., p. 136.
17 Ibid., p. 137.
18 Ibid.
19 Ibid., p. 138.
20 Ibid.
21 Ibid., p. 140.
22 Ibid., p. 141.
23 Ibid., p. 142.
24 Ibid., p. 143.
25 Ibid.
26 Ibid., p. 144.
27 Ibid.
28 Chetniks, more properly Chetnik Detachments of the Yugoslav Army, were the followers of former war minister Draza Mihailovic. Nominally loyalist, monarchist partisans, they frequently collaborated as auxiliaries of the Axis occupiers. The Allies quickly despaired of them and focused on Tito.
29 Lloyd Owen, p. 146.
30 Ibid., p. 148.
31 Ibid., p. 150.
32 Ibid., p. 152.
33 Ibid., p. 152.
34 Ibid., p. 155.
35 Ibid.
36 Ibid., p. 156.
37 For the Allied organization formed out of Force 133 (SOE) and jointly staffed by SOE and the Office of Strategic Services, see: http://www.oxfordreference.com/view/10.1093/acref/9780198604464.001.0001/acref-9780198604464-e-622 retrieved 25th January 2015.

CHAPTER 8
Garlic-Reeking Bandits, 1944–1945

Along the twisting terraces of broken view
The silent colonnades, the shattered arch
Look down on dust-masked things that pass
Tired, waving shadows in the ghostly streets,
Stumbling in rubble spewed from gaping mouths
New torn in tall, smooth walls, cool-drenched
I' the moon, up-stretched to the violent sky
Night blue with layering patterns of fire overlaid
Cool scent of sage in the scrub, with acrid fumes
From roaring, vicious flames, mix in the nostrils
And darkening, climbing pillars of dust
Mask from the cool, smooth sea and the plain
The placid farms and ominous, towering hills.

—E. Yates: *Salerno Fragment*

In my study of communist societies, I came to the conclusion that the purpose of communist propaganda was not to persuade or to convince, nor to inform but to humiliate; and therefore the less it corresponded to reality the better. When people are forced to remain silent when they are being told the most obvious lies, or even worse when they are forced to repeat the lies themselves, they lose once and for all their sense of probity. To assent to obvious lies is to co-operate with evil, and in some small way to become evil oneself. One's standing to resist anything is thus eroded, and even destroyed. a society of emasculated liars is easy to control.'

—Theodore Dalrymple

Communist duplicity and treachery was something LRDG would come to understand only too well.

A Very Balkan 'Do'

As a young man, I recall sailing from Corfu and approaching, as close as one dared, the Albanian shore. It was dark and deserted with what appeared to be barbed wire and bunkers guarding the beaches. There were no tourists. The contrast with bikini-clad Corfu could not have been more profound: 'us and them'; the communists shut away in their blank-faced tyranny. At this time Enver Hoxha, wartime partisan leader, was still alive and very much in control. He hung on till he died in 1985 and it took a while after that for the Cold War ice to thaw.

Albania is both wild and beautiful. The region was part of Rome's Dalmatian colonies in classical times and the historic connection appealed to Il Duce with his bold intentions to resurrect Italy's imperial glories. The country didn't gain independence from Ottoman rule until 1912, though its great medieval hero Skanderbeg had been a formidable bastion against the Turkish flood. From 1928 to 1939 the state was ruled as a form of constitutional monarchy by King Zog and his consort, Queen Geraldine. The King was inclined to be westward looking, encouraging his deeply conservative subjects to modernize. He even sent the royal princesses into the mountains dressed in, by rural Balkan standards, rather risqué outfits.[1]

The port of Vlore and its wide bay had attractions to Italian naval strategists both as a gateway to the Adriatic and a beachhead in the Balkans. From the mid-1920s Italian influence began to grow, as the country was dirt poor and debt ridden. Treaties were entered into in the 1920s but Zog was no puppet and stood fast against a blatant attempt at intimidation in 1934. With Hitler trumping Mussolini and annexing Austria and the Sudetenland four years later, Il Duce felt he was slipping behind in the *lebensraum* stakes. On 7th April 1939, despite King Victor Emmanuel's misgivings, Mussolini's new legions invaded in his name. Zog, whose queen had just produced an heir, fled – eventually to London. Count Ciano, Il Duce's son in law and foreign minister, had toyed with the idea of having the king murdered, but refrained due to a lingering fondness for Queen Geraldine.[2]

The King of Italy now also became King of Albania. Initial military resistance was non-existent, another easy coup for the Axis with no formal reaction from Paris or London. One of Ciano's aides sounded a warning note of skepticism, observing that had the Albanians possessed a half decent fire service, their firemen could have pushed the Italians back into the Adriatic.[3] The whole easy conquest fuelled Mussolini's delusions that he was the new Caesar and his army the new legions.

In October 1940, Mussolini used Albania as a balcony from which to begin his attempt on Greece. Here, plans for a Roman revival foundered badly until German intervention crushed the Greeks in 1941. The Italians remained as occupiers in Albania but several nationalist factions and a strengthening communist resistance, the National Liberation Movement ("NLM"), directed by Hoxha (these only commenced operations after *Barbarossa*), fought them, and latterly the Germans who moved into the vacuum after Il Duce's fall in September 1943.

In religious terms Albania was predominantly Muslim, and the Boche, for once, were content to rule with a greater degree of restraint. Several nationalist movements, being anti-communist, collaborated, and the SS raised a Muslim SS Division (an interesting extension of supposed Aryan supremacy and elitism). The war against the occupier also embodied a very nasty civil war. In total some 30,000 Albanians died at Axis' or each other's hands, and there was widespread devastation. On 29th November 1944, Hoxha's communist partisans took the capital Tirana as the Germans withdrew and, very quickly afterwards, brought the shutters down. They were to stay drawn for a very long time.

From early 1941, British missions had been trying to make contact with Albanian partisans. These attempts foundered once the Axis had also occupied neighbouring Yugoslavia, and it wasn't until April 1943 that Colonel W. 'Billy' Maclean[4] and Major David Smiley, on behalf of SOE, trekked in from Greece. By June, regular supply runs to the NLM had been arranged. Later in that year, a second mission under the left-leaning Brigadier Frank ('Trotsky') Davies and Lieutenant-Colonel Arthur Nicholls was infiltrated. Both Maclean and Smiley had reported that the NLM were keener to acquire weapons to use on their political adversaries than for killing Germans.

In January 1944, Frank Davies was netted in a German sweep. Though the Huns didn't have the same level of resources as previously, they could still bite. Nicholls escaped but later died from his exertions. Maclean and Davies were now working with the nationalist *Balli Kombetar* and complaining the NLM were waging war on them, using primarily British weapons!

LRDG in the Land of the Eagle

Bismarck once remarked, or is said to have remarked, that the Balkans 'weren't worth the life of a single Pomeranian grenadier'. Regardless of the accuracy, the sentiment is understandable. Nobody has ever penetrated the labyrinth of internal politics. Another apocryphal quip, attributed to General Michael Rose during the Bosnian war of the 1990s, delivered at the end of a briefing, goes something like 'anybody who now believes he understands what's going on here [Sarajevo] hasn't been paying attention'. LRDG were latecomers to the game in Albania. Happily, their path had been smoothed by a well embedded mission led by Lieutenant-Colonel Alan Palmer.[5]

An LRDG officer penned the following assessment of the worth and character of the Albanian partisans (author's paraphrase):

1. Unreliable and disorganised;
2. Only objective to extract as much equipment as possible from the Allies;
3. Rapidly succumbing to hard-line communist orthodoxy;
4. Would cheerfully cut our throats for a trifle;
5. Totally untrustworthy.[6]

As a succinct demolition, this is pretty good. Lloyd Owen, whilst fully aware of the partisans' abundant defects and limitations, was prepared to admit a limited seduction. They were wild and untamed, nineteenth century brigands, largely unaffected by the influences of Western civilization; *sanitation was a word unknown to them. Honesty was one with which they were barely acquainted.*[7] Those members of the former Italian garrisons, who came into their hands, fared very badly; starved and degraded. Few ever saw their homeland again. The partisans growing adherence to communism was not born out of any deep ideological understanding but more from a desire just for change. They'd had enough of elites with King Zog, and warmed to any creed that was different – *the peasants were too disinterested ever to oppose it, or too ignorant to understand its dangers. What a pity they never did.*[8]

LRDG's primary mission in Albania was to interdict German lines of withdrawal from Greece. John Olivey, after his dramatic escape in Athens, had been enjoying well earned leave in Rhodesia. Now returning to the fight, he was dispatched to the south of the country to spy out the enemy's grip on the Llogara Pass. This snaked along the coast, taking the road from Greece up through Valona. Olivey was duly infiltrated with his patrol and found the landscape bare, except for some local guerrillas who rather appeared to resent our intrusion.[9]

Next up was Stan Eastwood. His mission was to recce the ground north and south of Durazzo. The coast was bristling and a friendly LZ impossible to locate. It might be best to parachute his patrol in further south where they might hope for a friendlier welcome. The incursion was to prove something of an epic. On landing, Eastwood sought out Hoxha. Happily, Alan Palmer was with the self-appointed general and could offer a wealth of knowledge and advice. Mules, guides and Major Hare from the liaison team were duly enlisted, and the patrol began their march northwards.

The going was never easy, Albania is a mountainous country with few roads, a Tolkien-esque landscape as far removed from the war in Western Europe as could be imagined, enclosed, shut in, dark, primitive and treacherous in every sense. For weeks they marched, Eastwood himself laid low with a bout of malaria. It was mid-September before the patrol reached a village named Pajandra, south from both Tirana and Durazzo.

By now the Axis were in full retreat right across the board, in Italy, Greece and further east. This offered opportunities for Eastwood's patrol to be beefed up and act as a blocking force, which made good sense. German arms were everywhere stretched to the limit; holding key chokepoints could inflict booth delay and considerable loss. Killing Germans was a job for LRDG. Lloyd Owen rightly estimated that the partisans themselves might be less excited. For them, there was no profit in attacking Germans who were merely trying to escape.

All he had to do now was to sell the idea to the Balkan Air Force, and fortuitously Brigadier Davy was susceptible. Every dead German was a good return on an additional investment of air-supply. *Lochmaben* became the operational code name, and Lloyd Owen intended to lead in person with Stormonth-Darling and Ken Lazarus acting as joint chiefs of LRDG staff in Italy. Three more patrols were to be dropped in, but the partisans became truculent. They could see the operation might draw German fire in their general direction and their commissars feared a potential British takeover.

Penetrating the spider's web of Balkan politics proved tricky as ever. It took pressure directly from Alexander, 'leaning' on Hoxha, for anything to progress. John Olivey's falling out with his unwilling hosts didn't help. Hoxha prevaricated endlessly and Lloyd Owen decided to parachute in himself and join Eastwood. He might just succeed in animating the local resistors once on the ground. His first attempt at jumping, however, was foiled by the incompetence of the rather inexperienced US fliers who were providing the taxi service.

Although this initial sortie proved abortive, Hoxha had, at last, thrown in the towel and the whole crew, all thirty-six LRDG, was cleared for insertion. The three dozen commandos would be ferried in six planes. *I felt a little cold, as a tremor half of fear and half of thrill ran down my spine. My eye was on the red light, which had warned me to take up my position. Soon this light would turn to green, and then I must hurl myself into that forbidding rushing wind.*[10]

It turned out the parachutists had been dropped from a good two thousand feet above their expected ceiling. It's a long way down, in darkness, into an unknown, possibly hostile country. Lloyd Owen landed safely but took a fearful tumble in the blackness, crashing down a ravine and badly injuring his back. This was not an auspicious start. The height of the drop meant men and kit were widely dispersed. Providentially there were no other serious injuries, but getting everyone and their gear fully re-assembled took all night and much of the next day. For Lloyd Owen, his extremely painful back became a personal Calvary. Initial diagnosis from the unit's paramedics was confirmed through radio contact: his spine was severely damaged.[11]

Ken Lazarus arranged for Michael Parsons, the MO, to be dropped in. The good doctor was not an enthusiastic parachutist but Lloyd Owen's need was clearly very great. The weather was foul but the jump went ahead without mishap, immediately after grey-bellied, autumnal clouds closed in for the duration. Lloyd Owen was in a bad way and in a bad place to be incapacitated. Stan Eastwood too was still feeling the effects of malaria. Ron Tinker took over operational planning, and he and Tiny Simpson were soon cooking up a mission to cut the Elbasan–Tirana road. The LRDG base was a cannily improvised caravanserai of billowing hutments made up from their re-cycled parachutes.

Their liaison was a rugged bandit called Myslim Peza, who actually had an impressive track record of fighting the occupiers. Lloyd Owen thought he was probably too simplistic for a political role; wrongly as it turned out, as he later became Vice-President.[12] Another partisan leader appealed for direct help in seeing off an Axis sweep but, despite his weakened condition, Lloyd Owen demurred. Rightly so, LRDG had not landed just to fight as regular infantry. By now Eastwood was fitter so he and Tiny Simpson operated with their two patrols. They began a series of attacks against the main highway, establishing an effective block.

This proved a lively time. Having, on 4th October, 'beat up' a small convoy, despite an armoured escort, and killing many Germans, they then saw off the inevitable counter-attacks with élan. The road stayed closed and the Boche had lost eighty men. No prisoners were taken. Those Albanian fighters with them didn't do mercy. More explosives were now needed and these were dropped along with another Kiwi officer, Paddy MacLauchlan, who aside from being a welcome presence, brought Lloyd Owen a bottle of whisky to celebrate his birthday. He was 27.

Stan Eastwood was still holding his ground astride the severed artery of the main highway. Another attempt to bull through had been seen off with loss. The Hun still maintained a well fortified OP not far from his blocking position. Being otherwise unoccupied during a lull, Eastwood decided to take steps and eliminate this enemy presence. He led a partisan ground assault, backed by rocket firing Spitfires. The battle raged fiercely till the resistance succeeded in penetrating the perimeter wire and setting a barrack hut on fire. By the time the last shot was fired, three dozen Germans were dead at a cost of two wounded. For the partisans, booty, in the shape of ammunition, boots and gear was well worth having. Prisoners were not.

For all the LRDG patrols, food was always short, and the local turkey population suffered heavy losses. Expensive too, as all had to be paid for in gold, the only currency the Albanians were interested in. Disbursing more precious metal purchased a string of mountain ponies and an endless supply of Rakia, the local firewater. As Lloyd Owen underwent his slow recovery, Michael Parsons began to exercise his considerable skills in improving care for wounded partisans. That which already existed was rudimentary and filthy. Despite much truculence from their hosts, who resented being told to improve sanitation, miracles were achieved. Levels of care soared and female fighters were trained up as nurses. Operations were performed by flickering candlelight in squalid, rain-soaked bivouacs.[13]

Lloyd Owen was soon strong enough to visit Stan Eastwood's forward position. The main road had been kept firmly closed for a fortnight, but no sooner had he and Parsons arrived, the doctor continuing on his far flung rounds, than the partisan contingent upped and left. They had orders to converge on Tirana, and no amount of reason or shouting had any effect. Eastwood was now down to his twenty LRDG troopers, nowhere near enough to keep the back door as firmly bolted.

A visit to local partisan HQ proved a waste of time. Lloyd Owen found the party commissar less than helpful and uninterested in killing more enemy. The prize was Tirana. Aside from lice, the LRDG came away from the meeting empty-handed. The road watch had to be abandoned. Ron Tinker, MacLauchlan and Robin Marr had been interdicting another main arterial road, the Elbasan-Struga highway. The road was blown but the local partisans were lacklustre in their efforts and soon got bored. When the inevitable retaliatory blow fell, the LRDG were too few to contain the enemy and had to withdraw.

Undeterred, Ron Tinker decided to smash the road where a fast flowing river sped alongside, thus creating an impassable flood. The bangs were impressive but not quite biblical enough to incite the full deluge and the Germans soon returned in force, driving the raiders back up into the hills. Tinker gave the enemy a good fight as always, but was constantly finding his natural aggression checked by the lukewarm or obstructive attitudes of local resistance commanders. Their eyes were firmly fixed on what they considered the greater prize, and they were under the pernicious thumbs of their political masters.[14]

Stan Eastwood had more luck. He had intelligence that a big relief convoy was being mustered to reinforce Tirana. They'd be moving north/south so he selected a bridge to blow. This worked brilliantly and the convoy backed up, serpent like along the narrow road. Enter the RAF who Stan had primed by radio: they *sent over a large number of aircraft which together with the ground forces completely destroyed a convoy of 1,500 men, a few tanks, guns, M.T. and horse drawn vehicles.*[15] This was a very neat and productive bit of inter-services working and caused Eastwood's prestige with his hosts to soar.

The end for the Axis in Albania drew near. Tirana fell on 17th November. Stan Eastwood and his troopers lent weight to the final partisan offensive, calling down more airstrikes, delivered with impunity as the RAF enjoyed almost total hegemony in the skies. During one sortie, twenty-eight Beaufighters, equipped with rockets, blasted the enemy with pinpoint strafing. The city was liberated but LRDG were forbidden to enter. Their presence, in the modern idiom, would have been politically incorrect. Eastwood ignored the order and paraded anyway. He spent his last few weeks clearing the airfield, disarming mines and booby-traps.

Albania had provided exhilaration and excellent opportunities for biffing the enemy. However, it had thrown up more than its fair measure of frustrations. The same partisans, who might one moment be fighting like demons, might just as easily up sticks and be off the next. The cancer of political control was incurable. Nonetheless, the Albanian mission had been a success. A handful of LRDG had inflicted significant loss on the enemy, cut off his lines of escape and regularly hammered his transport of which he possessed a rapidly diminishing stock.

Lloyd Owen himself left by boat in the dying days of October. Their hosts gave the party a suitably lavish and completely hollow farewell:

> It was a cold night but our escort of partisans lit a good fire and we huddled round it to warm ourselves. They cooked the inevitable turkey and supplied us with quantities of raw and vicious Rakia, we had a happy evening. The Albanians sang some of their songs and we endeavoured to reciprocate by contributing in our discordant turn. They made speeches lauding our greatness and were able conveniently to forget the difficulties of the past. We were equally insincere and said a few feeble words.[16]

And so, LRDG went back to Italy but opportunities were also rife in Greece, where Britain's earlier involvement from 1940–1941 had not been auspicious.

Bronze Clad Achaeans

As early as the summer of 1940, German planners had considered the possibility of supporting an Italian invasion of the Greek mainland. The Greeks, in August, already alarmed by Italian sabre rattling and overt provocations had approached the British ambassador requesting assistance in the event, as now appeared likely, of an attack. The subsequent report prepared by the Chiefs of Staff Committee and delivered to the War Cabinet on 9th September was unequivocal and unfavourable.

The overwhelming weight of military advice was therefore, and from the outset, against any intervention in Greece. Salonika, Greece's second city and her great northern port, one which had seen much Allied military activity in the Great War, was the pivot upon which Anthony Eden's proposed Balkan alliance (Greece, Yugoslavia and Turkey) must turn. It was also the only harbour other than Piraeus that could provide a base for an expeditionary force. To hold the city however, the Greeks would have to base their defensive line on the northern chain of Macedonian passes.

The question of where best to stand on the defensive was discussed at the Tatoi Conference.[17] Here the bland eloquence of political assurance began to founder against the harsh reality of the topography. The first position was a line drawn along the Bulgarian Frontier, which would safeguard Salonika or a rearward position buttressed by the slopes of Mount Olympus and the Vermion range. This was the Aliakmon Line, stronger, but being some forty miles behind the first would mean the abandonment of Salonika. The Greeks, for understandable patriotic reasons, wished to hold the frontier and deny the Germans the soil for which they had already fought so hard.

But to hold this it was necessary to have the support of Yugoslavia, the second bastion of Eden's proposed alliance. Militarily, the British generals favoured the Aliakmon Line, as the forward position could easily be outflanked if the Germans attacked through Serb territory, a real possibility as the attitude of the Belgrade government had yet to be ascertained.

One of the main weaknesses of the strategy determined at Tatoi was the reliance on the Yugoslavs at a time when the mood in Belgrade was unknown, as indeed was the view in Ankara, the third capital in Eden's three great pillars. The Turks, whilst conciliatory, were not easily drawn. They had no reason to invite German aggression, and any vague assurances were clearly dependent upon them receiving quantities of aircraft and materiel which Britain was not placed to supply.

The situation in Yugoslavia was even more uncertain. The country was a political creation, born of the dismemberment of Austria-Hungary after 1918. This uneasy mix of peoples was dominated by the Serbs, who leaned toward Britain, their ally from the First War. There was, however, in Croatia a substantial minority who inclined more towards Germany and, in February 1941, Hitler had made it clear to the Yugoslavs that he expected them to ally themselves unequivocally with the Axis.

Prince Paul, the Regent, treading a delicate path between the two protagonists, was inclined to accept the German accord with the assurance that Italy would not benefit at his country's expense. He was cautious, as he intimated, as he feared too overt a move toward the Axis could produce a backlash that would unseat his government. The Germans were not minded to temporise – it was a question of whether the Regent preferred an alliance or an occupation. At the same time he was fending off repeated calls from Britain, with the result that his country stood unhappily poised in a continuing dichotomy.

By 13th December 1940 Hitler was outlining his plans for a Balkans campaign. This would begin in March 1941 and be expected to last no more than three weeks. Timing was everything, for the divisions would soon be offered fresh employment elsewhere. The invasion of mainland Greece and the occupation of Bulgaria, codenamed '*Marita*', would be an exercise intended to secure the southern flank whilst the main issue was settled on the Russian steppe. Even the deployment of Rommel and his Afrika Korps expedition to Libya was merely intended to bolster the Italians and keep the British engaged rather than advance into Egypt and capture Suez.

A dramatic development occurred on 26th March 1941 when an army coup unseated the Yugoslav Regent, took control of the person of the young King Peter II, and established a Serbian-dominated military regime. This course of events had been in part instigated by Big Bill Donovan, who had tapped into Serbian Nationalist, anti-Axis sentiment in Belgrade and the key garrisons. Although the junta leaned now toward the Allies the generals were not so foolhardy as to hazard their tenuous grip on power by defying Germany. Although there were discussions with General Papagos early in April, these broke up in confusion while the die was already cast. Outraged at what he perceived as standard Balkan duplicity, Hitler had, on 27th March, issued orders for the aptly named Operation Punishment.

It was now the turn of Yugoslavia to experience the full horrors of blitzkrieg with her air force shot to pieces on the ground and her capital subjected to a murderous aerial bombardment that left the city transformed into rubble and 17,000 of her citizens dead in the ruins. The Yugoslav army had disintegrated even before the panzers arrived, and on the morning of Sunday, 6th April, five full armoured divisions under General von List crossed the Greek frontier, together with two motorised, three mountain, eight infantry divisions and the Leibstandarte SS. There was no Balkan Alliance but there was now a Balkan War.

As Salonika was too exposed for disembarkation, the majority of British and Dominion troops came ashore at Piraeus or further north at Volos, which was closer to the forward post at Larissa. In total the forces dispatched totalled some 58,000 men, of whom roughly 35,000 were front liners with the rest support and administrative personnel. The initial Allied plan was that the three Greek divisions, under-equipped, under-strength and under-supplied, would be used as a blocking force to blunt the German onslaught.

The remainder of the available Greek forces were enmeshed with the three Italian armies operating in Albania. This attempt at a holding action was never really a viable proposition and the blow launched on the 6th April across the Bulgarian border and to the east of Salonika was delivered in overwhelming force, with full and close air support. Paratroops were dropped behind the Greek lines guarding the Rupel Pass, but this early deployment of airborne troops was not a success. Most of the detachment of 150 were killed or captured as the Greeks fought back with considerable gallantry. Nonetheless, Salonika fell within days.

Greece was, to all intents and purposes, a country with a near medieval infrastructure. A single railway line wound from Athens to

Salonika, a narrow and highly vulnerable ribbon that connected the two principal cities. Roads were little more than tracks, unsuitable for motor vehicles and impassable in bad weather. The Allied commander, General 'Jumbo' Wilson, was further hamstrung by the fact that, in order to satisfy the Greeks, still officially neutral, he was obliged to pretend he did not really exist, masquerading as a journalist!

By the middle of March, Allied battalions were digging in along the Aliakmon Line but the plan was already crumbling. General Papagos was unwilling and largely unable to extricate his divisions from Albania, while newly raised formations were hopelessly inadequate and under-equipped. Wavell's expressed concerns over the vulnerability of the Allied defences proved entirely well founded. The line was also very thinly held, and a vital corridor through which the Germans could penetrate and thus turn the whole position was virtually unmanned. Hitler was not blind to the strategic opportunities his sudden and violent occupation of Yugoslavia now presented.

Now there was no alternative but to withdraw, and Wilson extricated his forces from the trap which the Aliakmon Line had become to establish a new position which, in the east, would stretch from the anchor of Mount Olympus to the Serbian border. This proved to be the beginning of a series of extended rearguard actions into which the campaign deteriorated, faced with the continuous advance of an enemy with an overwhelming superiority of men, guns and armoured vehicles, and an advance closely supported at every stage by the siren wail of the Stukas and the murderous strafing runs of Me-109's.

On the ground Wilson faced the unenviable task of attempting a fighting withdrawal from the ruptured position around Mount Olympus to a shorter line of no more than fifty miles running from the heroic outpost at Thermopylae to the Gulf of Corinth. Even when they reached their new positions the Allies were as exposed as ever. On 22nd April the Greeks formally surrendered, and by the 30th evacuation by sea from the beaches was largely complete, despite a successful attempt by German paratroops to seize a vital crossing at Corinth by a coup de main. The Royal Navy, not for the first, or last, time had delivered the rump of the army, some 80 percent, from certain death or capture. Behind them the defeated army left all of their vehicles, heavy guns, armour and anti-tank weapons, with great quantities of small arms, spares and supplies.

Resistance

Resistance to the puppet regime established by the Germans in Greece took a while to get moving. When it did, it moved with gusto but, as ever in the Balkans, political infighting marred any form of concerted action. For generations, bandits cum guerrillas had operated against Turkish overlords from the mountain ranges. These colourful *Andartes* were not frightened of their Italian or Bulgarian occupiers. Much outrage was caused by the Quislings' secession of Greek Macedonia and Western Thrace, disputed lands seized by Bulgaria. The King of the Hellenes and his government in exile fled, first to Crete and, as that island was overrun, to Egypt. Many Greeks escaped to join Allied forces.

From the outset, left wing factions who eventually coalesced to form ELAS were at odds with more nationalist groups such as Zervas' EDES. The Allies, through British missions, sought to drag both elements into coalition. This enjoyed some success and the Italians were effectively driven out of certain areas. With their collapse, the Germans took over, as ever more thorough, more aggressive and more brutal. In July 1943, all factions had signed up to a 'National Bands Agreement' – putting political differences aside to pursue the common goal of victory and subordinating themselves to GHQ and 'Jumbo' Wilson. This did not long endure. By the end of the year, sectarianism led to clashes between rival groups, often very bloody. The seeds of the vicious post-occupation civil war were already sown.

> All of the army by that time was pretty well socialist. Everyone was of the view that the Conservatives were to blame for all sorts of ills that we had in the war, the general level of the economy and the way that people felt about the future, so that, by and large, they were all pretty well Labour. Even though people admired Churchill for his ability to lead the country, his politics were

> completely suspect – he was a Conservative. We felt that what the government was trying to do in Greece was to restore the monarchy, which we all surmised was really not what the people wanted, but was going to be imposed upon them. Therefore in the beginning there was a fair amount of favourable feeling towards this insurgency.[18]

Any incidental sympathy British troops may have felt for ELAS quickly dissipated on first acquaintance. For the firebrands of LRDG, it seemed that by the autumn of 1944 the war was drawing inexorably to a close. Allied armies had breached Fortress Europe and were poised to assault the Reich itself. The Red Army was closing in towards the River Oder and, in the Far East, the hard fought battles of Imphal and Kohima had turned the tide against Japan.

Lieutenant Michael Barker was the first to lead an LRDG patrol on the ground in Greece. He and his team were inserted by air to occupy or at least recce the island of Kithera, off the south coast of the Peloponnese. The notion was that if the place was empty of enemy, it could serve as a staging post for deeper raids into the mainland. As it turned out, all was clear; the Germans had pulled out beforehand.

In the early days of October, Moir Stormonth-Darling was parachuted into the Florina region with two full patrols, led respectively by Gordon Rowbottom and Jack Clough. Their reception on the ground was uncertain, but the jump was a success and LRDG were soon in action against retreating German forces. The enemy might be running out of time but not the will to continue fighting. As ever, *Wehrmacht* units were well organised, comprised of all arms and not shy about scrapping. Stormonth-Darling had taken one engineer, Bill Armstrong in with his teams. This was the sapper who'd cheerfully volunteered for the, happily, abortive assault on the Brenner Pass.

LRDG had prepared an ambush, the action to be triggered by the sappers blowing two culverts they'd mined. The fuse wire snaked into rough cover about a hundred and fifty yards back from the highway. Bill Armstrong was ready there with his box of matches. The rest of the raiding party was scattered amongst a riot of boulders, offering ideal fire positions. As the grinding chug of labouring engines approached,

Armstrong coolly bided his time till two trucks were passing over the first culvert and a third astride the rearward.

The explosions were timed just right. All three vehicles were engulfed in flames; a fourth driving in between was instantly disabled. The convoy ground to a halt and was systematically raked by sustained automatic fire. Fifty odd Germans were killed and there were no Allied casualties.[19] Just when the enemy thought it couldn't get much worse, it did, as the RAF, perfectly on cue, arrived and completed the work of destruction.

John Olivey too was back in Greece, though not as a POW. He'd taken his Rhodesians to support SBS mayhem in the Peloponnese. His other task, assisted by RAF personnel embedded with the patrol, was to seize Araxos airstrip. He had to fight his way over the narrow isthmus of the Corinth Canal before he made his second wartime entrance into Athens – this time as conqueror. Olivey's raiders were using ten jeeps and swept northwards to Florina to link up with the other patrols. This wasn't entirely bloodless. Two men were lost, including Alf Tighe, who'd endured the earlier epic in the desert, killed by a mine just past Corinth.[20]

The 'clean' war, one fought against an identifiable and repugnant enemy, was nearly over. Hostilities in Greece took a darker, shadier turn as the incipient civil war between communists and nationalists began to boil over into the streets, a developing conflict that would pitch Greece into a cycle of cruelty and violence. John Olivey found his second visit to Athens becoming as deadly as the first. During a routine jeep-mounted street patrol, LRDG was engaged by a sniper.

Olivey's driver was shot as a firefight erupted. In saving the wounded trooper, Olivey himself was twice hit, in head and arm. Undeterred, he managed to drag the injured man towards safety before a second bullet finished the driver off. John Olivey managed to reach a British armoured car ranging nearby and bring up additional firepower. He later had to be evacuated to Italy on account of his wounds.[21]

Other patrols were still active in Albania, where their major opposition came from the treacherous intransigence of the nominal partisan allies who were rapidly losing any interest in fighting the retreating Germans. David Sutherland and an SBS team were looking to harass the enemy's withdrawal along the country's eastern flank. Lack of cooperation became a constant frustration and mounting headache. LRDG patrol leader Jack Aitken, a Kiwi in classic LRDG mould, full of fire and determined to bring his two Rhodesian patrols in to biff the foe, also found himself thwarted by the intercnine squabbling and persistent duplicity of his theoretical allies.

Because the internal squabbling amongst the partisans was so byzantine, Aitken's teams had to be inserted onto a stretch of coast held by royalist/nationalists under Abas Kupe. Despite his waning prospects, Kupe still merited the presence of a small mission under Billy Maclean, but they were exfiltrated by the same schooners that dropped off Aitken's patrols.

'Jacko' Jackson, leading one of the LRDG patrols, was tasked to recce a German position near the village of San Dovani. This necessitated a quick dip in the Drin River, almost under the guns of the enemy and nearly two hundred yards across. The heavy, sluggish waters, swollen by autumn rains (this was November) proved treacherous. Jacko, a very strong swimmer, was first over but his two troopers following behind got into difficulties. One of them, Sergeant Ryan, he managed to pull clear but the other man was lost to the current.[22]

The next obstacle was a dense belt of mines covering the enemy defences. In the desperate race to save his two comrades, Jackson had lost his binoculars so had to creep between the mines to get close enough. Then there was the river again, *jolly cold for a time* as he modestly observed.[23] This form of guerrilla warfare has an aura of romance, though the realities were rather harsher; constant dirt and lice, exhausting marches in dangerous country, fear as much of one's supposed friends as the foe.

Yet, despite all the hardships the commandos often found great kindness among the very poor hill farmers they were billeted with. *They would dry our clothes and darn our socks. They might even stay awake the whole night through to watch for sounds which they knew to be alien.*

Then in the morning, when we woke from a stuffy slumber passed in an atmosphere of pine-savoured smoke, they would harness our mules and lend us their few implements with which to cook a meal.[24]

This was a very different war to that experienced by regular forces. For all its hardships and dangers, the comradeship and sense of adventure which had impelled LRDG veterans at the start didn't waver. Our allies at times might be questionable but there wasn't any 'bull', no murderous barrages of enemy guns. These Balkan lands were hard, unyielding, with centuries of endless conflict seemingly embedded in the stones. Moreover, the tide of history was already moving on, into a new era of Cold War. Would there be any role for LRDG in a changing political and military landscape?

Notes

1 Ball, p. 31.
2 Ibid.
3 Ibid.
4 Neil Loudon Desmond Maclean (1918–1986), latterly Unionist MP for Inverness, commissioned into the Royal Scots Greys in 1938, he moved to SOE in 1941, seeing service with Wingate's Gideon Force in Ethiopia.
5 Palmer, post-war, became chairman of the famous Huntley & Palmer's Biscuits Company.
6 Lloyd Owen, p. 180.
7 Ibid., p. 181.
8 Ibid., p. 182.
9 Ibid.
10 Ibid., p. 189 – the Balkan Air Force ("BAF") was composed of elements from both the RAF and South African Air Force under the overall command of Mediterranean Allied Air Forces command. It was active from 7 June 1944 until 15 July 1945.
11 Although his condition had improved, Lloyd Owen wasn't out of the woods. Back in Italy he'd need surgery and came close to being invalided home. He remained encased in spinal plaster for several months but managed to remain with the unit.
12 Ibid., p. 192.
13 Ibid., pp. 194–195.
14 Ibid., pp. 196–197.
15 Ibid., p. 197.

16 Ibid., p. 199.
17 Held to determine the defence plans for Greece, dominated by Foreign Secretary Eden's hopes for an alliance with Yugoslavia and Turkey.
18 Durham Light Infantry Sound Recording Project, courtesy of Durham County Record Office.
19 Lloyd Owen, pp. 202–203.
20 Ibid., p. 203.
21 Ibid., p. 204.
22 Ibid., pp. 205–206.
23 Ibid., p. 206.
24 Ibid.

CHAPTER 9
On the Shores of the Adriatic, 1944–1945

We are the D-Day dodgers out here in Italy,
Always drinking vino, always on the spree,
Eighth army skivvies and the Yanks,
We live in Rome and stuff our pants,
We are the D-Day dodgers out here in Italy.

We landed at Salerno, a holiday with pay,
Jerry sent the band to cheer us on our way,
He showed us the sights and gave us tea,
We all sang songs and the beer was free,
We are the D-Day dodgers out here in Italy.

Naples and Cassino were taken in our stride
We didn't go to fight there; we just went for the ride,
Anzio and Sangro were just the same,
We did nothing there to prove our fame,
For we are the D-Day dodgers out here in Italy.

On the way to Florence, we had a lovely time,
They ran a bus to Amalfi – through the Gothic Line,
Soon to Bologna we will go
When Jerry pulls back beyond the Po,
For we are the D-Day dodgers out here in Italy.

Now Lady Astor please listen to this lot,
Don't stand on the platform and talk a lot of rot,
You're such a sweetheart, the nation's pride,
But your damned mouth is far too wide,
That's from the D-Day dodgers out here in Italy.

If you look around the mountains, in the mud and rain,
You'll see a lot of crosses,
Some that bear no name,
Health, wreck and toil and suffering,
The boys beneath shall never sing,
That they were D-Day dodgers out here in Italy.

—Anon: *D-Day Dodgers* (sung to the tune of *Lili Marlene*)

In order to nip disorders in the bud the sternest measures must be applied at the first sign of insurrection. It should also be taken into consideration that in the countries in question a human life is often valueless. In a reprisal for the life of a German soldier, the general rule should be capital punishment for 50–100 Communists. The manner of execution must have a frightening effect.[1]

General Keitel's order, and he would be duly called to account for it at Nuremburg, reflects the stir that Tito's communist partisans had and were causing in Yugoslavia. After the lightning invasion and apparently equally rapid collapse, two very distinct and mutually antagonistic partisan groups emerged. Josef Tito, a convinced communist, was already a wanted man in his own country. Following *Barbarossa* he raised the red flag officially on 27th June. Well organised and highly motivated, his cadres recruited from their home bases. In Tito's case, this was Serbia proper. By September, he could count as many as seventy thousand fighters beneath his banners.

White Eagles in Serbia

Tito's recruits, unlike Mihailovic's Chetniks who were royalists and nationalists, were active in killing Germans. In Montenegro, Tito's forces routed the Italian occupiers, capturing four thousand of them, together with all their weapons and gear. Success brought retribution from the Germans – regular and damaging sweeps were scorched across the hills but Tito evaded conventional battle. Nonetheless, casualties were high and this spurred a need to reorganise.

Local militias were vulnerable to just this type of riposte, so he forged a more professional mobile force, some officers being recruited from those who'd fought with the international brigades during the

Spanish Civil War. Training was thorough, discipline strict; Tito even managed to build a fledgling navy which operated off the coast and among the necklace of islands. By November 1942 his re-branded People's Liberation Army ("PLA") could boast a complement of over a hundred thousand men and women under arms. Until 1943, the Allies had naturally inclined towards Mihailovic, but his total lack of any shadow of enterprise, and the favourable reports of SOE liaison teams persuaded Allied planners that Tito, for all his communist affiliations, was still the right horse to back.

As the invasion of Italy drew near, Tito's partisans were holding down half a million Axis troops. In the course of their fifth great anti-guerrilla sweep, the Germans nearly bottled up a large proportion of Tito's fighting strength in the harsh Montenegrin uplands. The odds were depressing but the partisans fought their way clear, earning well-merited plaudits from SOE. Attempts to broker an understanding between the rival groups failed. Their aims were too divergent and, this being the Balkans, a civil war between partisan factions was soon underway. By 1944, Tito was the clear favourite and, although a dedicated communist, would never be Stalin's stooge.[2]

Crossing the Adriatic

In Italy, putative LRDG missions were still being planned and then discarded at a furious rate – largely because the front line kept advancing. As the long attrition at Monte Cassino was finally drawing to a close, Stan Eastwood, at that point new to LRDG, was dispatched on a recce to a small island lying just off Corfu. The main island held a garrison of two and a half thousand Axis, and the patrol was to investigate a radar station on the northern side. The RN ferried them to the RV and they then rowed the couple of miles to Corfu itself.

Their contact had identified the enemy installation and one of Stan's troopers, Private Marc, went with him for a closer look. The enterprising Marc realised he would gain far more intelligence from inside the defensive ring. So he disguised himself as an impecunious local fisherman, eking a crust selling his catch. He made no sales and got booted around by contemptuous Boche but did discover much.

Eastwood himself had not been idle and had taken careful note of wire, mines and the rest, and the patrol was successfully ex-filtrated. They came back a man stronger – a young Greek volunteer, Spiro, who'd taken a shine to the patrol and the LRDG life, came out with them and was by alchemy taken on the payroll thereafter![3] Jacko Jackson, another new boy at this point, carried out a successful recce for an intended raid on Axis posts near Himara in Albania. In the event, once again, the raid never got off the drawing board.

Then there was, at last, movement in Italy. Two patrols were to be dropped in on 11th June. Bad weather delayed the flights but both went off next evening. Tragedy struck immediately when one young officer, again a relative newcomer, Simon Fleming, died when his 'chute failed to open. It was a very unlucky drop; another trooper was also killed, some were captured and the survivors trickled back empty-handed. Two additional patrols, led by Ashley Greenwood and Gordon Rowbottom, were due to be parachuted during the following night. Greenwood's team was dropped miles from their objective, right on top of an enemy-held village. He himself got snagged on the church roof and spent an exciting morning using the graveyard as cover. He escaped but most of his patrol went into the bag.

Gordon Rowbottom's men also ran into trouble. Though they landed safely enough, the patrol soon encountered an Axis post and split up. Rowbottom was unlucky and got caught. After so much ill-fortune, things improved radically when the truck taking him to captivity went off the road and overturned. In the confusion he grabbed his kit and bolted clear. Next, he managed to find Corporals Buss and Matthews and together they encountered a platoon of partisans. Rowbottom made up for lost opportunities over the next few weeks and was safely extracted before the end of July.[4]

One other member of his unit, Sergeant Morley, who had also evaded the net, undertook valuable solo reconnaissance before crossing the lines. He was instantly asked to return and guide 1/9th Gurkhas onto their objective. Their CO subsequently recommended Morley for an MM. John Bramley's patrol was the only one of the four to successfully undertake the intelligence gathering role they'd all been originally assigned: *Thus ended this unfortunate mission.*[5]

MFV La Palma

In May 2011 a group of ex-servicemen returned to the Dalmatian Island of Vis (now part of Croatia), Tito's wartime redoubt and Britain's 'unsinkable aircraft carrier' of the Adriatic War.

> With Marshal Tito camped in mountain caves, Winston Churchill decided to send a detachment to what is now Croatia, led by Royal Marines, to assist the partisans' mainland raids. The commitment quickly expanded, with the Royal Navy sending Motor Torpedo Boats to attack German supply ships and the RAF launching air raids.
>
> Churchill's decision to assist Yugoslavia's communist-backed partisans rather than the exiled royalists was controversial, even to Sir Fitzroy Maclean, of the Special Operations Executive. Peter Bickmore and Reg Ellis served on a Motorised Torpedo Boat that inflicted heavy losses on the German supply lines.
>
> "We weren't allowed off the pier," said Mr Bickmore. "We'd go out looking for the German boats between the islands during the day and returned at night for maintenance drill and rations cooked on two primus stoves before getting some sleep.
>
> "Even when we captured the Germans' supplies we'd hand them over to the partisans without dealing with them person to person." Pave Thomic, now 83, was a boy who played in the Hurricane workshop at the airstrip. The impact of the Allied force on local life has left a deep well of gratitude. "Before they came we had nothing, they gave us food and looked out for our basic needs," he said, "They were life-saving".[6]

After these costly frustrations in Italy, Vis offered possibilities. If a mini-air-force had been essential in the desert, boats were the key to the Adriatic. LRDG now added a converted fishing vessel to its inventory, stripped, up-gunned, decks cleared for shipping transport – MFV *La Palma* was fit to serve. She could carry a couple of jeeps lashed, in best Heath Robinson style, to her decks. Alan Denniff became skipper with 'Titch' Cave as bosun. She couldn't shift above ten knots an hour and took seven to complete her first passage to Vis, but was able to move a significant quantity of stores.[7]

Vis was an ideal raider's lair. LRDG could spot enemy shipping targets for the RN & RAF whilst, at the same time, mounting forays against Axis positions on the mainland. Road watch was replaced by shipping watch. Captain Stokes with a four-man team spent five months keeping tabs along the coast. A measure of Stokes' success was the huge bounty the Germans offered for his capture.

His tiny patrol was constantly on the move, could never relax its guard, and suffered frequently from hunger due to difficulties of re-supply. Their persistence, stamina and fortitude paid ample dividends, however, as Signaller Hansell kept the precious flow of sightings coming. Regardless of their many vicissitudes, damage inflicted on enemy vessels as a result was considerable. This was a classic example of LRDG excelling at their main forte.[8] Another patrol, led by Lieutenant Gatchell, worked with the partisans on Vis. They participated in the capture of a well-laden Axis schooner, brimming with supplies and two young ladies adrift from their concert party! The sequel to this agreeable bout of buccaneering does not seem to be recorded.

At Orso Bay by Valona on the Albanian coast, the Germans had a listening post of their own. Stan Eastwood did the recce and found a solid concrete blockhouse with pillboxes at both external angles, well sited, wired in and stripped of cover all around. Lloyd Owen, feeling stale from too prolonged an absence from the field, took charge and beefed up Eastwood's patrol with two more, under the leadership of Captain Browne, a Kiwi officer just re-lent by General Freyberg. By 28th June Eastwood's shore group was ready, though an inopportune RAF raid had alerted the enemy.

Crammed into a fast Italian torpedo launch, the three dozen raiders motored out of Brindisi in the early dark, another boat racing alongside as escort. Eastwood guided the party ashore in the timeless calm of a balmy summer's night. Dawn comes early and it was a hard slog, lugging all their gear off the beach and under reasonable cover. A nearby well provided sweet, clear spring water as Lloyd Owen, Eastwood and Browne set off to recce the target. The enemy, separated from them by a steep-sided ravine, appeared to be at ease, enjoying the warm sun. The plan was straightforward. The assault party would move up at dusk, closing to around seven hundred yards from the fort. As a spectacular curtain-raiser, the RN had offered massed broadsides from three destroyers (HMS *Terpsichore, Tumult and Tenacious*).

Everyone was in position by 23.00 hours, the warm, humming darkness of a Mediterranean summer seeming almost surreal given the impending barrage. The final signal was to be flashed twenty-five minutes later and shells would begin falling five minutes after that. The Navy likes to be on time and a brilliant star shell, bursting high up, showed the whole enemy post in stark relief. Ranging rounds punctured the dark. More star bursts followed, pulverising rock, shredding scrub and throwing up a dense wall of choking dust. A pause whilst the raiders assessed the damage; not yet sufficient, and another storm of screaming shot was unleashed. As the new dust settled, Stan Eastwood, way up front, led the assault party in. The stutter of small arms fire briefly rounded off the bombardment, then the signal for success.

A trio of traumatised prisoners was dragged down to the beach, their anticipated uneventful evening clearly ruined. There was a rather anxious and extended wait for the boats but the whole party was finally clear by 03.30. Only one of the LRDG had been wounded during the attack, a victim of 'friendly-fire'. Whilst the results of the raid might have been relatively trifling, the wider effect would send ripples of alarm along the enemy-held coast; nowhere was safe![9]

Vis

Moir Stormonth-Darling, indefatigable in spite of so many setbacks, was planning yet another proposal for seven patrols to operate in the north of Italy and support partisan groups there. Inevitably, after a great deal of fresh toil, this idea ended up in the waste-basket like so many of its predecessors. It was at this point that control of LRDG was transferred from Allied Armies in Italy to George Davy's Adriatic Command. The Brigadier was based at Bari while LRDG still had their principal HQ at Rodi.

Meanwhile, Mike Reynolds had returned to the scene at Orso Bay to find out how the enemy had reacted. This appeared rather bizarre; at one point the Germans seemed determined to rebuild their shattered blockhouse but then, for whatever reason, gave up the idea and blew up what remained of the ruins.[10] Vis became the FOB for LRDG patrols, and Archie Gibson was dispatched to keep an eye on the Axis aerodrome at Mostar.[11] The idea was to send back data on enemy planes with such rapidity the Balkan Air Force could scramble and intercept.

As ever, Tim Heywood ingeniously speeded up the receipt and decipherment of signals. Local partisans proved uncooperative and resentful; the Axis far more watchful, very aggressively so, than had been anticipated. Gibson was obliged to stand fast and fight alongside the locals who suddenly became far friendlier. He even became a godfather![12] It is most likely their earlier reticence was a top down order; British forces were not to fight in any attacking moves. These slight tremors of discontent, suspicion and growing dislike would multiply as the Axis withdrawal continued and political ideology came to outweigh military necessity.

In the sultry heat of August another two patrols, one commanded by David Skipworth and the other by John Shute, were infiltrated around Dubrovnik to identify suitable targets for the attentions of SBS. This was a similar relationship to that with David Stirling in the desert. LRDG were viewed, correctly of course, as primarily intelligence-gathering rather than blowing things up. Both SBS & SAS liked the blowing up part and were very good at it.

Skipworth experimented with carrier pigeons but the idea didn't work; he did, however, identify an important railway bridge so on the evening of 27th August an SBS detachment, commanded by the legendary Anders Lassen (later to win a posthumous VC), was landed. Two nights later, they attacked and severely damaged the bridge. Pursuit was swift and relentless, ending in a full-scale firefight with a weak battalion of *Ustachi* (pro-Axis guerrillas). As ever, the raiders fought with great gusto and most got clear away, but Skipworth,

Sergeant Leech and one of the SBS, together forming a rearguard, were captured.[13]

John Shute's patrol got off to a very bad start. Their overloaded assault craft capsized some four hundred yards from the shore. Much of their kit was lost and the radio damaged. They pressed on and identified a railway tunnel ripe for demolition, though this proved far too stout to suffer much damage from the limited amount of explosives they and their SBS partners had to hand. They couldn't be withdrawn until October by which time their gear was very much worn out. Field operations conducted over such harsh and unyielding terrain were as equally hard on men and equipment as their former desert habitat.

As the shipping watch had proved so rewarding, Tony Browne hatched a plan for him and a W/O to set up a watch on the west coast of Istria (the peninsula which juts out at the top of the Adriatic south of Trieste). Once in situ, the patrol would relay information to a flotilla of fast MTBs lurking offshore that could then pounce on any passing trade.

The mission began well. As Browne was being infiltrated, his MTB took on two Axis schooners, sinking one and boarding the other in best *Hornblower* style. Tony Browne quietly slipped ashore and set up his eyrie, so well camouflaged that locals working or passing nearby failed to notice. Jack Aitken, another returning Kiwi, went in to take on this watch. In fact, it proved less productive than hoped, but the RAF did score some hits based on his intelligence and, once again, the psychological and morale impact was likely to be far greater.[14]

Lloyd Owen was convinced, entirely reasonably, that the guerrillas' swelling successes could be fuelled by a constant supply, not just of guns and ammo but of specialist instruction and guidance – the 'force-multiplier' effect again. Fitzroy Maclean famously commanded the liaison mission[15] but he and his team were already totally overstretched. That August, a further four patrols, each led by a Rhodesian officer – Jacko Jackson, Joe Savage, Mike Reynolds and George Pitt – were infiltrated, three from the air and one overland.

Jackson's team had a relatively uneventful time and were able to get on with the job, but Joe Savage found his partisan allies less reliable. The commander of 19 Partisan Division was anxious to take all we'd let him have but offered nothing in return. Surly and recalcitrant, our allies veered firstly towards non-cooperation, then outright hostility. Petty, factional politics was never far away in the Balkans. Savage's patrol was ex-filtrated by sea on 19th October to the mutual relief of both parties.[16]

On 27th August, Mike Reynolds landed at a partisan strip near Fiume; for this run he only had three troopers with him. The Germans were clearly aware and on the prowl, probably guessing correctly that he would be trying to set up a coast watch between Fiume and Pola. The coast here is spectacular and beautiful, very difficult to defend but easily as hard for a raiding party to slip through from the landward side. It took him just over a month to get established, and even then the Huns hadn't given up, using portable direction-finders. The Rhodesians dealt with one enemy patrol which came dangerously close and were never caught. As ever, the emergent foe turned out to be their supposed partisan allies, sensitive that we had a presence, however small, so near Trieste which they coveted. Mike Reynolds, faced with increasing resentment, was pulled out on 17th October.

Looking out for enemy shipping in Trieste and Monfalcone harbours fell to George Pitt, *a big strong, friendly character whom no amount of toil deterred.*[17]. This was just as well for his odyssey was destined to be trying. Accompanied only by Signalman Wigens, his W/O, the duo was infiltrated by an American launch onto the small offshore island of Kria, from where they rowed to the mainland. Next, a hard week's marching north in the direction of Fiume. The September rain was pretty constant and one of their overnight halts proved very exciting when the Axis began a live firing exercise around them!

Their departure was both rushed and ungentlemanly as both had shed their wet clothes to dry them and thus fled with their manliness exposed to all![18] It was three hours before they could reclaim their kit. This was nothing compared to the intransigence of the partisans who ordered them out. Undeterred, Pitt pressed on, at one point with what appeared to be a whole Boche division on his case. Food was short and the pair never got as far as their intended objectives, not for lack of effort or determination. They were ex-filtrated on 20th October.

Gordon Rowbottom was also having a trying time. His patrol was tasked with shipping watch from the island of Vrgada. While taking a small craft across to another wee island, accompanied by three troopers, Sergeant Morley, Corporal Buss and Private McConnell, they ran into a bristling squadron of three E Boats – these were very fast, well armed, German motor launches. It was a singularly unequal contest and they were all captured. Rowbottom lied about his rank and Morley was mistaken for the senior man in the patrol. They were finally put ashore and incarcerated in Split. Here they were kept apart and each interrogated in turn, threatened with a firing squad. This went on for four days yet the LRDG men gave absolutely nothing away.

Finally they were marched into Split and bundled into the rear of a 3-tonner with five guards. The convoy, of around a hundred vehicles, set off just before dark. Soon there was wild shooting, possibly partisans were active or someone simply panicked. The Germans decided on discretion and headed for the nearest ditch. The LRDG men, in pairs, made off in entirely the opposite direction. All four were safely extracted.[19]

Command & Control

In the desert LRDG had operated over a vast, unmapped and hostile space, bare, stripped, empty and unadorned. Distances were terrific, supply a constant headache. On the shores of the Mediterranean it was very different. Here LRDG operated in Italy, Greece, Albania and Yugoslavia, in regions peopled by indigenous partisans who might or might not be friendly according to the season. Operations from the air and across the sea were required. The war being fought by the Allies in Italy bore little resemblance to that being waged by guerrillas in Serbia.

Planning was the essential first stage, and Ken Lazarus and his unit at Bari undertook these initial vital steps. It was the planner's job to liaise with the Navy and Balkan Air Force, and with Fitzroy Maclean's and other missions. Ken then had to determine the size of the unit to be infiltrated, what the team would need, their key objectives, who would command, the duration of the mission, obstacles, liaison and lastly, how the group could best be ex-filtrated at the end of their assignment. Weather conditions, dropping zones, re-supply and comms all had to be vectored in to the mix. As the LRDG would be putting very few men into very hostile territory, at a considerable distance, with uncertain allies, any slip up in these calculations could spell disaster.[20]

Communications, as ever orchestrated by Tim Heywood, were an essential component. Heywood had to be able to mesh the new stations into his network, incoming traffic had to be dealt with and the right signallers sent into the field. Radio was the core of good intelligence-gathering; obviously all the keenest observation goes for a Burton if the data can't be sent back. *To say Tim was a genius would perhaps be an overstatement but it is the nearest description I can find for his incredible ability as a signals officer. I don't think he will mind my saying that not everyone liked him; they couldn't, for Tim was hard and ruthless. But I am sure there was no one who did not respect him.*[21]

For the insertion itself, going in by sea was favourite. Fast MTB's proved the ideal marine taxis. They could cover a great space of water in a short time and were low profile, which greatly facilitated unloading. Usually the last few hundred yards of the approach would involve small boats rowed to shore. Clearly, the amount of kit didn't prove too great a hurdle. With a parachute drop, it was different. Loads had to be carefully packed and weighed, selection of dropping zones, the weather, light, visibility, enemy flak, the need for experienced pilots were all critical. For the patrol to be dispersed over a wide area in hostile lands, in the dark, separated from their supplies and comms, was clearly very disheartening and usually downright dangerous.

The same set of considerations naturally applied to re-supply. The patrol might be on the ground for days, more likely weeks, possibly for months. Getting them out could be another cause for heartache. Lloyd Owen recounts how, in attempting to get Mike Reynolds and his blokes out of a hot spot, he took an Italian launch over the Adriatic, her crew unenthusiastic, in a storm of biblical proportions, sufficient to completely un-man the pressed sailors. Though he could see the signal flashes from the patrol onshore and knew the Axis were close by, it proved impossible to get the craft inshore and the attempt had to be abandoned. The fury of the tempest caused considerable damage to the boat and they returned empty-handed.[22]

Psychology during the war years was, of course, not the advanced science it now represents. Conditions such as post-traumatic stress disorder ("PTSD") were not fully recognised. The stress of operations was intense, the drain on the men's physical and emotional resources enormous. Many thrived on the adrenalin burn, there is no greater intoxicant, but our stores are finite and the trick is to spot when someone is beginning to run low. Those who volunteered and passed LRDG selection were a special breed, born for the life. They had to be; otherwise it would have been intolerable. Time and again, LRDG personnel went far beyond the normal call of duty and kept on doing so. The scorpion badge was a byword for toughness and courage, something also to impress in the fleshpots of Cairo!

Men went from long periods of constant danger, physical discomfort, hunger, cold and exhaustion to the sudden luxury of warm baths, comfortable beds and billets, R&R and cheap booze. That some might O/D on the latter is hardly surprising. When in the desert, the fabled lights of Cairo took on an unearthly allure, a fleshy Shangri-la where the young soldier could be instantly transported from dirt, disease, death and terror into a world of instant hedonism. As far as this author is aware, no physiological and emotional assessments were made of former LRDG personnel, such as would be relatively commonplace with today's Special Forces. These would, had they existed, make very interesting reading!

As the end of the war drew nearer and the great German counter-offensive, *Wacht am Rhein* – the Battle of the Bulge – was repulsed, the scope for LRDG type operations appeared to diminish. It did seem likely that, as Allied armies ground down Axis resistance in Italy, there might be some trade to be had in northern Yugoslavia and Austria. This would surely involve mountain warfare, yet another fresh departure for LRDG. Moir Stormonth-Darling's squadron was withdrawn from the field for further training. In part this was frustrating for them but it did offer new horizons and the chance for some fresh exertions before the war finally ended.

By mid-February, the Scottish laird and his LRDG hooligans were enjoying the luxuries of Il Duce's favourite spa resort at Terminillo, some fifty miles north of the capital. LRDG took up lodgings in the five-star Caserna M hotel, a grand palazzo of fascist pampering, and offering rather better billets than they were used to! Here, they were under the tutelage of the Mountain Warfare School, though this was being run down and the squadron moved to another celebrity spot, the Gran Sasso.

It was here in the equally impressive mountaintop resort hotel, the Albergo Campo Imperatore, that the dictator had been incarcerated after his fall. Not for long, as an audacious raid led by Otto 'Scarface' Skorzeny had sprung Mussolini from this seemingly impregnable redoubt. In many ways a true Nazi, Skorzeny was still a remarkable operator, one with whom LRDG must instinctively identify. Like them the Austrian, who'd trained as an engineer, pioneered Special Forces operations and led numerous commando raids of great ingenuity, dash and daring.

The place was a wonderful base for mountaineering and ideal for training in load-carrying once the funicular had broken down. All stores had to be laboriously hauled up in backpacks, a full three thousand feet of near vertical ascent. The record was one hour twenty-five minutes with a forty-pound pack.[23] After all their intensive training, however, the would-be mountaineers never got to try out their newly acquired skills. The war ended beforehand and they spent VE day humping all their exhaustingly humped kit down the steep hill again.

Last Gasps

As both Allies and partisans advanced, Vis ceased to be a sensible base. The port of Zara, which Tito had taken at the end of January 1945, offered better prospects. It was ideally placed for air and naval support plus liaison with partisan friends, or at least sometimes friends, and handy for disrupting enemy activity by sea. This was a worry with Allied shipping coming so far north. For LRDG, this implied both more shipping watch and scope for active patrolling. The new command was rather grandly styled Land Forces Northern Adriatic. As well as LRDG and SBS it contained artillery and an RAF ground unit which was to provide weapons supply and support.[24]

Ken Lazarus would lead the Rhodesians and, as befitting his well-earned seniority, even had his own flagship, the MV *Kufra.* This addition to the fleet was an 80-ton schooner which Dick Croucher, one of Lloyd Owen's more experienced sailors, had very cleverly adapted into a floating HQ. LRDG might not be the senior service but, for landlubbers they did alright; *no small achievement with his music-hall crew of flatfoots.*[25] As ever, Tim Heywood had exercised his magician's touch on the comms. The Germans were everywhere retreating; they were beaten but not yet defeated. Though their cause was vile, nobody can deny the courage and resilience of the Wehrmacht. As the late Brigadier Peter Young, who would certainly know, once remarked – *if you haven't fought the Germans, you've never been to war.*

Even in February 1945, they still held all of Yugoslavia north of Karlobag and the islands offshore. The waters were extensively mined and Axis shipping could move, at least under cover of darkness, virtually unhindered. Shipping watch was still very much the order of the day. During daylight, patrols would seek out enemy lurking holes and introduce these to the attentions of the RAF while, by night, they would activate naval raiders.

Mike Reynolds would be leading the first of this current round of patrols. Contact and liaison with the partisans would have to be instigated afresh. His was a picked crew, including the highly experienced W/O Private Metcalfe. The patrol set out on 23rd February and would remain in the field for nearly two months. They were inserted by sea on the eastern coast of Istria close to the Arsa Channel. Here the enemy had utilised local coal staithes, loading supplies mined inland. An attempt to bomb the facility on 3rd March proved abortive due to bad weather.

Their time was far from being wasted. As a result of the patrol's activities, enemy vessels were hounded and sunk through March and early April, despite the best efforts of German ground forces. A number of tramp steamers and coasters were hit, most damaged, more than a few sunk. From Mike Reynolds' diary entries, we can appreciate the considerable amount of damage his team caused, not to mention the diversion of troops to hunt them down.[26] The Axis failed in this but our erstwhile allies did the job for them, corralling the patrol on 13th April.

Despite the nasty, sharp end of conflicting aims and ideologies, the locals themselves provided unstinting support, even going so far as to provide a night-time barber service![27] At one juncture, when it seemed a pair of LRDG, observing from an exposed hilltop, were bound to be captured by an enemy sweep, two young women used their local knowledge to find a safe hiding place till the danger had passed. The risks were very great; to be discovered would certainly prove fatal.

Tiny Simpson with a second patrol was infiltrated into Istria to link up with Mike Reynolds' crew. Simpson had troubles with his radio and Tim Heywood's deputy, Stuart Hamer, brought over the replacement set, and became something of a heartthrob and a great hit with the local girls! The war wasn't over though, and shortly afterwards two troopers, Corporal Waller and Private Edwards, who'd been detailed by Reynolds to deliver the replacement wireless to Simpson, simply appeared to vanish. Nobody knew where or how but there were disquieting rumours that they'd been captured and shot.

Thus far, LRDG had not been troubled by Hitler's infamous "commando order," but if the pair had indeed suffered such a fate, it raised serious questions for Lloyd Owen as CO. It is one thing to ask soldiers to take risks which might lead to capture, on the assumption that, being in uniform, they'd be treated properly as POWs. To do so in the knowledge that they will subsequently be murdered is a very different matter. If the operational hazards are raised to this level, then many operations might become questionable; a dangerous mission is still a far cry from a suicidal one.

Understandably, Lloyd Owen was unsure if he should warn patrols of this, especially as the reality remained unclear. All of the oracles up the chain of command were consulted and the instruction came back that men should be warned before being committed to action. This was still the LRDG, not one man demurred. As it happened, the missing men had been captured but not ill-treated, and both came safe home after the war's end.[28]

At one point, indeed for a time, they thought they might be shot. They'd been captured along with a partisan guide whom they knew would be roughed up by their interrogators. They maintained a strict silence and spent days in solitary confinement with only miserable rations. Eventually they were taken out through Trieste to a POW camp in Austria where they remained until the liberation. It seems the rumours of their deaths might simply have been a clever ruse by the Germans to damage morale. If so, it failed. Equally, our partisan 'friends' were not above a little rumour-mongering of their own.

Despite not getting his new radio, Simpson carried on, managing to get some replacement parts for the existing set. Soon he, like Reynolds, was transmitting a steady stream of data, enabling the Navy to locate and sink an enemy barge. The Germans took this very badly and exerted themselves to locate his patrol. Despite some very close shaves, they did not succeed. Both British officers shared fluency in the Rhodesian Chisona dialect. They used this to communicate by short wave 'walkie-talkie' radios. There are echoes here of the use of Navaho by the US in the Far East, albeit on a larger scale. Happily, the Germans in Istria possessed no Chisona speakers!

John Olivey was also active in Istria. His patrol set off on 8th March, their mission being to replicate and extend the shipping watch. He might also locate some suitable installations for David Sutherland's SBS squad to blow up. Reynolds's patrol provided a reception committee. This could disrupt their own work but it did mean the incomers would be getting ashore safely. Olivey's team was to operate around Fianona, a populous beat which proved very tricky.

Early next month, as spring arrived in Dalmatia, the last of the war, Olivey's patrol was re-assigned, back to their old routine of road watch, this time to the highway running between Fiume and Trieste. Stan Eastwood, with his squad, took over the coastal stretch from 8th April. LRDG now had four full teams in Istria, bolstered by half a hundred SBS under David Sutherland, who was appointed as local area commander. This was all good. Relations with the partisans, however, were turning all bad.

The Spring of Discontent

Mike Reynolds was the first LRDG patrol commander to get a foretaste of the Cold War. Without warning, at a routine morning get together, things turned nasty. He and his team were shanghaied at gunpoint. Providentially, his radio operator got out a distress call before he was scooped up. The entire patrol was threatened with ignominious deportation but was brought off by the Navy. Next to feel the freezing breath of the new east wind was Stan Eastwood, then David Sutherland and his SBS team. Our partisan allies had succeeded where the Germans had failed, to destroy all of the valuable work being done, in no small measure, on their behalf and to hopelessly compromise any future operations in the sector.

Trieste was the reason. For Tito, Istria with the city was the great prize. The presence of British forces could only detract from, if not hamper and delay, the great communist-led advance, the red and reds only finale. In fairness, the Yugoslavs were not alone in this politicized obsession. General de Gaulle was never too keen on having British SOE or SAS representatives mar his gloriously staged Franco-centric liberation parades.

Allied Force HQ lodged all of the appropriate protests. The bargaining chip was the continued flow of arms and equipment; Tito would have to decide how hard he wanted to bite the hand that was feeding him. In the meantime, Lloyd Owen issued orders that patrols were to obey local partisan instructions and not risk armed confrontation, however compelling the temptation. John Olivey's patrol was not yet corralled and the local partisan generalissimo, commanding their 4th Army, blandly denied any knowledge of arrests. As LRDG was learning, Nazis burned books whilst the communists preferred simply to re-write them as suited the moment. Tito's HQ issued the even more scandalous suggestion that the partisans in question were probably Axis forces in disguise![29]

The haggling continued at senior level, leaving Lloyd Owen and his patrols, literally in their case, out on a limb. David Sutherland had been driven beyond the point of patient diplomacy by the shifty intransigence of his hosts and asked for evacuation. Once tempers, including his own, had cooled, Lloyd Owen proposed one last operation. Senior command agreed, but he then found himself at odds with his elders and betters who were firmly of the view that the British presence in Istria had to be maintained beyond this for political rather than military ends.

Brigadier Davy went as far as to countermand Lloyd Owen's order for the withdrawal of patrols still in the theatre. This caused understandable friction within the chain of command. Air Vice Marshal Mills supported Lloyd Owen – *I am certain we would lose less face by leaving Istria under our own steam and with some dignity (if the position becomes impossible) than by having our men manhandled by a gang of ghastly garlic eaters.*[30] The patrols would have agreed wholeheartedly.

John Olivey meanwhile was playing the game like a master. He was rather older than the other officers and perhaps understood just how best to compete in this uncongenial sport. He acted as a bigger idiot than the most literal-minded idiot amongst the partisans – a significant challenge for even the most accomplished mummer. Any order he didn't like, which was all of them, he simply misunderstood and therefore ignored. He also grasped that many of the local Yugoslavs were simply obeying orders themselves, percolating down through an extended and highly politicized chain of command.

Lloyd Owen, as his own signals testify, was being goaded beyond endurance. The worry over the well being of those for whom he was responsible (at the age of 27) – *hope to avoid court martial but this unlikely and an inconvenience I must accept*[31] – was a heavy burden. This high level angst persisted till 21st April when authorisation to pull everyone out was finally issued, though the prevailing weather conditions meant this was, for the moment, impossible. Things in Istria were getting very sticky and an emergency ex-filtration loomed. However, this was all in the Balkans where the mood shifts with the clouds, and a left-dominated Balkans at that, one where yesterday's history becomes today's fiction.

With a fine instinct for brinkmanship, Tito backed down over the sad 'misunderstanding' – smiles, handshakes and drinks all round. Allied HQ was prepare to share this novel fantasy in order to save face, and therefore decided Sutherland and crew should carry out at least once more operation and thus leave on a suitably prestigious note.

On the ground nothing had changed; David Sutherland was deprived of viable local targets due to the enemy's continual withdrawal (the dire irony being that our allies were now covering the Germans backs very effectively). The SBS had about had enough of their surly and aggressive hosts and were ready for a showdown. Allied Forces HQ's woeful complacency could have triggered a most unpleasant incident, perhaps the first in the Cold War, even before the main conflict had ended!

At last, however, the penny dropped at AFHQ and they gave in. The order for evacuation was sent out. By the time the spring darkness had come down on 25th April, the SBS had been successfully ex-filtrated back to Zara. John Olivey, playing the canny fool till the end, was still operating in Istria when peace broke out, returning to base via Trieste. The whole sorry fiasco left a bitter taste, a very sour note for LRDG to end their eventful war on. Officers like Lloyd Owen, perhaps not overly political in outlook at the start, developed a distinct antipathy towards communism, which would plunge most of Eastern Europe into a continuing tyranny for the next half-century.

Not all was lost on the Dalmatian coast though. Whilst frustration and duplicity flourished on the mainland, several LRDG patrols were quietly conducting business as usual offshore. George Pitt had been inserted to identify coastal gun positions south of Karlobag. Next he crossed to the island of Rab for a spell of shipping watch. The place was crawling with Axis troops but he managed both to keep giving them the slip and to maintain the flow of intelligence. The RAF duly showed their appreciation in the usual way and even the local partisans remained on side. Pitt joined forces with them for attacks on the island garrison. Lieutenants Savage and Saunders were respectively active on the islands of Krk and Olib. Again they both watched out for enemy shipping and worked well with the resident guerrillas.[32]

Yet another offshore base was on Ist. By Dalmatian coast standards this was a 'cushy billet'; the enemy left the patrol alone and they settled into a routine, based in one of the islander's stone houses. Though the enemy might have been quiescent, they weren't entirely absent and certainly not complacent. On 10th January 1945, on a winter's night, they sent raiders of their own to engage in a 'beat-up'. It was a novel and disagreeable experience for LRDG to be the quarry rather than the hunter.

Signaller Kenneth Smith was the W/O, asleep at the time, LRDG occupying some rooms, the family still in others. Whether the partisan sentry was merely negligent or complicit could never be determined, but the enemy crept close enough to plant several explosive devices. One of these was placed by Smith's radio, an obvious target. Someone loosed off a couple of rounds which rather gave the game away and woke everyone including Smith, who discovered the bomb by his wireless. The thing was ticking, clearly about to explode so, to save everyone and his precious radio, he grabbed the IED and made a dash for open ground where he could safely chuck it. He didn't make it but everyone else did. For this act he was awarded a posthumous George Cross.[33]

The Final Curtain

> Peace? Peace. I hate the word...[34]

What to do with warriors when there's no war? LRDG was a cutting-edge fighting unit; it had never had a peacetime role. The post war expansion of Special Forces operations is discussed in the next and final chapter, but in May 1945 there seemed no need. As early as July 1944, foreseeing the end of the conflict in Europe, Lloyd Owen had made out a case for deploying LRDG to the Far East. Bob Laycock, by now Chief of Combined Operations, was minded to agree. The government of Rhodesia was prepared to allow its soldiers to remain with the colours, and the men were genuinely enthusiastic to see the job through.

On 16th June, Allied Forces HQ intimated to Lloyd Owen that the WO, in its infinite Olympian wisdom, concurred, and that a fresh round of training was to be undertaken. Barely a week later, the WO changed its mind and disbanded the LRDG: *Five years and fourteen days after its formation in Cairo, the Long Range Desert Group ended its active career. I believe that its days in the desert have made some mark in military history.*[35]

This typically modest claim turned out to be something of an understatement.

Notes

1. http://www.historylearningsite.co.uk/resistance_movement_in_yugoslavi.htm, retrieved 3rd March 2015.
2. Ibid.
3. Lloyd Owen, p. 159.
4. Ibid., pp. 160–161.
5. Ibid.
6. http://www.telegraph.co.uk/news/worldnews/europe/croatia/8529443/Croatian-island-of-Vis-remembers-World-War-Two-role.html – retrieved 3rd March 2015.
7. Lloyd Owen, p. 161.
8. Ibid., p. 162.
9. Ibid., pp. 163–165.

10 Ibid., p. 166.
11 Mostar was famous for its beautiful sixteenth-century bridge, later destroyed in the civil wars of the 1990s.
12 Lloyd Owen p. 166.
13 Ibid., p. 167.
14 Ibid., p. 168.
15 Fitzroy Hew Royle Maclean (1911–1996) was a celebrated author, traveler, soldier and MP, one of the very few who during the course of the war rose from private to brigadier. He is best remembered for his remarkable memoir, *Eastern Approaches,* and may have been one of those who inspired fellow Scot Ian Fleming to create James Bond.
16 Lloyd Owen, p. 169.
17 Ibid., p. 170.
18 Ibid.
19 Ibid., p. 172.
20 Ibid., pp. 174–175.
21 Ibid.
22 Ibid., p. 176.
23 Ibid., p. 211.
24 Ibid., p. 212.
25 Ibid.
26 Ibid., pp. 213–214.
27 Ibid., p. 215.
28 Ibid., p. 216.
29 Ibid., p. 222.
30 Ibid., p. 223.
31 Ibid., p. 224.
32 Ibid., p. 227.
33 Ibid., pp. 227–228.
34 Shakespeare, *Romeo & Juliet* (Act one, scene 1, Tybalt).
35 Ibid., p. 229.

Little Waco, lesser half of the LRDG's private air-force (photo courtesy of Long Range Desert Group Preservation Society).

A well armed and heavily laden LRDG truck, typically of the appearance of the average patrol, stowage and storage of kit, fuel and ammunition was, as ever, critical (photo courtesy of LRDG Preservation Society).

LRDG members in an improvised mess, figure on the left with LRDG shoulder badge is Alec Ross
(photo courtesy of Fliegel Jezerniczky Ltd).

Crashed Axis fighter
(photo courtesy of LRDG Preservation Society).

LRDG Patrol, unidentified location
(photo courtesy of the LRDG Preservation Society).

A Desert Diorama – 'the Patrol' (photo courtesy of LRDG Preservation Society).

Rhodesian LRDG Officer (photo courtesy of LRDG Preservation Society).

The figure on the right is identified as Hamed, an Italian POW who became an LRDG cook
(photo courtesy of LRDG Preservation Society).

Recreated LRDG Patrolman with the SMLE .303 rifle
(photo courtesy of LRDG Preservation Society).

Light patrol truck, thought to be in Greece after the end of the Desert War
(photo courtesy of LRDG Preservation Society).

George Pitt's R.1 Patrol
Top: Stopforth, unknown, Calder-Potts, Pitt, Utterton and Hawkins
Bottom: Robinson, Hogan, Marshall, Wood and unknown

George Pitt's R1 Patrol
(photo courtesy of LRDG Preservation Society).

Group of officers and men, possibly Kufra
(photo courtesy of LRDG Preservation Society).

Reading mail
(photo courtesy of LRDG
Preservation Society).

Patrol Car, Western Desert 1942
(photo courtesy of the LRDG
Preservation Society).

Crashed Blenheim bomber
(photo courtesy of LRDG
Preservation Society).

Signaller JC Whale and comrades
(photo courtesy of LRDG Preservation Society).

Well restored truck with mounted cannon
(photo courtesy of LRDG Preservation Society).

Ready for action!
(photo courtesy of LRDG Preservation Society).

Recreated Bren Gun team
(photo courtesy of LRDG Preservation Society).

CHAPTER 10
Ghost Patrols, 1945–2015

Are you ready, paratrooper? Said the sergeant looking up,
The paratrooper feebly answered, the dispatcher hooked him up.
But when he hit the atmosphere his chute became unstuck.
And he ain't gonna jump no more...

(Chorus)

Glory, glory, what a horrible way to die!
Glory, glory, paratrooper.
Glory, glory, what a horrible way to die!
And he ain't gonna jump no more.

—Sung to the tune of *John Brown's Body*[1]

Special Forces: operations conducted in hostile, denied, or politically sensitive environments to achieve military, diplomatic, informational, and/or economic objectives employing military capabilities for which there is *no broad conventional force requirement.* These operations often require covert, clandestine, or low visibility capabilities. Special operations are applicable across the range of military operations. They can be conducted independently or in conjunction with operations of conventional forces or other government agencies, and may include operations through, with, or by indigenous or surrogate forces. Special operations differ from conventional operations in degree of physical and political risk, operational techniques, mode of employment, independence from friendly support, and dependence on detailed operational intelligence and indigenous assets.

—US Department of Defense (author's emphasis)[2]

'No broad conventional force requirement' – for the purposes of this chapter I am working on an assumed definition of Special Forces based on the LRDG precedent. I am discounting larger commando-style or paratrooper formations. During the early stages of the war commandos were used for raiding, with mixed results, but like some of their Axis counterparts ended up being employed in the line as heavy infantry. Britain still fields both Marine Commandos and the Parachute Regiment. These are elite forces with a record second to none. but I do not include them within my particular definition of 'Special Forces'.

The LRDG came into being as a solution to a clearly perceived strategic problem, and as an opportunity for British arms to practise a peripheral, indirect role. In 1945 LRDG was disbanded, but the problems besetting the post-war world and the retreat from Empire threw up a whole raft of tactical challenges for which Special Forces offered an obvious remedy. Senior officers tend not to like irregulars. They're too much like loose cannon, disregard orders and hierarchies, tend to operate beyond effective control, and exhibit a tendency to siphon off the most able and daring men from regular formations. The prevailing staff college view was that the costs and risks far outweighed the dividends.

Ralph Bagnold and the LRDG, and David Stirling with the SAS had at least to a degree changed that. They had shown what highly trained and motivated raiders with the right tools and equipment could achieve. Nothing beats an endorsement from Rommel himself! As NATO settled into the largely passive routine of the Cold War, with the prospect of a major interstate Armageddon looming daily, there appeared to be little requirement for Special Forces. The Cold War was a kind of dry run of the Western Front, both sides dug in and facing each other, but otherwise little or no movement.

Warfare, post 1945, has tended to be a very different business. For half a century, industrial armies faced each other across the North German Plain, each driven by fear of the other. Both possessed vast arsenals of nuclear weapons which assured that neither side could possibly win – it was 'mutually assured destruction' or, very aptly, "MAD" for short. At the same time, Britain experienced the retreat from Empire sparking asymmetric conflicts across the globe, such as in Malaya, Kenya, Cyprus, Aden and Borneo. Simultaneously there was scope for expeditionary warfare in Korea, Suez, the Falklands, the two Gulf Wars and Afghanistan, with thirty years of domestic counter-insurgency in Northern Ireland.

It is remarkable to think senior commanders after 1945 envisaged a continuation of Industrial warfare without the need for Special Forces. Today, we tend to view our Special Forces as the front line is asymmetric conflict:

> the period 1946–1991 could well be defined as one of an overarching confrontation ... maintained by industrial structures, containing non-industrial conflicts, the parallel wars. It is within these conflicts that we see the first signs of the new paradigm, especially in the nature and objectives of the opponents, and in the constant adaptation of the existing means – the industrial military machines – to non industrial conflicts.... It was the beginning of a trend we live with to this day.[3]

Whilst the nature of the threat and the need for Special Forces' role has changed, in part at least, many of the core concepts underlying the creation of LRDG still hold good. Bagnold raised his force to perform a specific task in a very particular environment. Success in one sector, as LRDG discovered, did not guarantee a repeat elsewhere. LRDG was intended for deep penetration, reconnaissance and intelligence gathering. Much of this work, the dreaded 'road watch', was far from glamorous but vital in terms of overall strategic and tactical planning. 'Beating up' the enemy was a secondary function, giving plenty of adrenalin rush but often stirring up the hornets' nest, so compromising the primary role.

David Stirling had no qualms about riling the foe. That was the primary function of SAS – raiding enemy targets and creating massive havoc. The results were considerable, and the boost to battered Allied morale an important bonus, but sometimes the grim reaper approach made the work of LRDG more difficult.

It is axiomatic therefore that the formation and role of LRDG shows that defining the role of Special Forces in the theatre from the outset is crucial. The 'KISS' principle ('keep it simple, stupid') is not to be overlooked. Expansive combined commando-type operations such as Operation *Agreement* ended in disaster. This is a lesson which subsequent planners, say of grandiose Operation *Eagle Claw,* the 1980 attempt by the US to rescue hostages in Iran, failed to heed. That one also foundered, creating both a military and PR catastrophe.

It was the experience and success of LRDG that signposted some important features for successor Special Forces. Suitably built or modified vehicles, designed for heavy load carrying, rugged, reliable and not overly sophisticated, are essential. The failure of Axis forces to grasp this partly explains their own failures. A plethora of automatic weapons delivering a hail of fire way beyond the normal firepower of so small a group is frequently decisive in the vital opening seconds of the fight. Early fire supremacy not only kills enemy, it hastens their urge to disengage. It can also persuade them that they're facing a far superior force. Workable communications are a must. The tragedy of Arnhem in 1944 clearly shows just how horribly wrong things can go when the communications fail.

Any military unit depends upon the calibre of men it attracts. It has always been clear that you can't conscript Special Forces. They must, by definition, be volunteers. From those who come forward, only a small percentage will actually qualify. The current SAS selection is notoriously and rightly rigorous. None but the best will do. Bagnold established this principle from the outset, using the trusted cadre of those he'd explored alongside before the war. Those he recruited achieved prodigies. They were all ordinary men yet they were also magnificent men: resolute, resilient, courageous and bold.

Just to survive in the conditions LRDG regularly found itself required each man to have a steel core, officers doubly so. Being on patrol, hundreds of miles behind enemy lines in the harshest environment on Earth, made huge demands. Physical fitness and stamina had to be matched by emotional strength and motivation. There was no chain of command, no relief ever in sight, no backup and often no re-supply. The patrol was its own army. It carried whatever it needed. It had to care for its own sick and wounded, with no chance of a scapegoat when things went wrong; 'Corporals' wars' in army jargon. It is hardly any wonder that to the regular infantry, immured in their defensive 'boxes', harried relentlessly by the agility of the Desert Fox, these men appeared almost mythical – demi-gods drawn straight from the pages of Homer or Henty.

None of this has changed. For Special Forces to be able to operate successfully, only the bravest and the best can pass the test. Each man knows he can rely totally on his comrade. Officers have to muck in, to listen to the specialists whose combined skills determine unit effectiveness. There is no room for passengers, and service in the field will quickly and cruelly expose those not up to the mark. From the Maccabees to Desert Storm, this hasn't changed, nor ever will.

End of Empire

> The sharp end of SAS operations was arduous and dangerous work. An operation would be for up to three months with re-supply by parachute every fourteen days, security permitting. Fresh meat and bread would be dropped and consumed the same day before the beasties got at it. It was not unusual for supply 'chutes to 'whistle in' – plummet to earth without fully opening or become hung up in the trees or be otherwise inaccessible. These would invariably be the ones with the mail or rum ration onboard.[4]

The Malayan Emergency was a twelve-year counter-insurgency campaign against Communist Terrorists ("CTs"). At the outset CTs were able to strike almost at will from superbly camouflaged jungle bases virtually impossible to detect. Part of the riposte was to re-form the SAS, which took the fight to the enemy, a major factor in their final defeat. Obviously, the Chindit experience was invaluable, and expert practitioners in the art of jungle warfare such as 'Mad' Mike Calvert were brought in to train recruits. Malaya established the enduring value of a Special Forces component, one which despite the nightmare terrain could penetrate into the heart of enemy-held areas and direct telling air strikes.

> From Changi the squadron moved to the jungle warfare school at Kota Tingi in Malaya. British and Australian instructors taught basic jungle tactics with assistance from a company of Gurkhas. This course ended with the squadron's first operation, off the east coast of Southern Malaya. Landing from Navy

> MTBs, the squadron stormed ashore into flat, dense, sea-swamped jungle. Unfortunately nobody had considered the water supply (never usually a problem in jungle). Here the water was salty so we lived on coconut milk, a miserable experience....[5]

During the long and vicious years of the Troubles in Northern Ireland, the SAS learned to function in a covert, urban/rural environment. In temperament this sectarian conflict was the very reverse of *Krieg ohne Hass*. When an SAS detachment very publicly stormed the Iranian Embassy in May 1980, bringing to an end a violent siege and hostage scenario, theirs became a household name. In the thirty-odd years since, this status has been elevated to the iconic. Writers like Chris Ryan and Andy MacNab, who took part in the epic failure of Bravo Two Zero during the first Gulf War, have together sold millions of books since.

The killing of three Provisional Irish Republican Army ("PIRA") terrorists on the rock of Gibraltar during Operation *Flavius*[6] led to some disquiet. LRDG had only ever been called upon to fight in an honourable war, and took prisoners wherever possible. Shooting to kill is part of war but the lines are less clear-cut when facing terrorists or insurgents – 'war among the people' as General Smith would define it.

The retreat from empire – protracted, complex and not infrequently bloody – offered the perfect training ground for Special Forces. Each conflict threw up different scenarios, Kenya, Aden, the Radfan, and Borneo. All demanded that UK Special Forces learn to operate across a range of terrain, that they should work closely with local forces, and pursue the Holy Grail of 'hearts and minds'.

Despite the varying stresses of topography and demographics, the essential role is one LRDG would have recognised. In July 1972, a nine-man SAS patrol fought an epic fight against vastly superior communist forces at Mirbat in Dhofar. Stirling and Paddy Mayne would have approved wholeheartedly. SAS suffered three casualties but easily accounted for probably a hundred plus of the enemy.

On the night of 11th May 1982 during the Falklands War the SAS carried out a reconnaissance of an Argentinian air base on Pebble Island off the coast of West Falkland. This was classic LRDG/SAS territory. The enemy possessed significant air power and their Pucara ground-attack aircraft constituted a deadly threat to the expeditionary force. On the night of the 14th the SAS came back to Pebble Island, this time looking for a fight. The attack was pure textbook. Aided by supporting naval gunfire, the raiders pulverised the airfield and its planes, effectively destroying the place and were gone within a couple of hours. Only one man was wounded.[7]

One US officer, writing of the First Gulf War, described Iraq as a 'Special Forces Theme Park'. Robin Neillands comments that it was never seriously in doubt that the Coalition forces would defeat Saddam Hussein's army. Some 'experts' had predicted heavy casualties amongst ground forces when taking on the 'elite' Republican Guard, who in the event proved rather less than formidable. Saddam had begun shooting Scud Missiles into Israel, a flagrant provocation. Had Israel riposted then, Arab partners in the Coalition would have wavered. SAS and US Special Forces were tasked to seek out and destroy these Iraqi Missiles.[8]

> The SAS were born in the desert, fifty years before Desert Storm, so in many ways the regiment was returning to its birthplace in the Gulf War, albeit a few thousand miles further east from their old stamping grounds in the Western Desert of North Africa. The SAS were even equipped for this operation in a similar way. Long wheel-based Land Rovers replaced the traditional Willys' Jeep and the GPMG [General Purpose Machine-Gun] was mounted in place of the Bren gun or the Vickers 'K', but otherwise not a lot had changed since the desert campaigns of half a century before.[9]

In tandem with the hunt for Scuds, and reminiscent of the LRDG road watch, Special Forces were to interdict the major Iraqi internal supply routes – the saga of Bravo Two Zero came about in consequence.

The Hunt for 'Elvis'

Within days of 9/11, advance reconnaissance teams from the CIA's Special Operations Group (SOG) were in Afghanistan, essentially intelligence gathering and distributing bribes, followed by teams of Green Beret Special Advisors to prepare Northern Alliance warlords to take the fight to the Taliban.

These were joined for reconnaissance and target acquisition by SAS/SBS, who had far greater experience of such operations from Aden, Oman etc. At the time of 9/11, the UK was conducting Exercise *Swift-Sword* off Oman – deploying 22,000 personnel, 6.500 vehicles, twenty warships and close air support. The US already possessed a substantial forward base in Uzbekistan. The west had to respond swiftly once the ultimatums to the Taliban expired. Ground operations thus began on 7th October; it was essential to gain as much ground as possible before the onset of winter.

The Taliban (c. 50,000 strong), plus several hundred Al-Qaeda, pitted against the Northern Alliance, (c. 15,000 strong), had been conducting sporadic conventional warfare with massed forces on the ground, from fortress complexes and extended trench lines. The early phase of the conflict was thus a conventional war for which the Taliban were neither ready nor equipped. As the Taliban were attempting to fight a conventional war, they were massively outgunned and quickly routed; airburst munitions and strategic bombing by B-52s resulted in the destruction of fixed defences, supply depots, command and communications networks. Special Forces were directing and leading the campaign, doing 'hearts and minds' and looking at target acquisition; overall the Taliban put up a poor showing.

Al-Qaeda had its principal bases on the lower slopes of the southern Hindu Kush Mountains and circling Bagram Airfield. These were well concealed with heavily defended compounds and made full use of natural cave networks, very difficult to detect from the air. Reliance therefore fell on the SAS, providing close target reconnaissance ("CTR") and target acquisition. These were swiftly followed up by 'hammer and anvil' tactics; i.e. a main force with tanks and infantry approaches the target after reconnaissance with air support, while ground-attack aircraft bomb targets, obliging the terrorists to retreat away from the main assault into a carefully prepared ambush/kill zone where SAS are awaiting their arrival.

After the battle for Bagram Airfield, captured Taliban and Al-Qaeda were separated by Northern Alliance captors into indigenous

Afghan fighters, normally paroled or recruited, and foreigners, usually Pakistani, who could expect to be maltreated or killed. A large number of the latter were incarcerated in the ancient Quali-i-Janghi fortress for interrogation by the CIA while guarded by Northern Alliance. A revolt of the prisoners who seized arms occurred; the leading CIA operative and Northern Alliance bodyguards were shot down, and a major battle developed within the compound with CIA survivors and Alliance fighters getting the worst of it. The US appealed to a nearby SBS unit, six men, who stormed the fortress, weapons blazing, killing a large number of insurgents and restoring order – the senior non-com who led the group received the US Congressional Medal of Honor.[10]

This type of buccaneering action would have been instantly recognisable to those who served in the LRDG – daring and boldness, coupled with mobility and firepower. The enemy was clearly defined and visible.

Jihad

With the 'War on Terror', and the rise of asymmetric and now hybrid warfare, the perceived role of Special Forces has changed. Interstate wars are an increasingly rare phenomenon. International rivalries, as illustrated by the long decades of the Cold War, are often fought out vicariously. Conflicting ideologies, control of diminishing resources, and the rise of nationalism fuel modern conflicts which continue to proliferate. Special Forces are now deployed as the front line rather than purely for intelligence gathering and raiding. The clear and high moral plateau offered by the fight against fascism no longer exists. Civilians are very often first in the firing line, the 'enemy' a shifting, faceless chiaroscuro of changing factions and alliances.

Britons woke up to the reality of the Islamist threat at 5.50 am on 16th January 2013 when terrorists attacked the giant Tigantourine natural gas installation near Amenas, Algeria. The sudden eruption of the crisis, and the costly ruthlessness of the government's response, threw into stark relief the potential danger to British workers in the region. Such facilities are isolated, sprawling and virtually impossible to defend, apart from a massive military deployment. The terrorist will always have the advantage that only he knows where, when and exactly how he will strike. The incident left many hostages dead and injured, including a number from the UK.

On 28th January that year, French and Malian troops drove rebels from the fabled city of Timbuktu which, over a very long history, has seen its fair share of invaders. Islamist fighters, who had opted for a conventional, non-guerrilla response to the French deployment, had been easily routed and driven back from their earlier gains. Despite their major and pivotal role, the French have been keen to stress that their intervention was only part of a co-ordinated African response. Thus far, however, the hoped for Senegalese, Nigerian and Ivorian reinforcements have yet to arrive and demonstrate their capacity. It seems inevitable that the French will be staying for the foreseeable future. The lessons of Afghanistan clearly show that defeating the enemy in a conventional battle will certainly lead to a sustained asymmetric conflict, rather than to immediate and convincing victory.

What then will be the role of UK forces in this developing conflict? Earlier, Prime Minister David Cameron was too canny to respond directly to the question of whether British 'Boots on the Ground' in Africa would be needed. He did not rule out the possibility, and this is an eventuality which many may view with understandable alarm, given the fate of recent interventions in Iraq and Afghanistan, whose long-term effectiveness is still open to question.

At present there is not an answer to this quandary; in all probability the government is equally undecided, but the Malian intermeddling is a European, rather than US-led, deployment. France is Britain's ally; UK forces now train extensively with their Gallic counterparts and share operational capacities. France has 'form' in the region, a long period of colonial involvement and clearly, the established state governments, finding themselves under concerted attack, are more than willing to look to Europe for assistance.

The subsequent terrorist attack on the Westgate Shopping Mall in Nairobi offered a stark reminder of the vulnerability of 'soft' urban targets. Large retail parks present a complex labyrinth with built-in security features which may be used by attackers to thwart security forces. Such scenarios are, if we accept the arguments put forward by a leading expert in the field, David Kilcullen,[11] the shape of horrors to come. The murderous spree in Kenya bears similarities to the earlier attack in Mumbai, five years earlier.

In the past, guerrilla armies from David, seeking sanctuary in the Cave of Adullam, to Patrick Leigh Fermor and Stanley Moss spiriting Axis commander General Kreipe across the Cretan mountains, have sought refuge in the high ground. Geronimo led an entire US army on a merry dance through the sharp peaks and ravines of Arizona for decades with a mere handful of followers.

Now, modern surveillance and satellite tracking systems have largely stripped the hills of comfort. It is estimated that by 2050 some 75 percent of the world's population, which will by then have increased by another three billion, will be crowded into urban centres. In the developing world sprawling cities, an irresistible magnet to the rural poor, will grow exponentially in a riot of slums and shanties, perfect conditions for the rise of extremism. Kilcullen cites four main drivers priming the powder keg: huge growth in populations; concentration of people in cities; movement towards the world's coastlines; a spiralling revolution in technology-driven connectivity.

He foresees in some instances (Somalia being a case in point perhaps), doomsday outcomes where states and their governments fail and cities become a jungle and a battleground. The major powers, rather than deploying troops for counter-insurgency across barren plains and rock-strewn deserts, may find themselves fighting in the tangled rookeries of urban hives where all order has gone. The US experience in Mogadishu vividly recalled in *Black Hawk Down,* illustrates the perils such conflicts hold.

Street fighting is inevitably harder and costly, and demands infinitely more boots on the ground. Firepower, aerial observation and heavy weapons are far less effective. Ask General von Paulus. Worse, there is unlikely to be a defined 'enemy' as such, no Saddam or bin Laden to focus on. The current, awful civil war in Syria is being fought, on the rebel side, by a multiplicity of often-diverse groups, at best uneasy allies, very often mutually antipathetic, enmeshed in a quicksand of changing allegiances.

Conventional armies like conventional enemies, but Western forces could find themselves up against Al-Qaeda lookalikes or franchises, drug cartels, or sectarian mercenaries such as Hezbollah, fighting under the instructions and in the pay of a hostile or rogue state; war by proxy. The Nairobi attack, Kilcullen argues, like Mumbai, demonstrates how a small gang of well prepared, murderously ruthless terrorists can bring a whole city to a standstill.

No one anticipated the Arab Spring, fuelled largely by internet connectivity; nobody really understands how it may finally play out. Libya has descended into anarchy, and Egypt is balanced on the edge of chaos, the void of failure which provides an open door for extremists. Kilcullen takes a view that whilst huge areas of urban slum housing are nothing new, the internet changes everything, altering the dynamic in a way we have never seen before. Tinder for these volcanoes is provided by the deep wells of inequality, lack of opportunity, 'permanent exclusion and marginalization'. Awareness without hope is a dangerous pairing.

Je Suis Charlie

On the morning of 7th January 2015, two gunmen burst into the offices of the French satirical magazine *Charlie Hebdo,* a left leaning iconoclastic publication that was, ironically, struggling to stave off insolvency. Yelling their war cry *Allah Akbar,* the killers hosed the place with automatic fire, killing a dozen people. The massive hunt for the murderers, and an accomplice who held up a Kosher supermarket taking hostages, ended in much more gunfire and yet more deaths. *Je Suis Charlie* swept through the Western world, and the magazine's hitherto very modest sales soared to unimagined heights.

Like 9/11, this was a game-changer. There had been previous atrocities committed by jihadists claiming affiliation to ISIS or Al-Qaeda, but the carnage at 10 Rue Nicolas-Appert, in the 11th Arrondissement, focused the world's attention as never before. The continuing Islamic tyranny practised by ISIS in Syria and northern Iraq, characterised by mass murder and regular decapitations as spectator sports, may well define the decade. These are stateless enemies, and waging interstate, industrial war against them is, for the most part, impossible. Terror does not normally have a capital city or well-defined bases, or tanks, or planes or heavy guns.

> In times of crisis, the most reassuring call a prime minister can make is to the commander of Britain's elite Special Forces. Whether a terror cell in Yemen is plotting to blow up a passenger jet in mid-flight, or a group of al-Qaeda militants is threatening to kill British hostages, Downing Street can draw comfort from the fact that there is always a Special Forces unit ready to react at a moment's notice.
>
> The SAS certainly proved its ability to rescue British subjects in hostile terrain last summer when, with the backing of US special forces and Afghan troops, it staged a daring operation to rescue British aid worker Helen Johnston and three other hostages just hours before they were about to be murdered by their captors in north-east Afghanistan. A team of 28 special forces troops stormed the remote caves where Miss Johnston was being held, killing all four of the kidnappers while securing the aid workers' release.
>
> British Special Forces units were also very much in evidence during the Libyan conflict two years ago – despite Mr Cameron's repeated insistence that there were no "boots on the ground" in Libya. They helped identify potential bombing targets for Nato air strikes, as well as conducting classic behind-the-lines sabotage operations, such as cutting communications and energy supplies, to cripple the Gaddafi regime.
>
> Time and again the SAS and SBS have displayed a range of skills and levels of personal courage that have not only made them the envy of the world, but have also delivered spectacular results.[12]

Little Green Men

'Hybrid Warfare' is a new buzz expression. It involves warfare at every level, not the type of all-out industrial war we saw in the twentieth century, but a new breed of conflict where media manipulation and the use of the internet is as important as bullets and boots on the ground. The expression came into vogue when President Putin was manoeuvring to wrest Crimea back from Ukraine in 2014.

We heard of 'little green men', not from Mars but from Moscow. The expression may have gained something in translation but it derives from a colloquial term describing masked, military-looking types with no insignia but plenty of state-of-the-art weapons. President Putin naturally denied that these had anything to do with him, asserting they were purely locally raised militia units. This bland denial rather lost credibility when a Finnish expert (and the Finns have many reasons to be watching Russia), confirmed their kit was exclusive to Russian Special Forces.

None of this was particularly subtle, but the deployment represents an aspect of hybrid warfare. War isn't any longer a business of armies facing each other, relying on armour, airpower and battlefield tactics. Such confrontations will become much more rare. For one thing, industrial war is just too expensive. The UK campaign in Afghanistan, from the intervention in Helmand in 2006, cost £14m a day just to keep going.

We can't afford that. By and large, neither can anyone else. The new school of war embraces economics, IT and all manner of subterfuge. The recent drop in oil prices has hit Mr. Putin very hard. It's hit all producers, but Russia is especially dependent. Had the West organised this fall in prices rather than belatedly reaped the kudos (cue for conspiracy theorists), it would have been a clear and telling example of hybrid warfare in practice.

Some commentators suggest that Mr. Putin was rather quicker off the mark here than NATO. That may be right, but conditions in Ukraine perfectly suited this form of hybrid approach. Britain is now forming a bespoke unit specialising in the doctrine. This new 77th Brigade will have a complement of around 2,000. These will be military personnel but they'll be using words and media more than ammunition. Some 'civvies' may also be recruited independently to bring additional expertise in related fields such as psychology and marketing.

This represents a significant shift in strategic and tactical doctrine. Readers may recall the ill-fated attempts by David Cameron and

President Obama to get the West involved in Syria's fratricidal war. This would have been a deeply flawed policy had representatives on both sides of the Atlantic not vetoed the idea. In such conflicts – and Syria is very much the shape of things to come – it will be very difficult to identify clear factions. No more good guys and bad guys, but the shifting sands of fractious temporary allegiances, a mix of ideologies and theocratic doctrines, seasoned by ruthless barbarity. Nuclear submarines will have little or no role to play; aircraft carriers undoubtedly will.

Hybrid warfare will not replace military action, but may well dictate the timing and use of conventional forces. Those little green men might be there to quietly put some stick about or to harness and focus local militias. An ability to move and shape economic factors has always influenced warfare. Germany blamed its defeat in 1918 not on the superiority of the BEF but on a shadowy fifth column, a Jewish banking cartel which stabbed its generals in the back. Hitler knew all about hybrid warfare – using concentration camp victims, murdered and then uniformed, to create a myth of enemy action for his *casus belli* in Poland.

The designation 77th Brigade evokes the potent image of the original formation, far better known as the Chindits; a name to conjure with. Appropriate too, as Wingate's brainchild launched a new and unexpected type of jungle warfare behind Japanese lines. In such circumstances, the burden of the West's military response must fall on Special Forces. In the Western desert, LRDG were a tiny proportion of the whole Allied war effort, but today their successors very often *are* the war effort. What is certain in so uncertain a world is that the pioneers of LRDG created British Special Forces as we know them, and that resonance has a global implication. To that extent, the story continues.

> Certainly, as we prepare to tackle the wars of the future, it is clear we need more investment in our special forces, not ill-judged budget cuts. For, as George Orwell memorably remarked, 'People sleep peacefully in their beds at night only because rough men stand ready to do violence on their behalf'.[13]

The Last Post

As a young man, interested in desert travel and four-wheel-drive vehicles, this author was and remains an admirer of Colonel John Blashford Snell. In his autobiography Colonel Blashford Snell recounts a very odd and inexplicable experience that occurred, almost certainly, as Mike Morgan confirms, at the site of the Gebel Sherif skirmish. In the 1960s, working with fellow sappers and based at Kufra, the group was carrying out surveying and scientific work in the Fezzan. Blashford Snell was in charge of logistics. During one, otherwise unremarkable run, the supply team, who'd hoped to get back to Kufra before darkness, found they needed shelter for a night in the open. The ground was broken, with low indistinct hills, traversed by narrow wadis.

Their maps were poor and the wadi they drove down proved tricky. They got bogged several times and decided to call it a day under the lee of some rock buttresses. As he stepped out, in the gathering dark after a cold supper, for the purposes of nature, Blashford Snell heard a voice. None of the crew had called out so he turned in, thinking the sound a trick of the wind. Next morning, he awoke to the same internal imperative and stepped out a few paces from the camp. It was now just before dawn and a dull half-light was sharpening outlines. This was when he saw the truck. The ragged, wrecked but recognisable shape of an LRDG vehicle, the carcass surrounded by the detritus of battle: spent cases, ammo cases, rifle parts.

Daylight revealed a vehicle graveyard; the shells of more blitzed trucks littered the wadi. High up, almost hidden amongst the stones, they found a Pattern 37 canvas haversack, an old Kodak camera and a pile of spent .303 cartridges. Blashford Snell was sure this was the remains of Clayton's patrol and the residue of battle from 31st January 1941 with the Italian Air Force and Auto Saharan Patrol. The newcomers also found the remains of two graves, marked by simple wooden crosses, presumably the men Moore and the other escapers had buried. Blashford Snell and his team tidied up the graves, saluted, held their moment silence, and then drove away back into the present; but he never found out who it was who had spoken to him that night.[14]

Perhaps the ghosts, like King Arthur's knights, are out there still.

Notes

1 Quoted in Morgan, p. 141.
2 *Dictionary of Military and Associated terms* (2005).
3 Smith, General Sir Rupert, *The Utility of Force* Allen Lane, London, 2005, p. 197.
4 Bill Sculthorpe, a Canadian who served with 22nd SAS in Malaya, 1955–1957, quoted in Neillands, R., *In the Combat Zone* (Weidenfeld & Nicholson, London, 1997), p. 109.
5 Neillands, p. 109.
6 Operation *Flavius* in March 1988 involved the killing of Sean Savage, Daniel McCann and Mairead Farrell. At the subsequent inquest there was pressure on the jury to return a verdict of 'unlawful killing' – however they found the killings to have been lawful.
7 Neillands, pp. 253–254.
8 Ibid., p. 291.
9 Ibid., p. 293.
10 Ryan, M., *Battlefield Afghanistan* (Spellmount Stroud, 2007), pp. 42–48.
11 Kilcullen, D., *Out of the Mountains, the Coming Age of the Urban Guerrilla* (Talks at Google, retrieved 30th January 2015).
12 http://www.telegraph.co.uk/news/uknews/defence/9837238/The-SAS-a-very-special-force.html (retrieved 30th January 2015).
13 Ibid.
14 Retold in Morgan pp. 39–41.

GLOSSARY
Abbreviations and Acronyms

'AA' – Anti-aircraft
'AFHQ' – Allied Forces Headquarters
'AFV' – Armoured fighting vehicle
'AP' – Armour piercing
'A & SH' – Argyll and Sutherland Highlanders
'AA' – Anti-aircraft
'AT' – Anti-tank
'BAF' – Balkan Air Force
'BEF' – British Expeditionary Force
'Bir' – well, cistern
'Bivvy' – Bivouac
'BTE' – British Troops in Egypt
'CIA' – Central Intelligence Agency (US)
'C-in-C' – Commander in Chief
'CO' – Commanding officer
'CP' – Command post
'CSM' – Company Sergeant-Major
'CT' – Communist Terrorist
'CTR' – Close Target Reconnaissance
'DAF' – Desert Air Force (RAF)
'DAK' – *Deutsches Afrika Corps*
'DCM' – Distinguished Conduct Medal
'De-lousing' – minefield clearance
'DID' – Detail Issue Department

'Div' – Division
'DMI' – Director of Military Intelligence
'DSO' – Distinguished Service Order
'Erg' – Sand Sea
'FOB' – Forward Operational Base
'Fusti' – fuel drum
'Gebel' (Jebel) – mountain or hill
'Gilf' – cliff, plateau
'Goumier' – French irregulars
'GOC' – General Officer Commanding
'GSO1' – General Staff Officer 1st Class
'GSO2' – General Staff officer 2nd Class
'Hamada' – stony desert
'Hatiet', 'Hatiya' – patch of vegetation
'HE' – High explosive
'IAOC' – Indian Army Ordnance Corps
'IED' – Improvised explosive device
'IO' – Intelligence officer
'ILRS' – Indian Long Range Squadron
'ISLD' – Inter-service Liaison Department
'I-Tank' – Infantry tank
'KD' – Khaki drill
'Kebir' – large, big
'KIA' – Killed in Action
'LAF' – Libyan Arab Force
'L of C' – Lines of communication
'LRDG' – Long Range Desert Group
'LRP' – Long Range Patrol (forerunner of LRDG)
'LSF' – Levant Schooner Flotilla
'MAD' – Mutually Assured Destruction
'Ma'aten' – well
'MC' – Military Cross
'Mehariste' – Camel Corps trooper
'MG' – Machine gun

'MP' – Military Police
'MT' – Motor transport
'Mudir' – native official
'NAAFI/EFI' – Navy, Army and Air Force Institutes/Expeditionary Forces Institute
'NATO' – North Atlantic Treaty Organisation
'NCO' – Non-commissioned officer
'O Group' – Orders Group
'O.H' – Official History
'OKH' – *Oberkommand des Heeres*
'OKW' – *Oberkommand der Wehrmacht*
'OP' – Observation post
'ORBAT' – Orders of Battle
'PBI' – Poor bloody infantry
'PIRA' – Provisional Irish Republican Army
'POL' – Petrol, oil and lubricants
'PTSD' – Post Traumatic Stress Disorder
'Quaret, 'Gara' – hill
'QM' – Quartermaster
'Quibli' – hot, south wind
'RA' – Royal Artillery
'RAC' – Royal Armoured Corps
'RAF' – Royal Air Force
'RAP' – Regimental Aid Post
'RAC' – Royal Armoured Corps
'RAOC' – Royal Army Ordnance Corps
'RASC' – Royal Army Service Corps
'RE' – Royal Engineers
'Recce' – reconnaissance
'Regt' – 'Regiment
'REME' – Royal Engineers Mechanical Engineers
'R & R' – Rest & Recreation
'RN' – Royal Navy
'RSM' – Regimental Sergeant-Major

'RTU'd' – Returned to unit
'RTR' – Royal Tank Regiment
'RV' – rendezvous
'SAS' – Special Air Service
'Scarper' – Disorganised and precipitate retreat, verging on rout
'SDF' – Sudan Defence Force
'Shott' – salt marsh
'Serir', 'serir' – gravel desert
'SMG' – Sub-machine gun
'SMLE' – Short-magazine Lee Enfield
'SNCO' – Senior non-commissioned officer
'SOE' – Special Operations Executive
'Wadi' – watercourse, normally dry
'WD' – War Department
'W/O' – Wireless Operator
'W/T' – Wireless telegraphy
'VC' – Victoria Cross

APPENDIX 1
Weapons, Vehicles, Training & Equipment

Vehicles

In 1940, the era of specialised kit for Special Forces had not yet dawned. Much of what LRDG utilised was strictly on a 'make do and mend' basis, seasoned by chronic wartime shortages. As mentioned in the introduction, long after the war the shifting sands revealed a lost survivor, scorched by sand and wind but still recognisable – a Chevrolet WB 30 cwt two-wheel-drive truck. Found in and recovered from the desert like Ozymandias' bust, though this relic was not entirely forgotten. Its markings had survived sufficiently to be recognisable as truck 8 of W Patrol (New Zealand), though probably abandoned by G Patrol late in 1940 or early 1941. Despite new owners, the vehicle markings did not get updated, retaining their earlier Maori names, and we know that Trooper Clarkie Waetford branded this one *Waikaha* – the location his family hailed from.[1] The truck, still in its raw, scarred state, can now be seen in the Imperial War Museum, London.

It was of inestimable value that Ralph Bagnold had spent so many years engaged in desert exploration before the war. Optional extras such as sand tyres, water condensers for vehicle radiators, sand mats & channels, and the superb sun-compass (see below) became essential. Adapted, cannibalised and stripped, LRDG vehicles became *a mobile oasis in the desert for the troops who relied on them.*[2] Nominal weight limits were soon discarded and it wasn't uncommon for the 30 cwt truck to set off with over two tons (imperial) of fuel, supplies, ammunition and gear. Additional leafs were added to the existing suspension system to compensate. Each vehicle had a flexible crew of three: driver, gunner and commander. Each individual's roles might encompass a range of functions: wireless operator, medic, navigator and fitter. The ability to carry out running repairs was crucial; nobody was going to be anywhere near to a dealer or service station.

In the very early days officers were provided with Ford 01 (½ or ¾ ton) pickups. Additional air vents were added by the simple expedient of punching holes in the bonnet. New rear bumpers, affording better access for tyre-changing, were fitted together with swan-neck machine-gun mounts. Doors were removed and an ad hoc timber superstructure built up to house supply containers. Typical armament might be a .303 Vickers or Lewis Gun, or perhaps one of each, (see below). The advantage of these command or pilot vehicles was their relative lightness, far easier to dig out and so ideal for scouting.

Ford also produced the larger F30 truck – this had the apparent advantage of four-wheel drive but this was frequently offset by additional weight and a gas-guzzling V8 engine which could seldom offer more than six miles per gallon, a serious disadvantage on long-range missions where adequate fuel supply was a constant worry. This was the prime attraction of the Chevrolet 1533X2 30-cwt model, which had been specifically re-designed to military specifications. LRDG further customised these vehicles, which began to replace the older trucks from early 1942. To the standard rig troopers added the vital sand tyres and customised radiator grills to boost air-flow. Some were further modified for specialist support roles: engineering, light artillery and anti-tank capabilities.[3]

Heavier vehicles such as conventional 3-tonners were used for supply, and the 30-cwt trucks were augmented by their lighter brethren, the 15-cwt Pilot, also employed as a handy scout. Most of these were two-wheel drive, which was preferred as they used far less fuel. The idea of a four-wheel drive vehicle had to wait for the ubiquitous Jeep, the Willys MB. Perhaps the most famous images of desert raiders are photos of piratical-looking SAS troopers in jeeps which bristle with automatic weapons, a film-makers dream. LRDG, who'd first encountered the earlier Bantam BRC-40s, continued to refer to all jeeps as 'bantams'. The famous Willys were ideal for desert warfare; light, manoeuvrable, sure-footed, rapid and robust. Within LRDG, they swiftly replaced many of the earlier scout cars. Most LRDG jeeps carried less armament than their SAS contemporaries; say a single or twin-mounted machine-gun.[4]

A key innovation, unique to the desert and designed ingeniously by Bagnold himself, was the condenser:

> We realised that cars do not use much water by actually boiling it off in steam, but that the steam blowing violently down the narrow overflow pipe, provided in all radiators, carries with it a great quantity of water splashed up by the boiling. All this could be saved if the overflow were led into a special tank even if the steam itself were lost. So we blocked up the overflows of the radiators, and in their place soldered large copper pipes to the filler caps, joining them by other tubes down into two-gallon cans bolted onto the running boards of the cars, so that the only outlet from the radiator was at the end of a pipe immersed in cold water at the bottom of a can. When the water boiled in the engine a mixture of water and steam was carried over into the can where all the water was saved, and so, until at last the water in the can itself began to boil, the steam was condensed and saved.[5]

Getting around in the seemingly limitless wastes of the Western Desert, a region the size of the Indian sub-continent and with rather fewer inhabitants, wasn't just about having the right vehicles; it was very much about knowing how to use them. Again, the pre-war experiences of Bagnold and Clayton proved invaluable. The learning curve had already been met. Obviously, there was the ever-present risk that the heavily laden vehicles would get bogged in soft sand. The skilled driver soon learnt, usually the hard way, to judge the ground ahead. The use of sand channels and mats to ease trucks out of soft sand saved hours of sweat. The channels provided a hard surface for the rear (driving) wheels while the mats gave purchase for the front tyres. Much heaving and pushing might still be needed. If the truck was truly bogged then it might have to be first unloaded. At this point the driver might have few friends.

Over compacted ground, hard sand or gravel *serir,* the trucks could bowl along at respectable speeds, and might hope to cover over two hundred miles in a day. Progress across the treacherous shifting and undulating dunes, sometimes several hundred feet high, was a lot harder. A patrol leader had to know the difference between the hunched and passable 'whalebacks' as opposed to the hazardous 'razorbacks' where the unwary might come to grief over a blind summit and sheer drop. The favoured tactic was a 'balaklavering' (from the famous cavalry charges at Balaclava in the Crimean War, 1854): a rush at the slope, using speed, momentum and the grip of deflated sand tyres to get a bite. Pausing on the crest to consider the next move was advisable.

War generally is hard on military vehicles; desert warfare doubly so; and the distances and terrain traversed by LRDG on a daily basis, vastly more so. LRDG could not have functioned effectively without the unglamorous but vital work of the Light Aid Detachment. This was a trusty band of REME and RAOC fitters who looked after trucks, jeeps, weapons and all other things mechanical. Commanded by Captain Joe Braithwaite, they kept ships propellers and those of the trusty WACOs turning. Their work was the everyday mundane, no adrenalin-pumping contacts but, as David Lloyd Owen rightly points out, without them there would have been no action at all!

Weapons

Men of the LRDG, like most swashbucklers, valued their weapons. The choice could easily determine success or failure, life and death. Equipping the unit, however, was problematical from the outset as the whole theatre of war was bedevilled by a shortage of available firepower. Most of what was carried by patrols was standard British army issue. The most common sidearm was the .38 calibre Enfield or Webley, a tried and tested revolver; less sophisticated than its Axis semi-automatic counterparts, but rugged and dependable.

As the desert is as hard on kit as it is on men, reliability and durability were key. Rifle of choice was the legendary Mark III SMLE ('Smellie'), a .303 calibre, ten-round bolt action, box-fed rifle which served in both world wars and offered a grenade-launching variant.[6] In terms of sub-machine guns, the .45 calibre 1928 model Thompson, a variant on the gangster's favoured 'tommy-gun', was preferred to the mass-produced home grown 9 mm Sten. This American weapon could produce rapid hard hitting, 'man-stopper' rounds at close quarters.

For sustained automatic fire, the venerable .303 Lewis was widely carried, able to be fired from or off vehicles as circumstances dictated. This water-cooled weapon had been the standard British light machine gun from the second half of the Great War. Now obsolete and superseded by the air-cooled Bren, Lewis guns were, in 1940, more readily available in the Middle East. Much of the army's small arms and support weapons had been left in the shambles of Dunkirk. Indirect fire support could be provided by the handy 2-inch mortar.

Patrol trucks bristled with weapons. Whatever was needed for the fight had to be with the troopers as they took an enemy on. There would be no supporting fire from aircraft, armour or artillery. For desert raiders, being able to dispose massive firepower in an instant conferred an immediate and enormous advantage, likely to be decisive. Convoys of Axis vehicles could very quickly be deterred from resistance by a few well-directed non-lethal bursts. Those who were made of sterner stuff would receive the full deluge. This wasn't buccaneering; it was a micro-version of industrial warfare. In such sharp sudden encounters, he who shot first with accuracy and weight of fire would decimate his opponents and shred their vehicles.

The standard British medium machine-gun, the redoubtable Vickers in .303 calibre were mounted alongside the heavier .5 calibre weapon. Browning equivalents were also popular. A variant of the conventional .303 was the gas-operated Vickers K. These were essentially intended for use on aircraft, and when mounted in pairs could deliver a tremendous volume of sustained fire. Another survivor, carried in the early days, was the .55 calibre Boys anti-tank rifle, whose effectiveness was pithily summed up by Lloyd Owen: *a more useless military weapon has never been invented, either before or since.*[7]

For a weightier punch and taking on armoured vehicles, each patrol carried a truck-mounted 37 mm anti-tank Bofors[8] which could penetrate light armour and effectively shoot-up desert forts. Whenever possible, LRDG patrols would trade these in for captured Italian 20 mm dual-purpose Breda cannon.[9]

Communications and Navigation

Given the vast distances traversed by patrols, being away from any kind of base for weeks on end, good, reliable communications were an absolute essential. The raiders had to be able to transmit the intelligence they'd gathered and receive orders in return. British wartime radios have not enjoyed a good press, but the No. 11 set more than proved itself under desert conditions.[10] Though not initially intended to reach out over long distances, the No. 11 managed to operate at an extreme range of 1,400 miles. Sky-wave signalling[11] and key operating were used exclusively.

Security was obviously paramount. The Axis were good listeners and a single slip could spell disaster. Frequencies and call signs were varied twice daily. *All signal instructions were carried encoded; international commercial procedure was used and the known call signs of local commercial stations were employed wherever possible; and the controls of the set were always set to zero after every transmission was completed, thus avoiding the risk of compromise if the set were captured.*[12]

The sets were powered by two 6-volt batteries, one from the vehicle carrying the set and another with the radio itself, both charged by the truck generator. For distances up to 500 miles a straightforward six-foot rod aerial would do the job, but for transmission beyond that distance a Windom aerial[13] was needed. As a rule each patrol had three times slots in a day when they could radio in – morning, noon and evening. Due to the nature of the kit and the need to erect an aerial, transmission couldn't be managed on the move. It took time too to encipher and/or decipher the messages. As a result the midday slot was usually avoided.

Of course, the equipment was only as good as the operator, and veterans like Lloyd Owen have nothing but praise for the wireless operators who served with them. These men were the patrol's lifeline, the umbilical which linked them to a distant HQ. The radio-man carried a heavy burden, his hours were long and he needed technical skills to keep his set operational. The nearest repair shop was probably a thousand miles away.

Alongside the W/O, the patrol navigator was a key player. For the Axis, the desert was generally a place of terror, a surreal and threatening wilderness of seemingly infinite size. Operations were mainly confined to the coastal strip and, in the case of the Italians, isolated outposts at strategically vital locations. Many have likened the Western desert to an ocean. If so, then it was the British who were the sailors and LRDG the real pathfinders. Maps were either primitive or non-existent. The exploration undertaken by Bagnold and Clayton was, naturally, invaluable, not just because of the topography charted but on account of the specialist kit that they created. This wasn't confined to the simple genius of the condenser; Bagnold had also developed the sun-compass.

> Without going into details of exactly how the sun-compass worked, the principle can be briefly described as keeping the shadow from the sun of a vertical needle (which projected from the centre of a small circular table graduated into 360 degrees) on to the appropriate reading in order to maintain the direction required. If one was forced off this bearing it was still possible to read the direction in which the truck was then travelling. There were problems connected with the sun's azimuth at various times of day and seasons of the year, but these too were overcome by the inventive genius of Bagnold.[14]

On a day-to-day basis the patrol commander, at break of day, would decide upon the direction of travel and would set his compass accordingly. The navigator, riding in the second truck behind the C/O, would adopt the same setting. The compass itself was fixed between driver and front passenger so the former could steer to match his bearing. At the same time the navigator would take a speedometer reading and, should there be any deviation from the right bearing, he'd note the speedometer reading and the fresh bearing. As a basic form of dead-reckoning, this proved very robust, especially if augmented by the use of a theodolite to take an astrofix at night. The only difficulty here was getting hold of the instrument itself, which was in very short supply with Middle East Command.

Navigators needed skill and stamina, and like the W/O, theirs was not a nine to five job. When qualified as a Land Navigator, the War Office test of approval, the trooper was entitled to an extra shilling a day in pay. Needless to add, retail opportunities were not abundant during LRDG patrols.

Into the Air

Both Bagnold and Guy Prendergast had recognized the immense value of aircraft in desert exploration. The Italians had established their Auto-Saharan units (see Appendix 6), whose unit commanders were all trained pilots and actually had aircraft as an essential part of their overall establishment.

Guy Prendergast and a Kiwi NCO, Trevor Barker, were both qualified, as long as they had planes available to bridge the enormous gaps between HQ and forward patrols. Kufra to Siwa was a distance of some four hundred miles. Essential supplies, spare parts, radio gear, ammunition and mail could all be delivered by air.

Resourceful and determined as ever, Bagnold worked his contacts in Cairo to procure two small biplanes from local businessmen. The planes were essentially commercially produced WACO's (as in 'Weaver Aircraft Company of Ohio'). These aircraft were acquired from private, wealthy individuals and soon found themselves working in a more rugged environment. The better known of the two planes was a ZGC-7 (RAF Serial No.AX695). The other was a YKC (RAF Serial No. AX697). The main difference between them was the capacity of the motor. The ZGC-7 used a 285 hp engine while the YKC employed a less powerful 225 hp. The YKC dated from 1934, the ZGC-7 from 1937.[15]

Though the Desert Air Force had been unwilling to provide aircraft from its admittedly exceedingly slender resources, they took a very dim few of LRDG setting up in competition. Prendergast and Barker both flew and maintained the planes, assisted by a brace of trained-up navigators. Each of the aircraft could carry two, maybe three men and could be used to evacuate those seriously wounded. Flying both in tandem was something of a feat in itself as they had different cruising speeds, one at 115 mph, the other faster at 140 mph.

The WACO was a tough little plane with a typical short take off and landing distance, common to biplanes, ideally suited to the rigours of LRDG. They also bore a slight resemblance to the Fiat CR42 Falco (Falcon), one of the last Italian Fighter biplanes which may have provided a handy if unintentional element of disguise. (In any event the RAF had somewhat spitefully refused permission to paint roundels!)

Training

Being trained as a soldier and being trained as LRDG were two separate phases. Those who joined were already in khaki, they were simply not experienced in the Spartan rigours and tricky technicalities of surviving in and moving over the limitless, lunar wastes of the desert. Much of the training they did receive was very much 'on the job'. The unique proposition of LRDG was that the unit had a cadre of highly experienced desert explorers – Bagnold, Clayton, Lloyd Owen and Kennedy Shaw, who were also very good, if demanding teachers. They had to be. The cult of detail was never more valid than in an environment as harsh and remote, where you lived on what you could carry and how well you could navigate.

Survival skills, even as basic as correct water conservation, were building blocks of the curriculum. Navigation was the holy grail of desert travel, as discussed above. You had, like Hawkeye, to be able to read the spoor of Axis vehicle tracks, to recognise friendly and enemy, aircraft, tanks, armoured vehicles and transport. You had to know how to use and service the arsenal you carried on patrol. In a contact, firepower was the code for survival. If a gun jammed, as Clayton's did at the critical moment during the assault on Murzuk, fatal consequences could rapidly follow.

Patrols were not just small bodies of soldiers, they were teams of specialists. To be a good driver you not only had to learn how to move over soft and hard desert, to climb steep-sided wadis and tackle the forbidding expanses of sand sea, but you had to be your own mechanic and fitter. Every task required care, energy and judgement. There was no one to pass the buck to and nowhere to hide.

Once Group HQ was set up, training became more structured; detailed sets of training procedures were codified. Inevitably, not all would make the grade, 'returned to unit' or 'RTU'd' was code for not good enough. There was never a shortage of volunteers. Thousands of fit young men were stuck in tedious routines, in very out of the way places, mired in 'bull' and much 'mucked-about'. Being in the LRDG was a badge of elitism, and a chance for adventure with a hint of glamour. As one officer tersely observed when speaking of training, *there was only one way to learn, and that was to get on with the job.*[16]

Logistics

LRDG could only function with adequate supplies. Based in far-flung oases, hundreds of miles from the nearest depot, logistics were a constant headache. Unsung was the Supply and Transport Section. Their vehicles were heavy, lumbering trucks, wildebeests of the desert war, never as dashing as the sleek panthers of 30-cwts' or the leopard jeeps, but without which the predators would stall for lack of fuel. As patrols dashed out on daring missions, the convoys of 3-tonners and a scattering of heavier Macks would grind along the supply routes on their own regular and unsung epics.

Philip Arnold commanded the section for much of the desert war. He'd been a vehicle and transport manager in Civvy Street. *Half French, half-English, naturally perfect in both tongues and a good Arabic speaker too, there was little he did not know about getting trucks across the Middle*

Eastern deserts.[17] A born adventurer, he'd seen service with the Foreign Legion and had fought in Somaliland before joining LRDG in summer 1942. He was finally killed by a land mine just outside Hon.

Lieutenant 'Shorty' Barrett, a forty-year-old Kiwi and a lawyer in peacetime, was the LRDG Quartermaster. He was a founder member, returned to his unit for the abortive Greek expedition, then returned to LRDG in autumn 1941. Although troopers generally ate well, the job of getting rations in was Herculean. In the regulars, even up in the front line, the QM drew rations for his unit on a daily basis, collected from the Detail Issue Depot ("DID"). Shorty had a rather longer travel and had to plan ahead for a period of weeks, if not months. Whichever base LRDG was operating from would be a week at least away from any sizeable depot, and then patrols would be ranging over great distances beyond. Cairo would be at least a thousand miles off.

Shorty would be beset by demands way beyond the remit of the regular QM – a month's food and rations for two patrols; fuel for a thousand miles or more. A long-ranging patrol would require a series of dumps set up, needed thousands of gallons of fuel, hundreds of water. The list of stores was endless, food, fuel and ammunition for the whole diverse arsenal of weapons patrols might be packing, navigational instruments, clothing, tents and all manner of incidental gear.[18]

Medical treatment was always going to present problems. In addition to the normal fear of wounds from enemy action, LRDG troopers faced the threats of routine injuries, desert sores and a host of medical conditions, plus the unwelcome and hostile intent of local fauna. Just because LRDG took the scorpion as its cap badge didn't impress the real thing in the slightest. All these ills were compounded as ever by distance. Travelling over rock-strewn desert would be purgatory for an injured man, exposed to relentless heat and numbing cold in turn.

LRDG had its own MO, usually based at HQ, and a medical orderly/paramedic for each patrol. Kufra could boast a semi-decent hospital; most other places couldn't. The paramedics did wonders and became, like all LRDG masters of improvisation – *the use of a grease gun for an enema might find a place in the pages of the 'Lancet'.*[19] Dick Lawson, the MO in North Africa, was a remarkable character; his loss on Leros was a serious blow.

Notes

1 http://www.iwm.org.uk/collections/item/object/70000266 – retrieved 20th January 2015.
2 http://lrdg.hegewisch.net/lrdgvehicles.hmtl – retrieved 20th January 2015.
3 http://lrdg.hegewisch.net/lrdgvehicles.hmtl – retrieved 20th January 2015.
4 http://lrdg.hegewisch.net/lrdgvehicles.hmtl – retrieved 20th January 2015.
5 Quoted in Lloyd Owen, p. 22.
6 Grenades were the No. 36 Mills bomb, created by the inventor of that name, a native of Sunderland and introduced in 1915. The no. 36 was adopted in 1932.
7 Lloyd Owen, p. 18.
8 A Swedish pre-war design, the gun was used extensively in the early stages of the war and manufactured under licence in a number of European countries.
9 The Cannone-Mitragliera da 20/65 Modello 35 (Breda), also known as Breda Model 35, was a 20 mm anti-aircraft gun manufactured by the Società Italiana Ernesto Breda, designed in 1932 and adopted by the Italian armed forces in 1935.
10 The No. 11 Set comprised a radio transceiver featuring a single tuning unit and was designed in 1938 to replace the 1933 No. 1 Wireless Set. Originally intended to be used in tanks for short to medium range communications, it nonetheless served LRDG well.
11 Sky-wave refers *to the propagation of radio waves reflected or refracted back toward Earth from the ionosphere, an electrically charged layer of the upper atmosphere. Since it is not limited by the curvature of the Earth, sky-wave propagation can be used to communicate beyond the horizon, at intercontinental distances.* http://en.wikipedia.org/wiki/Skywave, retrieved 22nd January 2014.
12 Lloyd Owen, p. 20.
13 Technically this refers to an off-centre-fed Di-pole antenna fed by symmetrical open ladder line and co-axial cable via a balun – http://hamwaves.com/cl-ocfd/history.html, retrieved 22nd January, 2014.
14 Lloyd Owen, p. 19.
15 http://lrdg.hegewisch.net/lrdgvehicles.hmtl – retrieved 20th January 2015.
16 Quoted in Moreman T., & R. Ruggeri: *Long Range Desert Group Patrolman* (Osprey 'Warrior' Series no. 148), p. 17.
17 Kennedy Shaw, p. 138.
18 Ibid., p. 140.
19 Ibid., p. 214.

APPENDIX 2
LRDG Commanders and Patrol Designations*

LRP Commander

June 1940 – November 1940: Lt. Col. Ralph Bagnold

LRDG Commanders

November 1940 – August 1941: Lt. Col. Ralph Bagnold
August 1941 – October 1942: Lt. Col. Guy Prendergast
October 1943 – November 1943: Lt. Col. Jake Easonsmith
November 1943 – July 1945: Lt. Col. David Lloyd Owen

Patrol Designations

In the beginning R, T and W Patrols, all comprised of New Zealanders, operated as the LRP. With the formation of LRDG towards the end of 1940, the following patrols were operating through the war in the Desert and in subsequent campaigns:

G1 & G2 Patrols – Guards
Y1 & Y2 Patrols – Yeomanry
R1 & R2; T1 & T2 Patrols – New Zealand
S1 & S2 Patrols – Rhodesians

*Based on information contained in Morgan's *Sting of the Scorpion,* Appendix I.

M1 & M2 Patrols – British and Commonwealth
X Patrol – Italian Campaign

Heavy Section – supply and sustenance (mainly 3-tonners, delivering to desert drops and the principal oases)

APPENDIX 3
Patrol Commanders*

LRP Patrols

R (New Zealand) – Captain D.G. Steele
T (New Zealand) – Captain P.A. Clayton, Captain L.B. Ballantyne
W (New Zealand) – Captain E.C. Mitford

LRDG

G1 (Guards) – Captains M.D.D Crichton Stuart, A.M. Hay & J.A.L. Timpson
G2 (Guards) – Captain J.A.L. Timpson, Lieutenants the Honourable R.B. Gurdon, K.H. Sweeting & B. Bruce
R1 (New Zealand – Captains J.R. Easonsmith, A.I. Guild & L.H. Browne, Lieutenant K.F. McLauchlan
R2 (New Zealand) – Lieutenants C.H. Croucher & J.R. Talbot, Captain K.H. Lazarus
S1 (Rhodesian) – Captains C.A. Holliman, J.R. Olivey & K.H. Lazarus
S2 (Rhodesian) – Captain J.R. Olivey, Lieutenant J. Henry
T1 (New Zealand) – Captains L.B. Ballantyne, N.P. Wilder & Lieutenant J. Crisp
T2 (New Zealand) – Captains C.S Morris, N.P. Wilder, R.A. Tinker & Lieutenant R.A. Crammond

*Based on Morgan, Appendix IV.

Y1 (Yeomanry & others) – Captains P.J.D. McCraith, F.C. Simms, D. Lloyd Owen
Y2 (Yeomanry & others) – Captains D. Lloyd Owen, A.D.N. Hunter & E.F. Spicer

Indian Long Range Squadron

Indian 1 – Lieutenant J.E. Cantlay
Indian 2 – Captain T.J.D. Birdwood
Indian 2 – Captain A.B. Rand
Indian 4 – Lieutenant G.W. Nangle

APPENDIX 4
Daily LRDG Ration Scale*

Bacon, tinned – 9 ½ ounces
Bread – 16 ounces
Biscuits – 12 ounces
Cheese – 1 ½ ounces
Chocolate – 2 ounces
Curry powder – 1/8th ounces
Fruit, dried – 4/7th ounces
Fruit, tinned – 4 ounces
Herrings – 1 ¼ ounces
Jam, marmalade or golden syrup – 1 ½ ounces
Lime juice – 1/16th bottle
Margarine – 1 ½ ounces
Meat, preserved – 6 ounces
Pickles – 1 ounce
Chutney – ¼ ounces
Meat loaf or ham and tongue – 1 ¼ ounces
Meat and vegetable ration – 2 ounces
Milk, tinned – 2 ounces
Mustard – 1/100th ounce
Oatmeal or flour – 2 ounces
Onions – 2 ounces

---

*Based on information contained in Appendix 5 of W.B. Kennedy-Shaw's *Long Range Desert Group*.

Pepper – 1/100th ounce
Salt – ¾ ounce
Salmon, tinned – 1 ounce
Sardines – 1 ounce
Sausages – 1 ounce
Sugar – 3 ½ ounces
Tea – ¾ ounce
Vegetables, tinned – 4 ounces
Ascorbic tablets – 1 tablet
Marmite – 3/28th ounce
Rum – 1 ounce; as a rule the issue of a rum ration depended on the orders of a divisional commander, thus a Major-General. Obviously, in the course of LRDG missions there was a dearth of such high-ranking officers so it was normally on the patrol commander's say-so.
Tobacco or cigarettes – 2 ounces (per week)
Matches – 2 boxes (per week)
Total daily weight without containers – 4 pounds, 2 ounces
And with containers – 5 pounds

APPENDIX 5
LRDG Roll of Honour*

P.L. Arnold; L.C. Ashby; F.R. Beech; J. Botha; J.T. Bowler; W.H. Burton; D. Davison; E.J. Dobson; J.R. Easonsmith; J. Easton; S. Federman; S. Fleming; K. Foley; M. Gravil; R.B. Gurdon; J. Henderson; J. Henry; C.D. Hewson; A. Hopton; B. Jordan; H.L. Mallet; G. Matthews; L.A. McIver; L. Oelofse; N. O'Malley; A.J. Penhall; A. Redfern; G. Rezin; C. Richardson; R. Riggs; L. Roderick; R. Savage; D. Dinger; K. Smith; A. Tighe; H. Todman; J. Vanrensberg; P. Wheeldon; G.F. Yates & R. Young.

*Based on Morgan, Appendix V.

APPENDIX 6
A View from the Other Side – Axis Units

The Italians

Whilst it is fair to say that neither Italy nor Germany was ever able to field a unit comparable to the LRDG, they were not completely blind to the potential of desert raiders. And the Italians did have some form, having in the twenties created five combat units, the *Compagnie Sahariane.* In 1931, these units succeeded in taking Kufra Oasis. Seven years later Marshal Balbo moulded the separate columns into a single formation with substantial firepower, creating probably the most effective unit from among the Libyan colonial forces.[1]

O'Connor's tremendous successes following the start of Operation *Compass* meant that the newly designated *Comando de Sahara Libico* was denuded of many of its soldiers and much kit. The seemingly unstoppable advance of Western Desert Force and the fall of Kufra spurred a rapid reorganisation. In part, this was a largely defensive reflex, though in March 1941 General Dal Pozzo set up five new mobile columns to give the defence some teeth. This was still not an LRDG-type unit, beset as it was by supply problems and the questionable reliability of the predominantly Libyan troops. It remained equivalent to a weak brigade in strength with artillery, 20 mm guns and vehicles.[2]

Impressed by the performance of both LRDG and the Free French, General Dal Pozzo set up a new mobile column in November 1941.

He rightly deduced that mobility was the key. With Free French forces ranging, seemingly unchecked, throughout the Fezzan region, the Italian response was overhauled yet again, shedding men but adding weight of fire. Axis successes, coming fast in the wake of Crusader's stuttering climax, emboldened the Italians besides; there were now many captured British vehicles available to boost mobility.[3] From spring 1942, Dal Pozzo ushered in a more proactive raiding strategy in the area between Fort Lamy and Khartoum, beefed up with more aggressive patrolling between garrison outposts.[4]

The first real patrol unit, intended to match LRDG, was the superbly named *Pattuglia Vigilanza Terrestre Avanzata* (Advanced Land Surveillance Patrol) which came into being in late September. Three more patrols followed before the middle of the next month. Navigational training facilities were also established. These new and elite units were able to take the fight to LRDG, the first clash flaring on 17th November with another a week later. In both skirmishes the Italians acquitted themselves admirably.[5]

By this juncture, however, the writing for Il Duce's African Empire was indelibly on the wall, and units were progressively withdrawn and reorganised to assist in the defence of Tunisia. It must be one of the tantalising 'what if's' of the Desert War that had Dal Pozzo been in local command earlier, operations by both the LRDG and Free French might have turned out to be considerably more difficult and costly.

The Germans

Count Lazlo Almasy did not just inspire Michael Ondaatje's *The English Patient* but perhaps also *The Key to Rebecca* by Ken Follett. His real-life equivalent was even more colourful than fictional depictions. In the Great War he served as a Hussar, and latterly a fighter pilot. After the war he gained fame as a racing car driver, and this included taking part in a drive from Alexandria to Khartoum. He joined Robert Clayton-East in the search for Zerzura (the fabled 'White City'). Although the "Englishman" did die, it was due to natural causes rather than a plane crash. His wife Dorothy was killed when her plane came down in 1939. Romantic entanglements appear entirely fictional, as Almasy may have been homosexual.

When war broke out the Count, by now an experienced desert explorer, was obliged to leave Egypt as British Intelligence believed, probably wrongly, that he was spying for the Italians. Back in Budapest, he was certainly recruited by German military intelligence, the Abwehr. He served in a special commando unit, *Sonderkommando Dora,* established under the command of Major Niklaus Ritter, which had been formed to carry out Admiral Canaris' plan to infiltrate agents into Egypt and stir up national/anti-British sentiment. Ritter was not overly impressed by Almasy's plan to use vehicles to cross the desert, preferring air drops. Operation *Condor* nonetheless was a failure and the major was injured when one of the aircraft crash-landed.

Almasy now assumed command and instigated Operation *Salam* – a daring plan to use mainly vehicles captured from the British. A pair of *Abwehr* agents, Johannes Eppler and radio operator Hans-Gerd Sandstede, were successfully infiltrated into Asyut in Egypt after the group penetrated through the Gilf Kebir and Kharga Oasis. This was a daring and innovative raid, the nearest mirror to LRDG tactics the Axis achieved.

Though using British trucks, Almasy's men retained their German uniforms. Although the mission succeeded in its immediate objectives, the wider plan failed abysmally. Bletchley Park had already cracked the *Abwehr* hand cipher that the agents were using for wireless transmissions.[6] Operation Condor, the spy mission, proved completely abortive, and both Axis agents were rounded up six weeks after they'd reached Cairo. Blame for the fiasco could hardly be laid at Almasy's door; his tactics had been vindicated but the *Abwehr* and Canaris had lost their appetite for desert adventures. Almasy was soon back in Budapest and in search of employment.

The expression 'missed opportunity' which could be applied to Almasy's raid might equally be said to describe the whole German approach to Special Forces in the Desert theatre. Even when formed, units had a habit of being subsumed into the main order of battle, and there was generally a dearth of suitable vehicles apart from the handy *Kubelwagen.*[7] Hauptman von Homeyer, an officer with previous desert exploration experience, managed to interest OKH in an idea for a small raiding patrol, and although he was able to set his unit up, they disappear from view.[8] Other, larger units such as *Sondverband* (Special Formation) *288* and the *Tropen* (Tropical) *Kompanie* ended up fighting as conventional forces.[9]

Notes

1 Molinari, A., *Desert Raiders: Axis and Allied Special Forces 1940–43* (Osprey 'Battle Orders' no. 23), pp. 26–37.
2 Ibid.
3 Ibid.
4 Ibid.
5 Ibid.
6 An officer named Jean Alington at Bletchley had detected the signal trail. A warning sent to HQ ME in Cairo arrived too late (Rommel was attacking at this point and Afrikakorps messages had a higher priority in deciphering and analysis), and Almasy was able to return to his jumping off point at Gialo without interception. See: http://en.wikipedia.org/wiki/L%C3%A1szl%C3%B3_Alm%C3%A1sy, retrieved 27th January 2015.
7 The Volkswagen *Kubelwagen* was a light military variant of the famous Beetle, designed by Ferdinand Porsche. The name means 'bucket seat car' – the initial vehicles had no doors, and the seat design was intended to prevent occupants from falling out! The cars, though not four-wheel drive, were light, robust and durable.
8 Molinari, p. 45.
9 Ibid, pp. 45–46.

APPENDIX 7
Ultra in the Desert War

By mid-1942, the LRDG/SAS had developed into a major thorn in the enemy's side, striking at seemingly safe targets way behind the lines, destroying aircraft and fuel which Rommel could ill afford to lose. Alongside Special Forces, intelligence-gathering operations proliferated. The arrival of Rommel in the North African Theatre coincided with the establishment of a Special Signals Link to Wavell and Middle East Command in Cairo.

Hut 3 at Bletchley could now transmit reports directly to the GOC. Ultra intelligence was not able to identify Rommel's immediate counter-offensive, but Hut 6 had broken the *Luftwaffe* key, now designated 'Light Blue.' Early decrypts revealed the concern felt by OKH at Rommel's maverick strategy and indicated the extent of his supply problems. Though the intercepts were a major tactical gain in principle, the process was new and subject to delay to the extent that they rarely arrived in time to influence the events in the field during a highly mobile campaign.[1] Equally, Light Blue was able to provide some details of Rommel's seaborne supplies, but again in insufficient detail and with inadequate speed to permit a suitable response from either the RN or RAF.

Then, in July 1941 came a major breakthrough – an Italian navy cipher, 'C38m', was also broken and the flood of detail this provided greatly amplified that gleaned from Light Blue. Information was now passed not just to Cairo but to the RN at Alexandria and the RAF on Malta. Every care, as ever, had to be taken to ensure the integrity of Ultra was preserved:

> Ultra was very important in cutting Rommel's supplies. He was fighting with one hand behind his back because we were getting information about all the convoys from Italy. The RAF were not allowed to attack them unless they sent out reconnaissance, and if there was fog of course they couldn't attack them because it would have jeopardised the security of Ultra, but in fact most of them were attacked.[2]

Ultra thus contributed significantly to Rommel's supply problem. On land a number of army keys were also broken; these were designated by names of birds. Thus it was 'Chaffinch' which provided Auchinleck with detailed information on DAK supply shortages and weight of materiel, including tanks. Since mid-1941 a Special Signals Unit (latterly Special Liaison Unit) had been deployed in theatre.

The unit had to ensure information was disseminated only amongst those properly 'in the know' and that, vitally, identifiable secondary intelligence was always available to mask the true source. Experience during the Crusader offensive indicated that the best use of Ultra was to provide detail of the enemy's strength and pre-battle dispositions. The material could not be decrypted fast enough nor sent on to cope with a fast-changing tactical situation. At the front, information could be relayed far more quickly by the Royal Signals mobile Y-Special Wireless Sections and battalion intelligence officers, one of whom, Bill Williams, recalled:

> Despite the amazing speed with which we received Ultra, it was of course usually out of date. This did not mean we were not glad of its arrival for at best it showed that we were wrong, usually it enabled us to tidy up loose ends, and at least we tumbled into bed with a smug confirmation. In a planning period between battles its value was more obvious and one had the opportunity to study it in relation to context so much better than during a fast moving battle such as desert warfare produced.[3]

Wireless in the vastness of the desert was the only effective mode of communication, but wireless messages are always subject to intercept. The Germans had their own *Y Dienst* and the formidable Captain Seebohm, whose unit proved highly successful. The extent of Seebohm's effectiveness was only realised after his unit had been overrun during the attack by 26th Australian Brigade at Te-el-Eisa in July 1942. The captain was a casualty and the raiders discovered how extensive the slackness of Allied procedures actually was. As a consequence the drills were significantly tightened. If the Axis effort was thereby dented, Rommel still had a significant source from the US diplomatic codes which had been broken and which regularly included data on Allied plans and dispositions, the 'Black Code'.

Reverses following on from the apparent success of Crusader were exacerbated by *a serious misreading of a decrypt from the Italian C38m cipher*. Hut 3 could not really assist the British in mitigating the defeat at Gazala or, perhaps worse, the surrender of Tobruk. This was one which Churchill felt most keenly: *...a bitter moment. Defeat is one thing; disgrace is another.*

Until this time it had taken Bletchley about a week to crack Chaffinch but, from the end of May, the ace code-breakers were now able to cut this to a day. Other key codes, Phoenix' and 'Thrush', were also broken. Similar inroads were made against the *Luftwaffe*. 'Primrose', that employed by the supply formation, and 'Scorpion', the ground/air link, were both broken. Scorpion was a literal Godsend. As close and constant touch with units in the field was necessary for supply, German signallers unwittingly provided a blueprint for any unfolding battle.

On the ground, Eighth Army was increasing the total of mobile Y formations whilst the Intelligence Corps and RAF code-breakers were getting fully into their stride.[4] None of these developments could combine to save the 'Auk' but Montgomery was the beneficiary of high level traffic between Rommel and Hitler, sent via Kesselring, as the latter was *Luftwaffe*. The Red cipher, long mastered by Bletchley, was employed. Monty had already predicted the likely genesis of the Alam Halfa battle, but the intercepts clearly underscored his analysis.

By now the array of air force, navy and army codes penetrated by Bletchley was providing a regular assessment of supply, of available AFV's and the dialogue of senior officers. The relationship between Rommel and Kesselring was evidently strained. Even the most cynical of old sweats had cause to be impressed: *...he* [Montgomery] *told them* *with remarkable assurance how the enemy was going to be defeated. The enemy attack was delayed and the usual jokes were made about the 'crystal-gazers'. A day or two later everything happened according to plan.*[5] Ultra was dispelling the fog of war.

Notes

1 Smith, M., *Station X – The Code Breakers of Bletchley Park* (London, 1998) pp. 97–98.
2 Jim Rose, one of Hut 3 Bletchley Park's air advisers, quoted in Smith, p. 99.
3 Ibid., p. 100.
4 Ibid., p. 102.
5 Bill Williams quoted in Smith, p. 103.

Bibliography

Published Sources

Adair, R., *British Eighth Army, North Africa 1940–1943* (London, 1974)

Agar-Hamilton, J.A.I. & L.C.F. Turner, *Crisis in the Desert May–July 1942* (Oxford, 1952)

Alexander, Field Marshal the Earl, *The Alexander Memoirs 1940–1945* (London, 1962)

Arthur, M., *Forgotten Voices of the Second World War* (London, 2004)

Bagnold, R., *Libyan Sands* (London) 1935

———, 'Early Days of the Long Range Desert Group' in *the Geographical Journal,* Vol. 105 (Jan–Feb 1945 pp. 30–42

———, *Sand, Wind & War: Memoirs of a Desert Explorer* (University of Arizona Press, Tucson, 1990)

Bailey, J.B.A., *Field Artillery and Firepower* (London, 1989)

Barnett, C., *The Desert Generals* (London, 1960)

———, *Engage the Enemy More Closely: The Royal Navy in the Second World War* (London, 1991)

Barr, N., *Pendulum of War, the Three Battles of El Alamein* (London, 2004)

Beale, P., *Death by Design, British Tank Development in the Second World War* (Stroud, 1998)

Bennet, R., *Ultra and Mediterranean Strategy 1941–1945* (London, 1989)

Bidwell, S., and D. Graham, *Firepower, British Army Weapons and Theories of War 1904–1945* (London, 1982)

Bierman, J. and C. Smith, *Alamein, War Without Hate* (London, 2002)

Bingham, J., K. Wordsworth & W. Haupt, *North African Campaign 1940–1943* (London, 1969)

Bishop, C. & I. Drury, *Combat Guns* (London, 1987)

Braddock, D.W., *The Campaigns in Egypt and Libya* (Aldershot, 1964)

Bradford, E., *Malta 1940–1943* (London, 1985)

British Troops Egypt, *Official Handbook for British Troops in Egypt, Cyprus, Palestine and the Sudan* (BTE, 1936)

Bruce, C.J., *War on the Ground 1939–1945* (London, 1995)

Bryant, Sir Arthur, *The Turn of the Tide* Vols I and II (London, 1957–1959)

Carver, M., *El Alamein* (London, 1962)

———, *Tobruk* (London, 1964)

———, *Dilemmas of the Desert War* (London, 1986)

———, *The Apostles of Mobility: The Theory and Practice of Armoured Warfare* (London, 1979)

Chalfont, A.J., *Montgomery of Alamein* (London, 1976)

Churchill, W., *The Second World War* (London, 1951)

Clark, A., *The Fall of Crete* (London, 1962)

Clayton, P., *Desert Explorer: A Biography of Colonel P.A. Clayton* (Zerzura Press, 1998)

Connell, J., *Auchinleck: A Biography of Field-Marshall Sir Claude Auchinleck* (London, 1959)

Cooper, M., *The German Army 1933–1945* (London, 1978)

Cowles, V., *The Phantom Major: The Story of David Stirling and the SAS Regiment* (London, 1958)

Crawford, R.J., *I Was an Eighth Army Soldier* (London, 1944)

Crichton-Stuart, M., *G Patrol* (London, 1958)

Crimp, R.L., *The Diary of a Desert Rat* (London, 1971)

Crisp, R., *Brazen Chariots: An Account of Tank Warfare in the Western Desert, November–December 1941* (London, 1959)

Cruickshank, C., *Deception in World War Two* (Oxford, 1979)

Defence Operational Analysis Centre, *The Combat Degradation and Effectiveness of Anti-Tanks Weapons – Interim Analysis,* Vols. I & II, Study 670

———, *The Effectiveness of Small Arms Fire in Defence* Study no. M 83108

———, *Historical Analysis of Anti-Tank Battles – the Battle of Snipe*, Study N 670/201

De Guingand, Major-General Sir F., *Operation Victory* (London, 1963)

Delaney, J., *Fighting the Desert Fox* (London, 1998)

Die Oase – Journal of the Afrika Corps Veterans Association

Douglas, K., *Alamein to Zem Zem* (Oxford, 1979)

Eighth Army Weekly

Ellis, J., *Brute Force: Allied Strategy and Tactics in the Second World War* (London, 1980)

———, *The Sharp End of War: The Fighting Man in World War Two* (London, 1980)

Farran, R., *Winged Dagger* (London, 1948)

Fergusson, Sir Bernard, *Wavell, Portrait of a Soldier* (London, 1961)

Fletcher, D., *The Great Tank Scandal: British Armour in the Second World War,* Part 1 (HMSO, 1989)

Ford, K., *El Alamein* (Oxford, 2001)

Forty, G., *The Royal Tank Regiment – A Pictorial History* (Tunbridge Wells, 1989)

———, *World War Two Tanks* (London, 1995)

———, *The Armies of Rommel* (London, 1997)

———, *British Army Handbook 1939–1945* (Stroud, 1998)

Fraser, D., *Alanbrooke* (London, 1982)

———, *And We Shall Shock Them: The British Army in the Second World War* (London, 1983)

———, *Knights Cross: A Life of Field Marshal Erwin Rommel* (London, 1993)
Garret, D., *The Campaign in Greece and Crete* (HMSO, 1942)
Gordon, J.W., *The Other Desert War: British Special Forces in North Africa 1940–1943* (New York, 1987)
Greacen, L., *Chink: A Biography* (London, 1989)
Greenwood, A., *Field Marshal Auchinleck* (London, 1990)
Griffiths, P., 'British Armoured Warfare in the Western Desert 1940–1945' in J.P. Harris and F.H. Toase (eds), *Armoured Warfare* (London, 1990)
Hamilton, N., *Monty: The Making of a General 1887–1942* (London, 1982)
———, *The Full Monty: Montgomery of Alamein 1887–1942* (London, 2001)
———, *Master of the Battlefield 1942–1944* (London, 1983)
Harrison, F., *Tobruk: The Great Siege Reassessed* (London, 1996)
Harrison-Place, T., *Military Training in the British Army, 1940–1944: From Dunkirk to D-Day* (London, 2000)
Hinsley, F.H., *British Intelligence in the Second World War* (abridged ed. London, 1993)
Humble, R., *Crusader: Eighth Army's Forgotten Victory November 1941 to January 1942* (London, 1987)
Hogg, I.V. & J. Weeks, *The Illustrated Encyclopedia of Military Vehicles* (London, 1980)
Horrocks. Lieutenant-General, Sir B., *A Full Life* (London, 1960)
Irving, D., *The Trail of the Fox* (London, 1977)
James, M., *Born of the Desert–SAS in Libya* (London, 1945)
Jenner, R., D. List, P. Sarson & M. Badrocke, *The Long Range Desert Group 1940–1945* (Oxford, 1999)
Johnson, M. and P. Stanley, *Alamein: The Australian Story* (Oxford, 2002)
Joslen, Lieutenant-Colonel H.F., *Orders of Battle: Second World War* (HMSO 1960)
Kay, R.L., *Long Range Desert Group in the Mediterranean* (Wellington, 1949)
Kennedy-Shaw, W.B., *Long Range Desert Group* (Greenhill Press, London, 1945)
Kippenburger, Major-General Sir H., *Infantry Brigadier* (Oxford, 1949)
Landsborough, G., *Tobruk Commando* (London, 1956
Latimer, J., *Alamein* (London, 2002)
———, *Deception in War* (London, 2001)
Lewin, R., *Rommel as Military Commander* (London, 1968)
———, *Montgomery as Military Commander* (London, 1971)
———, *The Life and Death of the Afrika Korps* (London, 1977)
Lewis, P.J., & I.R. English, *Into Battle with the Durhams: 8 DLI in World War II* (London, 1990)
Liddell Hart, Sir B.H., *The Tanks: The History of the Royal Tank Regiment and its Predecessors, Heavy Branch Machine Gun Corps, Tank Corps and Royal Tank Corps, 1914–1945,* 2 vols. (London, 1959)
Lloyd Owen, Major-General D., *The Long Range Desert Group–Providence Their Guide* (Pen & Sword, Barnsley, 2000)
———, *The Desert my Dwelling Place* (London, 1986)

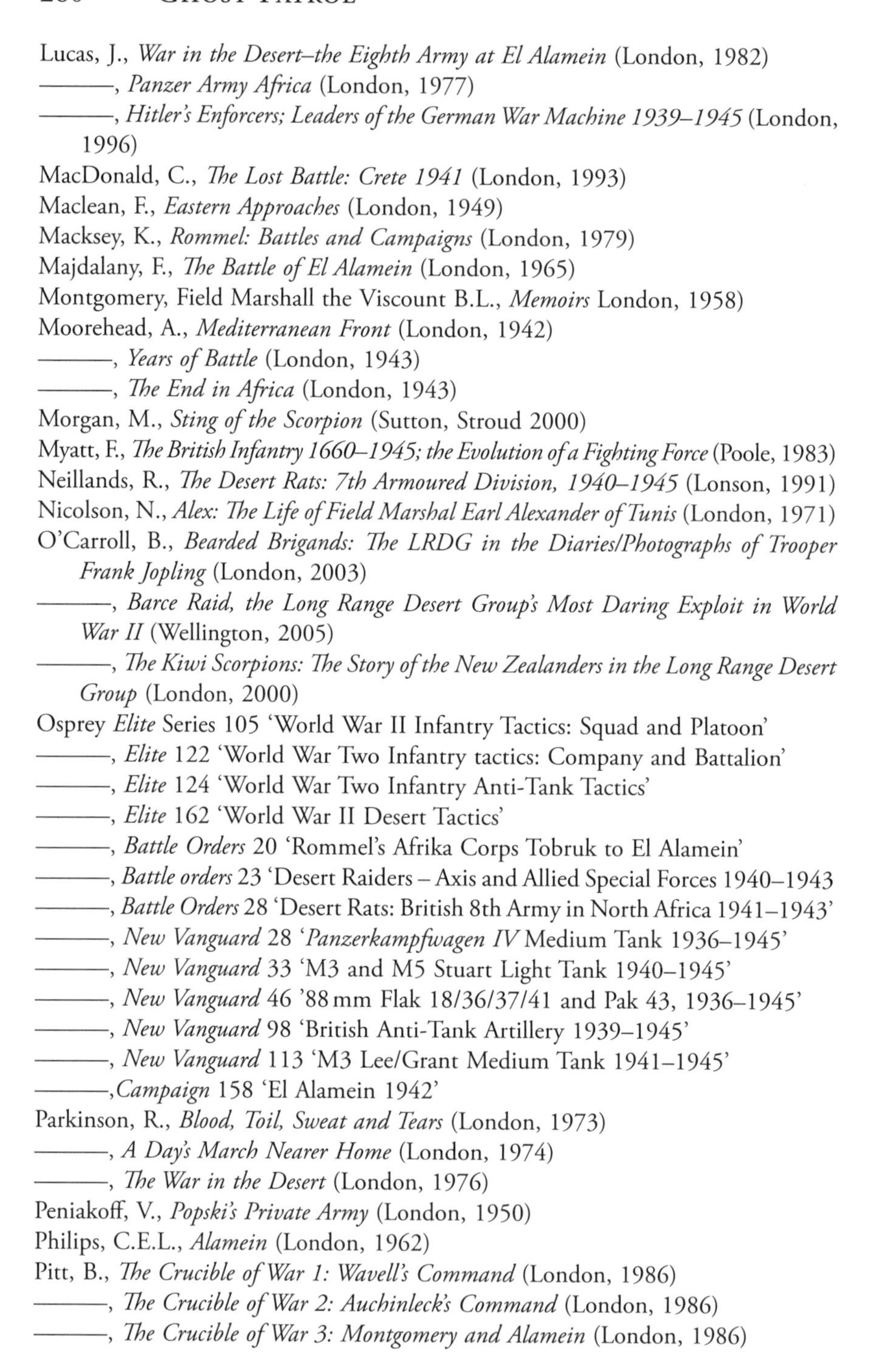

Lucas, J., *War in the Desert–the Eighth Army at El Alamein* (London, 1982)
———, *Panzer Army Africa* (London, 1977)
———, *Hitler's Enforcers; Leaders of the German War Machine 1939–1945* (London, 1996)
MacDonald, C., *The Lost Battle: Crete 1941* (London, 1993)
Maclean, F., *Eastern Approaches* (London, 1949)
Macksey, K., *Rommel: Battles and Campaigns* (London, 1979)
Majdalany, F., *The Battle of El Alamein* (London, 1965)
Montgomery, Field Marshall the Viscount B.L., *Memoirs* London, 1958)
Moorehead, A., *Mediterranean Front* (London, 1942)
———, *Years of Battle* (London, 1943)
———, *The End in Africa* (London, 1943)
Morgan, M., *Sting of the Scorpion* (Sutton, Stroud 2000)
Myatt, F., *The British Infantry 1660–1945; the Evolution of a Fighting Force* (Poole, 1983)
Neillands, R., *The Desert Rats: 7th Armoured Division, 1940–1945* (Lonson, 1991)
Nicolson, N., *Alex: The Life of Field Marshal Earl Alexander of Tunis* (London, 1971)
O'Carroll, B., *Bearded Brigands: The LRDG in the Diaries/Photographs of Trooper Frank Jopling* (London, 2003)
———, *Barce Raid, the Long Range Desert Group's Most Daring Exploit in World War II* (Wellington, 2005)
———, *The Kiwi Scorpions: The Story of the New Zealanders in the Long Range Desert Group* (London, 2000)
Osprey *Elite* Series 105 'World War II Infantry Tactics: Squad and Platoon'
———, *Elite* 122 'World War Two Infantry tactics: Company and Battalion'
———, *Elite* 124 'World War Two Infantry Anti-Tank Tactics'
———, *Elite* 162 'World War II Desert Tactics'
———, *Battle Orders* 20 'Rommel's Afrika Corps Tobruk to El Alamein'
———, *Battle orders* 23 'Desert Raiders – Axis and Allied Special Forces 1940–1943
———, *Battle Orders* 28 'Desert Rats: British 8th Army in North Africa 1941–1943'
———, *New Vanguard* 28 '*Panzerkampfwagen IV* Medium Tank 1936–1945'
———, *New Vanguard* 33 'M3 and M5 Stuart Light Tank 1940–1945'
———, *New Vanguard* 46 '88 mm Flak 18/36/37/41 and Pak 43, 1936–1945'
———, *New Vanguard* 98 'British Anti-Tank Artillery 1939–1945'
———, *New Vanguard* 113 'M3 Lee/Grant Medium Tank 1941–1945'
———,*Campaign* 158 'El Alamein 1942'
Parkinson, R., *Blood, Toil, Sweat and Tears* (London, 1973)
———, *A Day's March Nearer Home* (London, 1974)
———, *The War in the Desert* (London, 1976)
Peniakoff, V., *Popski's Private Army* (London, 1950)
Philips, C.E.L., *Alamein* (London, 1962)
Pitt, B., *The Crucible of War 1: Wavell's Command* (London, 1986)
———, *The Crucible of War 2: Auchinleck's Command* (London, 1986)
———, *The Crucible of War 3: Montgomery and Alamein* (London, 1986)

Playfair, Major-General I.S.O., Official History, UK Military Series, Campaigns: *Mediterranean and Middle East* Vols. 1–4, (London, 1962–1966)
Quarrie, B., *Afrika Korps* (Cambridge, 1975)
———, *Panzers in the Desert* (Cambridge, 1978)
Rommel, E., *Infantry Attacks* (London, 1990)
Salmond, J.B., *The History of the 51st Highland Division* (Bishop Auckland, 1994)
Samwell, H.P., *An Infantry Officer with the Eighth Army: The Personal Experiences of an Infantry Officer During the Eighth Army's Campaign Through Africa and Sicily* (London, 1945)
Schmidt, H.W., *With Rommel in the Desert* (London, 1951)
Smith, M., *Station X–The Code Breakers of Bletchley Park* (London, 1998)
Special Forces in the Desert War (HMSO, 2001)
Stewart, A., *The Eighth Army's Greatest Victories: Alam Halfa to Tunis 1942–1943* (London, 1999)
———, *The Early Battles of Eighth Army: 'Crusader' to the Alamein Line 1941–1942* (London, 2002)
Strawson, J., *The Battle for North Africa* London, 1969)
———, *A History of the SAS Regiment* (London, 1986)
Terraine, J., *The Right of the Line* (London, 1983)
Toase, F.H., & J.P. Harris, *Armoured Warfare* (London, 1990)
US Command and General Staff College–Selected Readings in Tactics, Vols I & II, April 1974
Van Creveld, M., *Supplying in War: Logistics from Wallenstein to Patton* (Cambridge, 1977)
Verney, G.L., *The Desert Rats: History of 7th Armoured Division 1938–1945* (London, 1954)
War Office: *Military Report on the North-Western Desert of Egypt* (London, 1937)
Warner, P., *The Special Air Service* (London, 1971)
———, *Alamein–Recollections of the Heroes* (London, 1979)
Wynter, Brigadier H.W., *The History of the Long Range Desert Group June 1940–March 1943* (National Archives CAB 44/151, 2008 edition)
Young, D., *Rommel* (London, 1950)

Unpublished – Defence Academy Shrivenham

TRDC 02954; Notes from Theatres of War, Vol 1; Cyrenaica, November, 1941
——— 05407; The Retreat to El Alamein, 22nd June 1942–30th August 1942
——— 05408; The German Assault on the Alamein Position, 31st August 1942–7th September 1942
——— 05408; The Battle of El Alamein part II–Opr. Lightfoot
——— 05408; Campaign in the Middle East Part 3, September–November 1942
——— 05889; Defence in the Land Battle
——— 06347; Tactical Deception

——— 07315; Charles Turner Saga
——— 08225; Pace of Operations
——— 09153; The Battle of Snipe
——— 09657; Engr. Aspects of N.Africa 1940–1943
——— 09787; Battle of El Alamein
——— 09995; Passage Operations, El Alamein 1942
——— 10728; Culminating Points
——— 11964; The Manoeuvrist Approach
——— 12114; Tactical Handling of Artillery
——— 12274; AFM vol. 4, part 3, Historical Desert Supplement
——— 12374; " " " " " "
——— 12546; El Alamein BFT
——— 12686; Armour in Battle 1939–1945
——— 13054; The Battle of El Alamein, Part III
——— 13535; Info. Brief on Tactical Deception
——— 13711; Conquest of North Africa
——— 13846; North Africa Extracts
——— 14118; Air Power at El Alamein
——— 14221; Desert Warfare: The German Experience of WWII
——— 14258; Effectiveness of Anti-Tank Weapons in Combat vols. 1,2, & 3, parts A & B
——— 14543; Breakthrough and Manoeuvre Ops, vols. 1 & 3, parts A & B
——— 14903; Exercise Sphinx Ride–JFHQPXR
——— 75123; Air Power at El Alamein

Unpublished Private Sources

Pinkney, M., *Maurice and Mary*
Akam, E.A., *A Memoir*

Online Sources

Long Range Desert Group Preservation Society – http://www.lrdg.org
Long Range Desert Group – http://www.lrdg.de/main.htm

Index